At Large

BEHIND THE CAMERA
WITH BRIAN LARGE

by Brian Large and Jane Scovell

IMPRINT

Written by Brian Large and Jane Scovell
Edited by Brian Large
With contributions by Renée Fleming and
Mary Lou Falcone
Designed by Michael Balgavy
Type Setting by Birgit Seese
Proofread by Michaela Alex-Eibensteiner

PUBLISHED BY

VfmK Verlag für moderne Kunst GmbH
Schwedenplatz 2/24, 1010 Vienna, Austria
www.vfmk.org

© 2025, Brian Large, Jane Scovell,
photographers, and
Verlag für moderne Kunst, Vienna

Printed by Gerin in Austria
ISBN 978-3-99153-127-2

BIBLIOGRAPHIC INFORMATION PUBLISHED BY THE DEUTSCHE NATIONALBIBLIOTHEK

The Deutsche Nationalbibliothek
lists this publication in the
Deutsche Nationalbibliografie;
detailed bibliographic data are
available on the Internet at
http://www.dnb.de.

DISTRIBUTION

Europe: LKG, www.lkg.eu
USA, worldwide: D.A.P.,
www.artbook.com

In memory of Zdenka Podhajská

Table of Contents

Foreword

by Renée Fleming

Brian Large's masterful videography and compelling story-telling ensured that, during a period when they were facing an avalanche of competition from new forms of entertainment, opera and classical music could continue to engage audiences. I can think of no other director who had such an impact.

I met Brian in 1995, when he televised my first Metropolitan Opera *Otello*. Previously, videography of opera had been slow to develop, and standards for the capture of live performance were rudimentary. I experienced something like despair at my viewing of the initial "scratch" taping. Brian took time to help me understand camera angles and use of lighting, and he worked with me to achieve the effect I had hoped for. What I learned on that occasion has benefited my work in dozens of other televised performances. My collaborations with Brian have included performances in great opera houses and concert halls from Los Angeles to St Petersburg. For these ephemeral live events, Brian created compelling telecasts and video recordings, giving audiences exciting experiences of the performances and, I firmly believe, sparking their interest in attending in person.

One of the most memorable projects for me was a programme in which I was paired with the great Dmitri Hvorostovsky, *A Musical Odyssey in St Petersburg*. We performed music with both orchestra and piano, shooting in palaces and locations all around the city, and in places where I think video hadn't often been allowed. Brian was brilliant, guiding the local crew toward what he wanted, and, in effect, giving a master class in production along the way. With a shoestring budget, he worked miracles, and the result was a beautiful document that we were all proud of.

Ultimately, what distinguishes Brian's work—apart from painstaking preparation—is that he always wields his cameras in the service of the story and the music. No shot is superfluous, and audiences are inexorably swept into the experience of the performance. One can well understand why he has been a favourite creative partner for Leonard Bernstein, Pierre Boulez, Carlos Kleiber, Lorin Maazel, Christian Thielemann, and Franz Welser-Möst—to name but a few major conductors—over the last fifty years.

Introduction

by Mary Lou Falcone, Public Relations Strategist

First and foremost, Brian Large is a pioneer. The ebb and flow of music touched his heart and soul long ago. He knows music inside out. He parlayed that knowledge into an art form captured on video and over which he reigned for fifty years. It started in the 1960s when Brian worked for the BBC in London. Absorbing all the existing techniques of video recording, he made them his own and enlarged them, no pun intended. Brian had the vision, the technique, and the inventive spirit to make himself indispensable for half a century. Under his guidance, all aspects of videography seemed sharper and stronger. Among his non-technical achievements, he developed a person-to-person connection that allowed performers to feel comfortable enough in his presence to appreciate and follow his counsel. "Feel the light", he'd advise them, "… whether you're being photographed or whether you're being filmed doesn't matter. Just make sure you're in the light."

Brian is both consummate gentle man and a gentleman. His mild but incredibly determined manner made it clear that "it will get done and it will get done right". And it's all about style and the long, expressive arc of the line. Over the last twenty years, we became a society eager to chop things up; we wanted rapid vignettes, we wanted to rattle the cage. Brian doesn't rattle cages; Brian follows the music. Other directors may be equally as good in their own genres, but theirs is a different skill, more a combination of MTV and sitcom, where the cutting is quick, quick, quick.

Brian wouldn't do that, he could have, but he wouldn't. Asked to continue with *The Three Tenors* after its initial success, Brian declined. That franchise went on for years and earned millions, but Brian felt he'd done it right the first time. It's a matter of integrity and the authenticity of his chosen style.

Brian once was told that he was "too musical", and that's actually a good phrase because it's dismissive and complimentary at the same time. Which brings us back to style. You're either into the chop, chop, chop or you follow the long, legato line. The fact is, you have to serve the music, that's the bottom line. And whatever Brian has done in his career always has been in the service of music. He's probably one of the most private human beings on the face of the earth and really doesn't show much emotion, except with the camera.

The State Opera Prague

OVERTURE

Big Ben during the Blitz, World War II

I.

War and Peace

I was born within the sound of London's Big Ben and the first music I ever heard was its comforting chime. From that moment music has played a dominant role in my life. Not surprising considering that both my parents were musicians—my mother, Ruby Eileen Willis, a pianist; my father, John James Robert Large, a violinist. My parents themselves had no musical background whatsoever. Londoners born and bred, they came from disparate baking families; my maternal and paternal grandfathers were master bakers. My father's predecessors came from Norfolk; my mother's ancestors were London-based. The Willises owned a shop in South London and my grandfather delivered bread and cakes throughout the neighbourhood in a horse-drawn cart. The dough, however, stopped there. Although my mother was a gifted amateur baker, neither she nor my father cared to continue the family trade. As for myself, I inherited zero baking skills.

Ruby Willis and John Large came of age during the heyday of jazz and swing bands, popular ensembles which, in the 1920s and 1930s, provided music for tea dances, dinner dances, ballroom dances, and radio broadcasts. Bands were all the rage and the Savoy Orpheans, the resident orchestra of London's Savoy Hotel, topped the list. That group captured my father's imagination, inspiring him to create his own orchestra. In search of a catchy title, he took advantage of the Orpheans' popularity by appropriating the "Savoy" and flipping it. The result? The Yovas Dance

Band, ten or so musicians who, although they could be hired for a lot less than their Savoy counterparts, had a similarly jaunty repertoire. While the Yovas Dance Band never reached the heights of the Savoy Orpheans, they were well respected and kept busy in a variety of venues, from dance halls to hotels, and for a variety of celebrations, from weddings to bar mitzvahs. My father, the front man, became known as John of Yovas. My mother, like most young ladies of the day, regularly attended dance parties and during one of them noticed the jaunty violinist at the front of the stage. She looked up, he looked down, and in a matter of weeks they were seeing eye to eye. Ruby Willis and John of Yovas married in June of 1931. Six years later, on 16 February 1937, my father's 27th birthday, I arrived at the historic General Lying-in Hospital on the south side of Westminster Bridge and was later taken from there to our home in Lambeth.

During the year of my birth, several diverse events took place in the UK that, one way or another, influenced the world I was entering and, in some instances, my life in particular. To name a few: The British Broadcasting Corporation, the world's oldest and arguably largest national broadcaster, initiated BBC Television (BBC TV). The widely popular network would acquire two affectionate nicknames, "Auntie" and "The Beeb". "How's Auntie doing tonight?" and "What's on The Beeb?" soon entered popular jargon. In the classical music world, twenty-four-year-old composer Benjamin Britten's *Variations on a Theme of Frank Bridge* premiered at the prestigious Salzburg Festival, thrusting his name into international prominence. At the same time, pilot and inventor Frank Whittle was testing the world's first jet engines designed to power aircraft. And, the durable musical comedy, *Me and*

My Girl, opened in London's West End. "The Lambeth Walk", a song and dance number from that show, became an international hit, putting my hometown on the musical map. These are a mere smattering of many 1937 highlights, yet all were dwarfed by a singular event. After barely a year as reigning monarch, Edward VIII gave up his throne, received the title Duke of Windsor, and married the woman he loved. On 12 May 1937, his younger brother Albert became King George VI thus dramatically altering the line of succession. (His daughter-successor, Elizabeth II, the longest reigning monarch in British history, died in September of 2022.) Using the indispensable mobile control van, the coronation of George VI in Westminster Abbey became the fledgling BBC TV's first outside broadcast. Fatefully, the wedding of the Duke of Windsor to the American divorcee, Wallis Warfield Simpson, would be the second. No question, my birth year included many considerable occasions, but for Ruby and John Large my appearance was 1937's crowning achievement.

I was an only child and ours was a harmonious household. While my father led his band, my mother gave piano lessons. Their combined income was enough for us to live comfortably. Life was good save for one ugly instance, the relentless rise to power of Adolf Hitler and his Nazi Party. When England declared war on Germany in September of 1939, harmony shattered and Londoners prepared for the worst. Many of them, including our neighbours, built bomb shelters in their gardens. Later, larger spaces, such as the underground passages of Lambeth's Waterloo Station, would become public refuges. On 7 September 1940, German bombers and fighter planes began the first of fifty-seven consecutive days of bombing raids on London. *Blitzkrieg* ("lightning war"), the German word for this kind of attack, was shortened to Blitz by the British press. Too young to fully realize the horror of the London Blitz, I do have distinct memories. For one, the screeching of the air raid sirens is fixed in my mind's ear. There were two different siren sounds; the warning alert and the all-clear. The deafening high and low shrieks of the former terrified while the steady drone of the latter comforted. My mother used to sing the signals to me so that I'd become familiar with them. Ultimately, I learned that the warning siren's squeal meant run like hell. Whenever it blared my parents would scoop me up and rush to our neighbour's garden shelter where we were welcomed in. As chaos rained down, we'd huddle together in the damp, torch-lit quarters waiting for the second siren's release. At its cry, my mother would look up, smile, and say, cheerfully, "Ah, there's the all-clear. We're safe, for now."

Under a constantly menacing sky, life went on. To keep our spirits up, the British Ministry of Information began poking fun at the Third Reich. A good example of this was a short propaganda film entitled *Lambeth Walk—Nazi Style*. In this celluloid spoof, footage from Leni Riefenstahl's *Triumph of the Will* shows Hitler reviewing the German armed forces. The newsreel soundtrack, however, was edited to make it appear that the soldiers were marching to "The Lambeth Walk". Theatre audiences roared as they watched the goose-stepping troops "doing the Lambeth Walk". The film, which reportedly enraged Reich Minister of Propaganda Joseph Goebbels, can be seen on YouTube.

One evening, after a particularly relentless bombing, my parents and I left our neighbour's shelter and walked over to what a few hours earlier had been our home. We found a mountain of rubble, a confusion of chunks and bits of ceilings, floors, walls, curtains, pictures, beds, chairs, tables, books, rugs, toys, clothes, everything we owned, smashed into nothingness. The sight was unbearable and the three of us stood there stunned. In the blink of an eye, like thousands of other Londoners, we were homeless. I began to wail. My mother quickly gathered me in her arms. "Don't cry, Brian", she said, tears spilling from her eyes. "It's all going to be fine, you'll see. Everything will be fine." My dad stood by silently as my mother rocked me back and forth. Eventually, he shook his head, heaved a sigh, and put out his arms. "Give the boy here", he said, and I was passed into his sturdy embrace. Exhausted, we returned to our neighbour's untouched residence, a matter of steps that took us from utter ruin to status quo. Leaving my mother and me with the neighbours, my dad went off to arrange for our living quarters. Previously, his parents had survived a direct hit on their home and had returned to Norfolk. My Willis grandfather's house also was struck yet somehow remained standing. We had no alternative other than to move in with him. The shocking irrevocable loss of place played itself out as I got older. For me, security meant a roof over my head; consequently, for most of my adult life I have maintained multiple residences in Europe and America.

The Blitz continued but now when the alert sounded, instead of going to our snug shelter, we sat out the mayhem in a nearby tube station where multitudes gathered hundreds of feet below the surface. I had never seen so many human beings, as well as assorted animals, jammed under one roof. Jagged rows of people and pets were piled up on the unyielding cement. Frightened that we might somehow be separated, my mother sewed together a little purse into which she put some money and a piece of paper with my name, my birthdate, our address, her name, and a brief note at the end: *If anything happens to me, please use this money to look after my little boy.* That purse hung around my neck every time I left my grandfather's house.

The Blitz showed no signs of stopping and Londoners, advised to get their children out of the city, dutifully sent them to the countryside or overseas to America and Canada. My parents long deliberated those alternatives. Ships transporting children across the Atlantic were regularly torpedoed and the mortality statistics were enough for them to reject the transatlantic option. Nonetheless, it was obviously best to get me out of town. In due course, like so many other city kids, I was sent to the country. My destination was the village of Marsworth in Hertfordshire in the northwestern part of the Chiltern Hills, a chalk escarpment covering more than six hundred square miles. An elderly couple generously agreed to take me in. They were kindly but old, and likely overwhelmed. Everything was on a "keep calm and carry on" basis which was rough going for a barely five-year-old. I yearned for my mother's loving attention, but there was no recourse other than to stick it out. My story is not unique, nearly two million children were evacuated from London. And while slogans exhorted us to *Be Strong, Dig for Victory, Stand Firm,* and *Be Like Dad; Keep Mum,* we were a nation of homesick kids. It was a horrendous time. But you learn to become grateful for what you have and you learn to become stronger. You must because if you don't fight to become stronger, you're lost. Stiff upper lip and all that.

Once I'd settled in Marsworth, my parents followed their own paths. My father had been conscripted into the service. Keenly interested in radio communications, he'd mastered Morse code early on and became an amateur radio operator, a ham. Because of this knowledge and skill, he was assigned to military communications which kept him from being sent to the front lines. A blessing. My mother wanted desperately to accompany me to Hertfordshire, but family obligations got in the way. When she was eleven, her own mother had died leaving my mum to be raised, lovingly, by her Aunt Eila. Just as I was about to leave for Hertfordshire, Eila became ill with cancer and required full-time care. My mother was torn. Realizing that I would be safe but her second mother wouldn't, she made the difficult decision to stay and look after her aunt. For nearly a year, she remained by Aunt Eila's side while contenting herself with a handful of visits with me. She'd take the train to Tring, nearby Marsworth, and we'd spend a couple of days together. The visits seemed to be over before they began, yet she always was cheerful and urged me to keep my chin up. "We'll be together soon", she'd promise, and I believed her. I had to believe her because I missed her so much. I'm sure my mother never bargained for such an extended stay, but she would not desert her aunt. When Eila died my mother put her aunt's affairs in order and immediately joined me in Hertfordshire. Soon, she found us an end-of-terrace cottage in New Mill, a semi-rural village not far from Marsworth.

Our home consisted of two very small rooms, living space and kitchen below, and above, two very small bedrooms. We had no electricity, no heat, and no plumbing. All the cooking was done on the fireplace grate. An outside pump provided water and, rather than a proper toilet, a rickety loo stood at the end of the garden. Friday was bath night and my mother would boil water in a large pot and pour it into an aluminium basin, a poor stand-in for a tub. At war's end, the three of us were reunited in that rough-hewn hovel in the middle of nowhere. By then, electricity and gas had been installed. We no longer had to rely on candle or lantern light after dark, and a gas stove took care of the cooking needs. We never had running water, though, and continued to fetch and carry from the outside pump as well as trip down the garden path to the loo. A shower, rigged outside the house, took care of our bathing needs. Here we lived for nearly a decade. A long way from Lambeth, for sure.

I started school in 1944. Teachers were scarce as many had been called up to serve in the military, thus instruction came from retired pensioners, most in their seventies. With their professional lives long behind them, not a few, understandably, had lost their enthusiasm for pedagogy. Some were simply no longer capable. Looking back, I realize how difficult this must have been for them. At the same time, the situation was oppressive for us kids. The teachers had little patience. They barely could control the older children, who at least understood "yes" and "no" and "stop" and "go". Younger students were rambunctious, though, and didn't take orders easily. Basically, I was a quiet child, a loner, and my goal was to make myself as unobtrusive as possible. Compounding the pedagogical problems, school supplies were nearly non-existent. Everything went into the war effort and the entire country was long on shortages. Because we had no pencils to write with and no paper to write on, we had to make do with bits of chalk and battered slates, not easy for me. I am naturally left-handed; each time I wrote, I inadvertently smudged or erased with my sleeve what I'd just written. At the end of the exercise, the teacher would ask to see our slates. I'd hand over mine and, invariably, was reprimanded. "You lazy little brat. Look at this mess! You'll never amount to anything. Get up and bend over." Obediently, I'd rise from my chair, turn around, lean forward, and await the sharp smack of a thin wooden stick on the back of my bare knees. In those days, English schoolboys wore short trousers until they reached their teens. I received a goodly share of those stinging raps and, at the same time, had to endure taunts about my indolence and inability to do the work. As for my classmates, perhaps if I'd participated in sports, they might have tolerated me but I really wasn't very interested in playing games. Besides, my parents forbade me to join in. They'd determined that I was going to be a pianist and my mother didn't want me doing anything that might injure my hands. Even bicycling was verboten. Later in life, I tried to play tennis and golf. I didn't take to the former and found the latter utterly boring.

Whether or not my school was as Dickens-like as I remember, it was not a pleasant place. Home was far better, but it, too, remained a hardscrabble existence. Everything was rationed and necessities were scant, consequently, people were encouraged to grow their own food. My mother had a small vegetable garden where she cultivated lettuce, tomatoes, and cauliflower. Once the seeds were in the ground and the shoots began to flourish, we made a daily check for progress. My mother would lean over, gently touch the leaves, and say, "Almost, but let's give it one more day." All too often we'd go out the next morning only to discover that the garden, while not quite ready for us, had been picked clean by strangers. My mother rationalized, "Don't fret, Brian, someone needs the food more than we do." I always appreciated my mother's indomitable spirit. Whether it be gardening or guidance her unflagging spirit remained intact.

To keep her skills sharp, she decided to teach me to read music, somehow managed to find a dilapidated piano,

On the left side, a wedding photo of my parents, John Large and Ruby Willis, 1931. Both my grandfathers were bakers. On the right, grandfather Willis and his horse-drawn delivery cart; grandmother Large in front of the bakery; a wedding photo of my maternal grandparents

25

and had it brought to our humble home. Positioning me on her lap, she'd sit at the (barely) upright and my lessons began. Long before I could read the alphabet, I read music. My mother accomplished this through an ingenious method of her own devising. She'd tear endpapers out of books (the paper shortage was ongoing), draw five-line staves and fill in the notes. Next, she'd hang little animal cut-outs, a dog, a cat, an elephant, on the notes. Then, she'd take my right-hand index finger and place it on the animal. "See this doggie, Brian? That's a D note." Moving on, she'd put my finger on the next animal. "Look where this cat is sitting; that's a C." As she pointed out the notes, she'd gently press the index finger of my other hand on the corresponding piano key. Her method immediately pitched itself to me. I learned to read music as though I was playing a game of cats and dogs. What could be more fun? Inspired, I began to poke out melodies on the decrepit instrument in front of me. Who cared what it sounded like? I was making music. Thereafter, music continued to weave its way into my life. Here's a well-remembered example: Terrified of thunder storms, at the first peal I'd run for cover, or mother, whichever was nearer. One time, I huddled against her sobbing away until I finally blubbered, "Mummy, what is that horrible noise? It's scary." "Calm down, Brian," she said as she wiped away my tears, "there's nothing to be afraid of; it's only the giants who live in the clouds. They're moving pianos around so they can play music." Pianos? Music? That did it. Those words, piano and music, completely reassured me. Thunder never again frightened me. Snow, however, did. When it began to fall, I panicked. Again, my mother calmed me down. "It's just those giants", she'd say. "They're making up their beds and the soft white feathers from their eiderdown duvets are drifting down."

After the Japanese attack on Pearl Harbor, America, which heretofore had remained neutral, joined forces with Britain and the Soviet Union against Germany, Italy, and Japan. American bases were set up in England, one of them near New Mill; World War II was in full swing. One rare sunny afternoon, I was playing outside when a jeep carrying four American GIs lurched down the dirt road and came to a screeching stop not far from where I stood. "Hey, kid", called out one of the soldiers. "Kid?" I thought to myself. No one had ever called me that before. "Bloody Nuisance", yes, but kid? Never. I walked over to the jeep. "Where's the American Army base?" the soldier asked. "Just keep going straight that way and you'll get to it", said I, pointing down the road. "Thanks, kid", replied the soldier. The driver revved the engine, the jeep jolted forward. Suddenly, the soldier who'd been talking to me cried out, "Hold it!" The driver slammed on the brake and once again the car abruptly came to a standstill. My soldier friend stood up, reached into his pocket, and pulled out a bright yellow cylinder. "Here, kid," he said as he waved the golden object, "take this as a thank you." I shook my head and called back, "I'm sorry, but my mother told me never to accept anything from strangers." The soldier laughed, tossed over the mystery item which landed a few feet away from me, and sat back down in the jeep. Off went the GIs in a cloud of dust. Slowly, I walked over and gazed down at the proffered gift. What could it possibly be? My mum would know. Gingerly, I picked it up and, carrying it straight out ahead of me, walked into the house. My mother looked up from her sewing, saw me, and cried, "Brian, where on earth did you get that? Who gave it to you?" I told my tale and at the end tentatively asked "Is it a bomb?" "No, no, dear, it's not a bomb, it's a banana." I didn't know what she was talking about. "What's a banana?" "It's a fruit, dear, a lovely fruit." She took the banana from me, showed me how to unzip it, and I had my first bite. It remains my favourite fruit to this day.

The banana incident was a momentary bright spot. I wouldn't taste one again for at least a year, maybe longer. Meanwhile, the bleak routine continued. The war raged and, aside from my *moments musicaux* and the comfort of being with my mother, life went on, monotonously the same and with a steady diet of darkness. The minute the sun went down, curtains were drawn. We lived in a perpetual blackout with no light anywhere. And then, suddenly, the war was over. We'd won, and the whole of England was given permission to light bonfires and celebrate. Crowds frolicked in the streets, shouting, cheering, and singing popular war songs. Stuffed rag effigies of Hitler were hung on broomsticks and flung into the flames. I had never seen a bonfire before and stared in awe as they lit up the skies on that victory evening in September 1945. The war ended but recovery took its time; food rationing, for example, continued until 1954.

After my father returned, he quickly took notice of my musicality and decided that I should follow in his footsteps and become a violinist. My mother did not agree. She favoured the piano. A tug of war ensued, each parent wanting me to carry on his or her tradition. The fact that I'd already started on the piano and, more relevantly, that I showed a true aptitude for the instrument, was the deciding factor. My dad yielded and my path was set. The piano was a godsend. Put me at a keyboard and I was no longer the lazy school kid. Rather than being chided by my schoolteachers, I was nourished by my mother's instruction and enthusiasm. As time went on, she would have me play for children's parties which gave me a good idea of what it was like to perform in front of others. It didn't hurt that at the end of each performance there always would be an offered sweet or a piece of cake. On one level it was bribery, but the results were worth it. What's more, though I never turned down a sweetie, I'd have played for nothing save the sheer joy of making music. Regarding those early musical endeavours, while I studied at university my mother and I sometimes reminisced about life in New Mill. On one such occasion I brought up something that always had bothered me. I told her that every December the piano seemed to go wrong. "The piano? Wrong? What are you talking about?" I explained. "Well, for weeks the piano sounded muffled. I thought it might be on its last legs, but by the end of the year it miraculously recovered and sounded just fine, till the next December." My mother smiled. "Oh Brian, I know exactly what you're talking about. You see, everything was so cramped in the house, your dad and I had no place to hide your Christmas presents so we put them inside the piano."

Another vivid, non-musical, memory of our New Mill days remains. Each year at the end of October, we began making Christmas puddings. It was a major undertaking. My mother would put down a huge bowl in a corner of the kitchen and once a week, ingredients were added. First came flour and fruit, then nuts, after which beer was poured in. The ingredients were gently folded together with a large wooden spoon and the bowl was covered. Seven days later, the routine was repeated, flour, whatever fruit was available, and nuts would be added, and beer poured in. And so, it went until the second week in December when my mother would divide the ingredients into three small bowls, place cloths over them, and tie them round. On 24 December, the bowls were put on the stove hobs and steamed. The result? On 25 December, a perfect Christmas pudd awaited each of us. A warm, lovely remembrance.

The war was done, but things were not the same, not for a long, long time, and, even at that, they never were quite the same again. Some things, however, didn't change. Parents still wanted their children to study piano, consequently my mother continued giving lessons. It was different for my father. When he returned, there were no calls for anyone to lead a band. There were no calls for bands. The era of the dance orchestra had ended and John of Yovas was no more. My father didn't agonize over the situation. A man who wore many hats, he quickly donned another. Unable to earn a living playing the violin, he focused on his expertise in radio communication and that led him to electronics. He developed an interest in television and the timing was perfect; using his electronic skills, he got into television repair and made a decent wage. We lived not quite as comfortably as before the war, but we were in tune with the rest of the nation.

Although the glory days were over, music-making continued in our home. On Christmas, New Year's, birthdays and Sundays, my parents played duets together for an appreciative audience of one, me. My father's violin-playing days only ended when arthritis made delicate fingering impossible. As I've mentioned, my father possessed many skills as well as a talent for adapting. Although he could no longer play an instrument, he'd always been interested in the making of them. Eager to keep music in his fingers, he decided to build instruments. He left the television repair business and began his final career as a luthier, specifically, a maker of violins, violas, and the occasional cello. Carving did not require the same precise touch as did fingering the violin. He worked at home and stored his tools in an attached shed which served as a workshop. When I grew older and became a wage earner, I'd always ask him what he wanted for his birthday. "Wood. Get me some wood", was ever the answer. And that's exactly what I'd do. At least once a year I managed to visit Mittenwald in Bavaria where the forests provide some of the finest spruce and maple for musical instruments. I'd buy a block, wrap it up, and present it to my dad who couldn't have been more pleased. While my father sold most of his work, he kept the first piece he ever made, a violin, which remains in my possession.

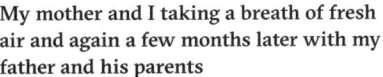

My mother and I taking a breath of fresh air and again a few months later with my father and his parents

2.

Small Screen/Big Picture

On 2 November 1936, the British Broadcasting Corporation had launched the world's first regular television service, four hours of programming each day available to set owners. At the onset of World War II all technical resources were allocated to military purposes and commercial transmission ceased. Once victory was declared, the BBC again became active in the electronic phenomenon and from the mid-to-late 1940s, like Great Britain itself, the BBC attempted to get back into step, especially with television transmissions. Broadcasts began and television sets were sold.

By 1947, there were fifteen thousand television households in Britain; in 2021, that number topped twenty-seven million. The early black-and-white Cathode ray sets were primitive, but my father had to have one. Soon, our modest home contained not only a piano, electricity, and gas but a nine-inch television set as well. Size doesn't seem to mean much to current generations. They're content to view programmes on wristwatches, mobile phones, or tablets. Still, most have an alternative since home screens now range up to sixty-five inches and more. We had no such luxury. Back then, a big screen meant twelve inches.

Tiny as it was, I remained glued to our 9-inch TV, watching anything that appeared, which wasn't much as the BBC was the lone channel and, basically, government controlled. Programming was geared to family living. Weekdays, the BBC could televise between 9 a.m. and

Alexandra Palace in North London, known round
the world as the birthplace of television

11 p.m., only two hours of which could be shown before 1 p.m. On Saturdays, a mere eight hours could be televised and on Sundays that precious interlude was shaved to seven and three-quarter hours, for God knows what reason. Actually, God was the reason; nothing could interfere with attending church. Moreover, lest it interfere with Sabbath Bible studies, no children's programmes could be televised between 2 p.m. and 4 p.m. on the Lord's Day. Finally, and with Orwellian overtones, a complete blackout, dubbed "the toddler's truce", occurred between 6 p.m. and 7 p.m. every single day of the week on every single television receiver in the United Kingdom. Ostensibly, this break allowed parents to get the little nippers to bed. And this was "social media" for my generation.

My own personal recollections include the often-comical decorum of those early TV days. Every programme was introduced by a formally dressed "speaker", either a gentleman in a dinner jacket and black tie or a bejewelled lady in an elegant dress. (I vividly recall the 1953 coronation transmission wherein the lady speaker, not to be outdone by the monarch, sported a glittering tiara.) The BBC quaintly ended its daily transmissions at 11 p.m. by playing the National Anthem as an image of the Union Jack filled the screen. From the mid-forties to the mid-fifties, the most popular children's programme had to be *Muffin the Mule*. Muffin, an animal puppet, was teamed with a live presenter, Annette Mills (sister of actor John Mills and aunt to Hayley and Juliet). She played a grand piano on top of which, Muffin danced, sang, and chatted with the lively hostess-cum-pianist. I, like most young viewers, watched spellbound. Later in the afternoon came news coverage, not so interesting, followed, after the daily break, by variety and dramatic shows. I particularly enjoyed *Café*

Continental, a live Saturday night programme set, appropriately enough, in a café. The show opened with a host/speaker, in this instance called the "Maître d'hôtel", smiling into the camera and welcoming the viewing audience. "Your table has been reserved as always", he'd cordially coo. The camera then followed him as he led us onto the set. Tables and chairs were placed in a semi-circle around a dance floor, at the back of which a band was positioned. Patrons in evening dress were seated at the tables, pretending to eat, drink, and chat. Once they were "settled", the show began. The roster of performers included singers, dancers, jugglers, ventriloquists, conjurers, etc. When an act finished, the patrons applauded, got up from their tables and, as the band played, did a brief waltz or a foxtrot around the dance floor. The music stopped, they returned to their seats and awaited the next act. The minute that act was over, the patrons applauded, stood up, and again returned to the dance floor. And so it went, for nearly an hour. There was nothing extraordinary about the presentation and yet I was hypnotized by the entire process. So were many others. *Café Continental's* popularity also was strengthened by the occasional appearance of well-known entertainers. I first saw Folies Bergère star Josephine Baker on the *Café Continental* show and was entranced by her bubbly charm. The novelty of watching performances in my own home never lessened; I became addicted to that miniature screen. Considering that my life's work would begin in the BBC's television studios, I must have been subliminally influenced by all that viewing.

We might have remained in New Mill forever if it hadn't been for me. I, who was the reason we were there in the first place, became the reason we left. The war had turned our world topsy-turvy. My dad had had to change his profession and no longer tied to the Yovas Dance Band, could do what he did anywhere, as could my mother. Although they would like to have returned to London, we had no place to which we could return. Thousands of displaced Londoners were in the same predicament. The government responded by hastily putting up prefabricated dwellings that weren't much to look at or to live in. Still, the waiting lists were extensive and it took years to get into one. Per force, my parents decided to settle into country life. That life did not enthral them but they made the best of it until the time came for me to be educated properly. In the back of the beyond where we lived the effects of wartime lingered and education remained rudimentary. I needed to be correctly schooled and my parents realized it wasn't going to happen in New Mill. So, just as we had left the city for my sake, we went back for my sake.

The Large family returned to London in 1949—not to Lambeth, however, way too pricey. We settled, rather, in the outer borough of Croydon, a large commercial district eleven miles south of Central London. Inhabited since pre-historic times, Croydon had gone from Cro-Magnons to Saxons to Normans to present day. Before Heathrow and Gatwick, Croydon was home to London's airport and be-cause of that, the area was subjected to intense bombings. When we arrived, Croydon still was rising from the residue of war, albeit at a far quicker pace than Hertfordshire. I was immediately enrolled in Selhurst Grammar School, an all-boys (ages twelve to nineteen) day school. Selhurst had pencils and paper, and best of all, a school orchestra and choir. I was twelve years old when I started to be educated properly, which is quite late. I knew how to read and write, and how to unzip a banana but I wanted to know more about music, and I yearned to learn languages. Because of my lackluster schooling in the country, I began at a disadvantage, except in music. Also, for whatever reason, the headmaster took a dislike to me and bombarded my parents with written reports some of which they shared with me. One, a particularly harsh evaluation, stuck with me. I can recall the last line verbatim: *Your son will end up playing piano in a bar or someplace like that because it's all he's good for.* The headmaster, whose name I've totally forgotten, may have been against me, but the music teacher, Stanley Spratt, was one hundred per cent for me, and that made all the difference.

Stanley Spratt (could there be a more Dickensian appellation?) was the right person at the right time and instrumental in broadening my musical horizons. Most teachers just want you to buckle down; this man saw potential and wanted me to excel. Mr Spratt did not train in musicology; his graduate work had been in English literature. Nonetheless, he led the school's choir and orchestra with fervour and invention. He brought in outside musicians to fill the ranks of the latter and to enhance its sound. As for the choir, while we sang traditional choruses from Haydn's *Creation* and Handel's *Messiah*, Mr Spratt also presented us with challenging pieces such as the Fauré *Requiem*. He had a fine library of 78 rpm records as well as the beginnings of an impressive LP collection and allowed me to listen to many of them. Thanks to Stanley Spratt, I became acquainted with composers I never had heard of before: Palestrina, Vivaldi, Bruckner, and more. At the same time, he reinforced my appreciation of Mozart, Beethoven, and Brahms. What a difference it makes to have a teacher who believes in you and wants you to achieve the very best. As I advanced in school, Mr Spratt cheered me on and gave me the confidence to go forward. I became a piano soloist with the orchestra and played concertos at many school concerts. With my parents and Mr Spratt urging me, I successfully applied for a scholarship to study piano and composition at London's Royal Academy of Music. My parents' willingness to help plus the assist from my music teacher made everything possible.

Years later, after I was well established as a video director, I contacted Stanley Spratt. We had a good long chat on the phone and, as we were saying our goodbyes, he told me of his plans, "Brian, I'm retiring this year, and I've given it a lot of thought. Even though I won't be teaching anymore, I've decided to return to university and get my music degree. You know, I've always regretted not having the proper qualifications to teach music. Now, I have the time to do it." His desire to keep on learning impressed me, and I told him so. His response somewhat surprised me. He thanked me for my commendation, adding "I wonder, Brian, if you could help me?" "Help? How?" "I want to register as an external student at London University. You have a prominent position in the musical world and I'm hoping you might be willing to sponsor me. Please if it's ..." I cut him off. "I would be honoured to sponsor you!" Mr Spratt was touched by my quick reaction. Being able to do something for this man who had done so much for me was a distinct pleasure.

When I began classes at the Royal Academy of Music adjacent to Regent's Park in Central London, I was assigned a composer/tutor to coach me in composition and theory. He had little time for me as he was actively involved in a work of his own, an opera based on Somerset Maugham's novel *The Moon and Sixpence*. The opera's premiere at London's Sadler's Wells Opera was barely six months away and my tutor fiercely focused on its completion; I was in the way. I rarely got to see him and, when I did, he couldn't hide his desire to get rid of me and get back to *The Moon and Sixpence*. Understandable yet decidedly unhelpful. Realizing I had to act quickly or be deficient in an essential subject, I screwed my courage to the sticking place and went to the principal's office. I explained that while I liked my piano teacher and all my other courses, I needed a new composition tutor, someone who had the time to teach me. By golly, I got one. When I met my new instructor, he smiled, shook my hand and said, "I'm here and I'm going to prepare you for your degree." And, that's exactly what he did. With his guidance, I sailed through my theory and composition courses and in 1959 graduated from the Royal Schools of Music. In 1960, I received a bachelor's degree in Music from the University of London where, in 1963/64, I also received a doctorate. Not bad for a "brat" who was supposed to end up in a bar.

This is how we watched TV in 1945—on a 5 × 7 inch screen

The Davis Theatre, Croydon. My childhood Shangri-La.
Here I saw my first opera and heard my first concert

3.
The Food of Life

While all music inspires me, opera holds a special place. I fell under its spell as I approached my teens. Predictably, my mother, who had introduced me to music, brought me to opera, as well. She was eager for me to see a live production, but opportunities did not abound in the hinterlands. Once we settled in Croydon, prospects brightened. Throughout the 1950s, opera companies toured in select cinemas and, in one of those grand movie houses, the Davis Theatre on the High Street in Croydon, I saw my first opera. When it was built in 1928, the Davis was the largest cinema in England and the second largest in the UK, bettered only by Green's Playhouse in Glasgow, Scotland. The Davis's stage was huge, thirty feet deep, and the dressing rooms could accommodate more than one hundred artists. A sizeable central dome covered an auditorium decorated with a mélange of classic Greek and Italian Renaissance styles and a café/restaurant, complete with dance floor, nestled in its interior. In short, the Davis was over-the-top magnificent. While the Davis had survived the Blitz, it took a hit in January 1944 when a bomb dropped through the roof and landed in the stalls, killing six and injuring twenty-five. The half-dozen deaths were a tragic loss but had the bomb exploded it would have been an utter disaster of death and destruction. Damages to the structure were repaired and the theatre reopened. Along with films, the Davis hosted live shows ranging from performances by Sir Adrian Boult conducting the London Philharmonic Orchestra to the Bolshoi Ballet on its first tour outside Russia, from solo concerts by stars such as Jeanette MacDonald, Mario Lanza, and others, to musical productions such as *Peter Pan* and *Annie Get Your Gun,* and live drama such as *Pygmalion* and *Harvey.* The pop music offerings included appearances by Buddy Holly and Bill Haley and the Comets. Of my own visits to the Davis, two concerts, one given by pianist Eileen Joyce, the other by pianist Myra Hess, stand out.

Eileen Joyce, an attractive, red-haired Australian, toured the UK extensively during World War II and throughout the 1950s. Her status was secured when she played the second movement of Rachmaninov's *Piano Concerto No. 2* on the soundtrack of two popular films, *Brief Encounter* (1945) and *The Seventh Veil* (1946). Joyce was esteemed not only for her pianistic skill but also for her glamourous presence, to which I, personally, can attest. Reviews of her performances were equally divided between praise for her playing and bravos for her costume changes. One unforgettable evening at the Davis, Eileen Joyce played, brilliantly, three piano concertos—the Grieg *A Major,* Rachmaninov's *Second,* Tchaikovsky's *First*—and in the process wore three different ball gowns, a green one for Grieg, red for Rachmaninov, and blue for Tchaikovsky. Apart from being a splendid evening musically, it was dazzling to behold. (Eileen Joyce's haute couture musical singularity may have been outdone by Yuja Wang on 29 January 2023. Changing outfits for each selection, the astonishing pianist fashionista played all four Rachmaninov concerti for piano and orchestra as well as his *Rhapsody of a Theme of Paganini* at New York's Carnegie Hall.)

On stage, Eileen Joyce glittered, Myra Hess, on the other hand, quietly glowed. A still, commanding presence at the keyboard, most often garbed in conservative dark concert attire, Hess, a handsome rather than beauteous woman, specialized in Mozart and Beethoven but was equally eloquent in Brahms and Chopin. Born in London, her fame soared throughout the UK during World War II. When the Blitz began, concert halls went dark for fear of German bombers. To get around the ban, Myra Hess organized Monday to Friday lunchtime concerts at the National Gallery that went on, without fail, for six-and-a-half years. She herself played in one hundred and fifty of those concerts and for all her efforts, both patriotic and artistic, was created a Dame Commander of the Order of the British Empire.

At an early age, I fell under Dame Myra's spell through her recordings. Seeing her in person at the Davis was bliss. Later, when I attended the Royal Academy, I was introduced to her. My joy and excitement knew no bounds. Eventually I was privileged to study privately with her. The lessons took place in her Hampstead home where she helped me with Bach Preludes and Fugues. Sometime clad in a long-sleeved black velvet housecoat, other times in a simple dress, Dame Myra would greet me at the door and usher me over to the piano. Although she never lit up during our lessons, Dame Myra smoked like a chimney and the stale, sticky aroma of long-dead cigarettes choked the air. I'd also heard that she enjoyed her whisky, but never was privy to any of those scenes, either.

To put her pupils at ease, Dame Myra favoured a relaxed atmosphere. A perfect teacher, kind and generous, she had a down-to-earth sense of humour. Occasionally, she'd make remarks that verged on the risqué. For example, she compared the crossing of hands and intertwining of fingers, used when playing Bach's Fugues, to "two pairs of legs grappling together". To me, a rather naive nineteen-year-old, statements like that sounded a bit bawdy.

But Dame Myra spoke in an off-hand way so I let it go. All told, as serene and noble as she appeared on the concert platform, at home, I got a feeling that, with the smoking, the rumoured nips and the provocative chatter, on some level Dame Myra wanted to be "one of the boys". Whatever she thought or said, though, nothing ever got in the way of making music. She was steadfast in her tutelage and her support. If I bobbled a passage and chastised myself for being clumsy, she'd respond with comforting words. "Gosh, Brian, that is difficult to play. You know, my dear, I always had, and still do have problems with that passage. Trust me, you are not alone." The idea that Dame Myra Hess and I shared the same tribulations provided a tremendous boost to my ego. I only wish I could have studied longer with her.

Myra Hess and Eileen Joyce were but two of the outstanding performers I was fortunate to see at the Davis. Truly, there was something for everyone in that treasured theatre which continued as a mecca for musical events until May 1951 when another venue, the Royal Festival Hall, entered London's musical world, as part of the Festival of Britain.

Well-nigh forgotten today, the Festival of Britain had tremendous impact in its time. Six years after the end of World War II, the UK hadn't fully recovered. Shortages and rationing had become an expected and accepted way of life and areas of London remained piled with debris and dotted with gaping holes in the ground. A sense of gloom pervaded the nation. No question, the country badly needed a shot-in-the-arm. To shake off the war doldrums and proclaim that England was once again a power to be reckoned with, the Labour Government harkened back a century to recreate a splendid and uplifting event of Queen Victoria's reign, the Great Exhibition of 1851. However, the

Dame Myra Hess
(1890–1965)

Australian pianist
Eileen Joyce
(1908–1991)

updated affair, the Festival of Britain, differed from its predecessor. The Great Exhibition had been an international occasion, a World's Fair of exhibits and attractions from many nations. The Festival of Britain celebrated indigenous industry, science, design, and the arts.

On the South Bank of the Thames, a stone's throw from where I'd been born, a site was created which included the Dome of Discovery, a display of exhibitions related to discoveries, the Skylon, an aluminium and steel tower, and the Telekinema theatre, which showed films and large screen television attractions. Musical and performance events were given in the newly erected Royal Festival Hall, a much-maligned edifice. Late in its construction, Sir Thomas Beecham happened upon the Festival Hall and, appalled by its appearance, dubbed it "an exotic chicken coop". The name stuck. London was the main site of the festival, but cities and towns throughout Britain had exhibitions of their own. Government sponsored and government funded, the Festival of Britain had its detractors and defenders. The former called the project a waste of money which should have been spent on necessities such as housing reconstruction. The latter believed the Festival gave the country a needed jolt out of the past and into the future. I, too, had my likes and dislikes. I found the Dome of Discovery a big bore. On the other hand, the "chicken coop" completely captivated me, not because of its appearance but for what it housed: music. My dad frequently took me to concerts there and best of all, we'd often go from the Festival Hall to the Festival's Battersea Park amusement section with its rides, restaurants, fast food stands, boats for hire, and all manner of funfair delights. We'd take a ride or two, perhaps rent a boat, and then pick up some fish and chips or frankfurters in a bun, always followed by ice cream. As a special treat, my father would take me to the Lyons Corner House at Marble Arch where waitresses, wearing their distinctive black and white uniforms and headbands, served what to my palate was the best food ever.

The Festival of Britain was an enchanted time but good things end and, after the scheduled five months run, the exhibition closed. When it was over, Winston Churchill, newly reinstated as Prime Minister, ordered the entire site razed to the ground, especially the Skylon. (Churchill particularly hated the tower, which was said to resemble one of his cigars.) Mr Churchill made no bones about his belief that the Festival represented Socialist propaganda fostered by the Labour government. The Festival of Britain was wiped out save for one building, the forever ugly duckling Royal Festival Hall. No one admired the look of the place, but it was functional, deemed necessary, and allowed to stand. Ironically, they're still trying to pull it down and until that happens, the exotic "chicken coop" is all that remains of the Festival of Britain. The Davis Theatre, on the other hand, suffered a worse fate. Before, during, and after the Festival, the Davis persevered, presenting its reliable array of films, concerts, and live theatre. As the decade advanced, television gradually assumed the entertainment mantle and theatre audiences began to dwindle. Finally, to make way for a building complex and parking lot, and despite concerted efforts to save it, the Davis was demolished in 1959. An incalculable loss to the people of London, especially Croydon, who would not see its like again.

I was twelve when my mother read in the paper that a touring Opera Company was coming to the Davis. She quickly checked the repertoire to find the best opera for me. Because I loved animals, she chose *Aida*, which customarily included a horse or two pulling the hero's chariot during the extravagant "Triumphal March". On the appointed day, my mother gave me exactly enough shillings for a gallery ticket, tram fare, and an ice cream. I raced out of the house, grabbed a tram, reached the theatre, and stepped up to the box office. "I'd like a ticket to *Ada*, please", I said, not realizing that I had botched the opera's name. The lady in the booth smiled. "Where do you want to sit?" "I only have enough money for the gallery." "Oh dear. I hate to disappoint you, my lad, but the gallery's sold out." I was crushed. "Don't be upset, sonny, there are other operas being performed. Tell me, was there a particular reason you chose *Ada*?" I clearly remember that she pronounced the opera's name as I had done. I don't know whether she was kindly humouring me or didn't know how to pronounce *Aida*, herself. "Well, I love animals and since I've never been to an opera before, my mother thought I should see one with animals on the stage." "Hmm. Well, I can't help you with *Ada*, my lad, but we do have another opera with a horse in it, and it's being performed tomorrow afternoon. What's more, I have a gallery seat. If you buy your ticket now, you can come back and see it. How about that?" Elated, I quickly purchased the ticket and caught the tram home.

"What are you doing here?" my mother asked as I walked in the door. "I couldn't get a gallery seat, but the lady in the booth told me there was an opera with a horse in it tomorrow, so I bought a ticket." "What opera is that?" I wasn't sure how to pronounce the name and showed my mother the ticket. She took one look and cried out, "*Die Walküre*! My God, you must be joking. You're going to *Walküre*? Brian, it's not exactly the opera to … I mean, it's very, very long and very, very … uh … heavy. I really think you should try and exchange this ticket." "But Mum, it has animals and the ticket lady said I'd like it." Try as she might, I would not be swayed. The following day, convinced that my opera-going would begin and end that afternoon, my mother sent me forth.

Die Walküre, the second of the four operas comprising Richard Wagner's monumental tetralogy, *The Ring of the Nibelung*, clocks in at four hours not counting intervals, and for that reason alone might be near the bottom of a list entitled, "Best Operas for Young People". Undaunted by my mother's doubts and fears, I climbed up to the gallery, took my seat, and sat there for five hours. I was utterly and completely blown away. Forget the horse, which was led onto the stage by Brünnhilde and in the same instant led off by a chorus member, I was totally consumed by the music and the story. The following day, I went to the library and took out a piano/vocal score of *Walküre*. I was a good enough pianist at twelve to be able to read and play it, which I did, over and over, until I knew every note, or close to it. Thus began my love of opera and my passion for Richard Wagner. Indeed, my infatuation with Herr Wagner was such that I decided to learn German, not an easy effort, especially back then. After the war, German remained the "language of the enemy" and, in general, was not taught in schools. The only languages Selhurst Grammar School required and offered were Latin and French. Latin was useless, or so I thought, while French was the popular romance language choice because we were just a channel away from France. Frustrated, I went back to the library, took out a German grammar book and began to study on my own.

George Bernard Shaw coined the term "the perfect Wagnerite" and, as a teenager, I became one of them, with *Walküre* at the nexus of my obsession. In those days, while you could hear excerpts from it, especially the "Ride of the Valkyries", there were no complete recordings of *Walküre*—it was simply too long. The first recording of the entire opera would not appear until over a decade later. To make up for the lack of a commercial recording, I'd sit at the piano and play and sing (howl) along until I became as familiar with the score as I could be. Soon, my interest expanded to include the rest of the *Ring—Rheingold, Siegfried,* and *Götterdämmerung.* One by one, I took those scores out of the library and gave them the *Walküre* treatment on the piano. Coming to the *Ring* was life-changing. I may have missed a lot of fine points, still, I was hypnotized by the music, the stories, and the striking cast of characters so convincingly depicted in Arthur Rackham's illustrations. I was completely under Wagner's spell. The more engrossed I became, the more concerned my mother became; she wanted me to enter the universe of opera, not just the Wagner world. The antidote? My mother hoped that an infusion of Italian opera would do the trick and forthwith took me back to the Davis.

My first exposure to the Italian repertoire was Giuseppe Verdi's *La Traviata* performed by a touring Italian opera company. The antidote did not take. Compared to *Walküre, Traviata* seemed pallid. I hated it. I couldn't have been more wrong. Subsequently, I grew to love and admire Verdi's tender masterpiece and, in the process, learned to love all operas, German, Italian, French, Russian, Czech, English, whatever. In my inmost heart, though, Wagner always will hold a special place. I think it's because immediately after seeing *Die Walküre,* I began playing it on the piano and the music came to me through my fingers. Just as my father had told me, the sheer physicality of learning through touch, as well as through sound and sight, is intoxicating. That distinctive introduction, and the fact that I would become the first person to video direct the entire *Ring* in colour from Wagner's iconic theatre in Bayreuth, secured his pre-eminence in my opera pantheon.

I

——

ACT

Leonard Bernstein conducting the London Symphony
Mahler's *Eighth*, Royal Albert Hall, 1966

Prague: Dawn rising over
the Charles Bridge

4.

Czechpoints

I'd long planned to continue my studies and go on for a doctorate, but before beginning the final phase of my formal education, I decided to take a break. Never having been beyond Britain's borders, I yearned to see something of the rest of the world. The question was, where to go? Rome and Paris were tempting but, in the end, I chose Vienna. I wanted to immerse myself in the city where Mozart, Beethoven, Schubert, Brahms, and Mahler had lived and where I could study and improve my German. Serious musicians need to be familiar with languages, particularly German, French, and Italian. Thanks to Selhurst Grammar School, my French was passable; but my self-taught German needed polishing. Ergo, Vienna. I have never regretted my choice. I fell in love with that city the minute I arrived there—the imposing Baroque buildings, the grand tree-lined streets, the lush parks, the food, the wine, the people, and above all, the music, which is everywhere. To this day Vienna remains *die Stadt meiner Träume*. I maintain a residence there and *the city of my dreams* has become my second home. Most significantly, it was during my first visit to Vienna that my professional life took an unexpected and major turn.

I settled in quickly, studying during the day, and spending evenings in cafés, theatres, and concert halls. I became a regular in the *stehplatz* (standing place) of the Vienna State Opera where I made friends. Together we would go to recitals and concerts, especially those of the Vienna Philharmonic Orchestra given in the glorious Musikverein. Traditionally, Vienna hosted some of the world's finest orchestras and I was particularly intrigued when reading a placard advertising a visit by the Czech Philharmonic Orchestra. Aside from the Overture to Smetana's *Bartered Bride* and Dvořák's *New World Symphony*, I knew very little about Czech music. I was curious, consequently I attended the performance. Naturally, Dvořák and Smetana were on the programme. However, I'd never heard of Bohuslav Martinů whose *Fifth Symphony* also was presented. Martinů proved to be quite a find. I was beguiled and deeply moved by his music, an intricate weaving of rhythms, colours, and Czech folk melody. I wanted to know more about him. A decade prior I'd gone in search of Richard Wagner and now, though Martinů's draw was nowhere near as intense, I determined to track him down, too. The next day I was in a library. Unlike Wagner, entries on Martinů were sparse and contained more biographical facts than musical analyses. I read *Martinů* by Miloš Šafránek, the first biography of the composer published in English. However, Šafránek was a Czech diplomat, not a musician, and the book concentrated on Martinů's life rather than his art. His life was fascinating.

The Martinů family came from Polička, a small Czech town bordering Bohemia and Moravia. Martinů's father, a shoemaker, was the town's fire watchman and bell ringer for services and special occasions in St James's church. The Martinů family—father, mother, sister, and Bohuslav— lived in the church's bell tower flat, one hundred and ninety-two steps above the ground. Weak and sickly as a child, Martinů was both born, 8 December 1890, and bred in that aerie loft which had no running water or sanitation. For the first six years of his life, whenever he did go out, his father had to carry him on his back, up and down the stairway. Later, Martinů wrote about his bird's eye view of the world. *People were like ants scurrying around. I couldn't see their small interests, their cares, their hurts, or their joys. What I did see below me was the space between them and me. I have that space in front of me always.*

Martinů's view of *space* remained with him throughout his life and profoundly influenced his ideas of composition.

Intrigued by the Czech composer's oddball early years as well as his colourful music, I made a rather madcap decision when I returned to London. I, Brian Large, would rescue Bohuslav Martinů from obscurity by writing his biography. I, who had never written a book, would just do it. Crazy? Perhaps. But I was two-and-twenty and possessed of more chutzpah than even I had realized.

I began by sending a letter of intent to Martinů himself, advising him that I wished to write his biography and asking if he would participate. I sent the letter in care of his London publisher, Boosey & Hawkes, requesting that they please forward it to the composer. Months passed. I heard nothing. Hooked on Martinů's music and his story, I wanted to write about him, but, without his input, I was stymied. Deeply disappointed, I reluctantly put aside my grand plan. Ah well, at least I'd tried.

More months passed when, unexpectedly, I received a letter from the composer's wife. She apologized for the delay in her response explaining that her husband had died in August of 1959. Shortly thereafter, she left Switzerland where they had been living and where her husband was buried, to return to France. My letter had been forwarded there. I was shocked to learn of Martinů's death. If there had been any announcements of his passing, I never saw them, glum evidence of his lack of renown in the west.

Despite her husband's demise, or maybe because of it, Madame Martinů was enthusiastic about my proposal. So much so, she invited me to meet her in Paris to both discuss the book further and to attend the premiere, a radio performance of her husband's opera, *Juliette*. I couldn't believe my luck.

Within the week, I boarded the Boat Ferry train at Victoria Station. Eleven hours later I disembarked at the Gare du Nord in Paris where Charlotte Quennehen Martinů met me. An attractive woman in her early sixties with beautiful white hair done up in an elegant bouffant, she was simply but smartly dressed. Although her English was limited, she was cordial and welcoming and spoke quite eloquently when we switched to French. Madame Martinů was born in Vieux Moulin, in the forest of Compiègne, thirty-odd miles from Paris. She came from a humble background and had been a seamstress. She'd met her future husband in Paris at the Cirque Medrano, a popular entertainment palace as well as a gathering place for artists of all disciplines. Married in 1931, the Martinůs escaped the Nazi occupation of Paris in 1941. A year later, the couple arrived in the United States where they lived for the next seventeen years. While residing in New York City in the fifties, Martinů taught at the Mannes School of Music where an up-and-coming young composer named Burt Bacharach studied music theory and composition with him. At the time of our meeting, I was unaware of the ins and outs of the Martinů's marriage. According to contemporary accounts, Madame looked after her husband and took care of his daily needs, but they were not "compatible culturally". He strayed and had at least two major affairs with ladies who were quite compatible, culturally and otherwise. His wife stayed the course, though, and he always returned to her. Charlotte Martinů struck me as a good person, unpretentious and selfless, whose one wish seemed to be for her husband to receive the recognition she believed he deserved.

It's difficult to describe my feelings at that initial meeting with Madame Martinů. Nervous, excited, I desperately tried to maintain my cool as we sat together in the Salle Pleyel concert hall. And then the performance began and I was completely taken out of myself. *Juliette* is a stunning work that many consider to be Martinů's greatest. After the performance, I escorted Madame Martinů to a nearby café where we were joined by various cast members from the opera, and Charles Bruck, the conductor. I don't believe I ever closed my mouth that evening and I wasn't talking; my jaw hung open in awe at the company I was keeping. Later that night, in my hotel room, I found it impossible to sleep. I could not get over being in the presence of such illustrious and knowledgeable personages. With Martinů's music resounding in my head, I resolved, at once, to make the book happen and fortify his musical legacy. It would take many years, but happen it did. Not only did I get the book done, later I would translate *Juliette* from French to English and fashion an updated singing version. In April of 1978, thanks to conductor Charles Mackerras, a longtime Martinů enthusiast, my version of Martinů's *Juliette* was given its British premiere by the New Opera Company in the London Coliseum. Sadly, Charlotte Martinů was unable to attend this performance but I brought a tape of the BBC Radio 3 broadcast to her later that summer. That was the last time we met; she died in November 1978. Charlotte Martinů was a good soul and I am gratified to have helped her accomplish what she most wished to do, ensure her husband's musical heritage.

The morning after the broadcast premiere of *Juliette*, I accompanied Bohuslav Martinů's widow to her home in

Vieux Moulin where she lived with an older sister. Madame Martinů accommodated me, fed me, and conferred with me in a parlour piled high with documents, letters, papers, photographs, and scores. She told me that I would have access to all her memorabilia, but that her items constituted a fraction of the abundant material. "You need to go to Prague and Polička where my husband was born. You must speak to the people who knew him while they're still alive. I'll give you the address of a woman in Prague who can help. She's a former dance teacher who knew my husband before I met him. He played piano for her dance classes and they became good friends. She's trustworthy and will give you many contacts that I do not have." Madame Martinů went over to a desk and took out a worn address book from the top drawer. She then copied the name and whereabouts of the trustworthy lady on a piece of paper which she handed to me. I glanced down, saw "Zdenka Podhajská" written at the top, and tucked the paper into my pocket. I had no inkling then that Zdenka Podhajská would become an essential part of my life.

Upon my return to London, I wrote Madame Podhajská explaining that Charlotte Martinů had given me her name with the hope that she would assist me. She immediately wrote back affirmatively, urging me to come to Prague where she promised to provide as much information as she could and to "take me around" to meet those who knew Martinů. A bonanza! Madame Podhajská and I agreed on a starting date and I began to make travel plans. I had no idea what I was getting into. While my interest and enthusiasm surely played a part and while I did have a vague imprimatur from Boosey & Hawkes, to this day, it remains hard to believe how willing those two women were to put Martinů's story into the hands of an unproven literary stripling. I had no illusions. I knew I was the chosen one because I was the only one. Still, the endorsement of the composer's widow and the promised access to all the composer's material struck me as a tangible achievement.

My first visit to Prague took place in 1961 during the height (or depth) of the communist rule. Three London-based music students, Charles Mackerras, Christopher Hogwood, and I, were "exchange students" admitted into Czechoslovakia. Charles would study with Václav Talich, the renowned Czech conductor; Christopher would work with the brilliant Czech harpsichordist, Zuzana Růžičková (the first person to record Bach's complete works for keyboard); while I did independent research on Martinů. With hindsight, and based on what was going on at the time, it's incredible that the Czech government let us into the country. Like all Soviet satellites, the country was strangling in Red tape but I guess even a Cold War must yield to culture.

Blissfully ignorant of the ways of autocracy, I set about making my travel plans. First, I called the Czech embassy in London and was informed that I needed a visa. A visa? What was that? The clerk begrudgingly explained, and advised me that visas could be obtained through the Czech tourist office in Kensington Palace Gardens. At the tourist office I was further informed that to get said visa I had to buy, with British pounds, a minimum of a hundred Czech crowns for every day I spent in Czechoslovakia. Moreover, my hotel had to be reserved and paid for in advance. I did as I was told. After my visa was issued, my Czech crowns secured, and my hotel, the Zlatá Husa (Golden Goose) booked, I cheerfully set off on my first trip behind the Iron Curtain, a long and arduous journey from London to Prague via Brussels and Frankfurt am Main that took twenty hours to complete.

I arrived at Prague's dazzling Art Nouveau railway station, *Hlavní Nádraži,* and must admit that, just as Charlotte Martinů had appeared at the Gare du Nord in Paris, I fully expected Zdenka Podhajská would be on hand to greet me. She wasn't. Only the fact that I knew the name of my hotel kept me from mild panic. I found a station attendant who spoke a bit of German and was able to give me directions to the hotel. With luggage dangling from either hand, I walked from the train station to the Golden Goose. That fifteen-minute stroll was a revelation. The architectural beauty surrounding me was breathtaking— magnificent Baroque buildings with façades decorated in stucco reliefs, some simple designs, others showing scenes of patron saints protecting against evil and pestilence, or victorious battles waged long ago. The spires, towers, and turrets of Gothic cathedrals and churches loomed over huge squares and medieval lanes, every nook and cranny of this fairy tale city was layered with history and lore. And, miraculously, everything was intact. Prague, like Paris, had been occupied by the Nazis during the war and thus spared the bombings endured by London. I had come from England, a civilized environment, and was now in a repressed communist regime. Yet, ironically, Prague stood whole while my city remained pockmarked with bomb sites and other scars of war. All the same, as magical as this wonderland appeared, something dark and oppressive enveloped the cityscape. To begin with, a preternatural silence was everywhere. After six at night, except for the rattle of an occasional tram, no vehicular noise could be heard. There was no traffic simply because there were no automobiles other than the black limousines of communist party members. Who could imagine a capital city with so few cars? At night the streets were practically empty and so were the sidewalks. During the day, the people who were active didn't look at each other and didn't talk to each other. Heads down, glancing neither right nor left, they ploughed straight ahead to wherever they were going without uttering a word. I have never forgotten that peculiar and unsettling quietude. Predictably, goods were in short supply, consequently long lines filled the sidewalks. When you spotted a row of people standing silently, you automatically got in the line and then waited to see what you were waiting for, and whatever it was, you bought it. Food was scarce, restaurants were few and those that existed offered little choice. If you were lucky, you might find a bit of sausage buried under a mountain of onions. Coffee, black coffee with a half-inch of grounds at the bottom of the cup, was always available. So was beer, which one drank at all times of the day, anything to avoid drinking the coffee. Prague's glory was obscured by a leftist layer of grime and want. Yet, somehow, the underlying spirit of the city, an incandescent artistic and cultural spark, was ever present and, happily, that spark inspired an artistic and cultural awakening in me.

In time, I immersed myself in the city of Prague. I got to know the five historical districts, the Old Town, the New Town, the Jewish Ghetto, the Lesser Town and Prague Castle where the Castle itself overlooked the Vltava (Moldau) River. I also delved into Prague's rich cultural and artistic life. On the banks of the Vltava stands The National Theatre, opened in 1881, where I saw operas from the standard repertoire as well as Czech operas most of which I had never heard of, nor ever could hope to see in the West. While all productions were sung in Czech, opera companies were dependent upon guest singers from Hungary, Poland, Slovenia, and Russia. Usually, these artists either sang in their own language or the language in which the opera was written. As a result, you'd have multi-lingual performances with the chorus and small roles sung in Czech while the principal parts might be sung in German and Russian. Going to the opera and hearing a Babelish mixture of tongues could be an unexpected lark. Try to imagine Act II of *La Bohème* with Mimi pouring forth in Czech, Rodolfo answering her in Russian while Marcello accuses Musetta in Slovenian. While no performance ever reached quite such ludicrous heights, it remains a tantalizing thought. In pursuit of musical and theatrical presentations I went to every one of Prague's theatres including its oldest, the Estates Theatre (Stavovské Divadlo). Built in 1783, the Estates Theatre is a beautifully preserved jewel box whose heritage includes the world premiere of Mozart's *Don Giovanni* in 1787.

Along with opera, I was keenly interested to know what Czech theatre and films were offering and discovered the Black Light Theatre, and Laterna Magica. Each astounded me. The Black Light Theatre uses a technique that can be traced back to eighteenth-century Asia and incorporates a darkened stage, black curtains, and actors in head-to-toe black costumes making them invisible to the audience. The costumes are covered in fluorescent paint which UV (black) lighting illuminates thus making it possible for the performers to create all sorts of magical movements. The Laterna Magica was invented in 1958 for the Brussels Expo by Alfréd Radok, a Bohemian theatre director. (Josef Svoboda, the innovative Czech scenic designer, and Miloš Forman, the Oscar-winning Czech director, were among Radok's collaborators.) Laterna Magica is a multimedia show combining live action and film projection. Actors, mimes, and dancers are interspersed on screens that are operated with a multimedia laser technique. All of which creates a dreamlike enchanted theatre, a completely different form of entertainment and one that had a profound effect on me. Black Light Theatre and Laterna Magica broadened my theatrical horizons, colouring my own work and greatly influencing what I later tried to do.

I made many friends in Prague, people who looked after me and opened doors to historical musical corridors which I took every opportunity to explore. I recall lively get-togethers where, after a simple supper of bread and soup, we'd listen to old 78 recordings of Czech music, most of which was completely new to me. After hearing the music I'd seek out the scores in second hand bookshops. Among the riches were choral pieces such as Dvořák's *Requiem* and *Te Deum* and Josef Suk's huge *Asrael* and *Zrání* Symphonies. I never would have come across these treasures if it hadn't been for those special at home evenings. I also was introduced to a number of notable Czech musicians such as Karel Ančerl, chief conductor of the Czech Philharmonic. Ančerl was Jewish and had survived Theresienstadt and Auschwitz, his wife and son had not. A kind, thoughtful gentleman, he spoke to me about Czech music in general and Martinů, in particular. Ančerl had been working for years to bring the composer's music to a wider audience and generously shared with me his enormous insights into conducting Martinů's symphonies and concertos.

The composer and poet Jan Novák was another welcome source. He'd known Martinů in New York and, like Ančerl, shared many relevant anecdotes. At first, Jan and I spoke to each other in German but he was nervous talking aloud, even in a foreign language. "There are microphones everywhere", he'd whisper. He was right, of course. Prague was totally wired; you weren't even safe in your own bed. To keep Jan calm, we began speaking to each other, as well as writing notes to each other, in Latin. Although many members of the *Státní bezpečnost* (Czech secret police, 1945–90) knew German and Russian, few were familiar with *latinae linguae*. It's incredible how much you can say in that "dead" tongue. I once joined several phrases together to create a word for "television". Not that the ancient Romans had TVs, then again, neither did most Czechs, but if you simply put together the Latin for "moving pictures flown on a wire through the air to a box in a room", the result is "television". Alas, I'm too far away from Latin now to recreate the idioms I used back then. Enough of things to come! I'm getting ahead of my story. Back to Wenceslas Square and the Zlatá Husa Hotel.

During my walk from the railway station to the hotel, I absorbed much of Prague's character. I soon learned that everything came with a story attached. For example, my hotel's original owner, a very wealthy widow, had a homely daughter who, despite her vast fortune, never married. She was called *zlatá husa*, "golden goose" and that's how the hotel got its name. When I arrived at the Zlatá Husa front desk a letter from Zdenka Podhajská was handed to me. In French, she wrote to say that she was sorry she wasn't there to meet me, but that I would be contacted by a friend of hers who would tell me how and when we'd get together. I found this a bit unnerving. She was, after all, my lone contact, my one link to this strange old world. I spoke no Czech and was totally relying on her. Frankly, I didn't know what to do. Likewise, there was nothing I could do. So, I went to bed.

The next morning, the reception rang and announced that a gentleman was waiting to speak to me. I went down to the front desk and a nondescript fellow stepped forward, introducing himself as Zdenka's friend, Pavel. I didn't know whether that was his first or last name. He spoke English serviceably rather than well, and immediately insisted that we step outside to talk, a nod to the ubiquitous listening devices stippling the city. We stood in the street yet even in the open air Pavel spoke very quietly as though wary of being overheard. "Zdenka is not in Prague. She is in Polička. You need to go there and meet her at the Hotel Poličan. "How do I get to Polička?" "You take the train. Leaves tomorrow at twelve." "Can you help me?" "Yes, I come back and get you eleven o'clock in the morning." Pavel put out his hand, shook mine, turned on his heels, and walked off down the street.

I spent the rest of the day exploring the city after which I had a dull dinner in the nearly empty hotel dining room and then retired early. The next morning, I re-packed the few articles taken from my suitcase and checked out. Pavel was waiting for me in the street and we walked, side-by-side, to the station. Notwithstanding the initial "good morning", not a word passed between us. I was already in the non-communicative communist groove. At the ticket counter I gave him enough Czech crowns for a ticket which he purchased and then handed over to me. "When you get to Polička, go to the Hotel Poličan and Zdenka will meet you there." He shook my hand, muttered goodbye, and was gone. The train ride took about four hours with a change at Svitavy/Pardubice, the transportation hub of the area. Passengers were few and no one looked at me, let alone tried to talk to me. I was obviously a Westener, consequently people shied away from me even more than they did from each other.

I arrived in Polička and, surprise, couldn't find an English, German, or French speaking person. I did a bit of hand signalling while repeating the name of the hotel till someone figured it out and pointed the way. I arrived and found the Poličan even more basic than the Golden Goose. I checked in and asked if there were any messages. "No", answered the clerk. Hmm. I had to assume that Zdenka eventually would get to me. I went to my tiny room, un-packed and, unwilling to spend anything other than sleep time in such cramped quarters, went down to the empty lobby. I took a seat at the dingy bar and ordered a beer from the barman who nodded his head and said not a word. Imagine, a closemouthed barman. I was on the verge of ordering another beer when a woman entered the hotel lobby. She looked around and, spying me, waved her arm and headed towards the bar. I knew I was in the presence of Zdenka Podhajská.

Well built, neither thin nor heavy, Zdenka moved with a dancer's grace. Attractive rather than conventionally pret-ty, with strong, even features, she wore a green silk coat which had seen better days but still provided the only touch of brightness in the darkened vestibule. Like Charlotte Martinů, Zdenka Podhajská was in her early sixties but totally unlike the self-effacing widow, Zdenka was glamour personified, albeit slightly faded. "Vous devez être Brian", she said when she reached the bar. I stood up as she slid onto the stool next to me. We ordered drinks and began conversing in French. She wanted to know all about me. I began to tell her but at one point couldn't come up with a particular French word. Frustrated, I muttered, "Shit", under my breath. "Ah," said Zdenka instantly switching tongues, "you speak English." "Alas, and so do you", I responded, embarrassed by my potty-mouthed slip. We both laughed. Zdenka, in fact, spoke four languages. Her French was perfect as was her German. Her English, how-ever, was heavily accented. Among other vocal hiccoughs, she pronounced g as k and to the day she died continued to address me as "darlink". I never quite got used to hearing that jarring endearment.

We spent an hour or so at the Poličan during which, at Zdenka's request (command), the barman produced a couple of sausages in buns. The buns were stale, the sausages were tasteless, and the beer was flat, but the conversation sparkled. Suddenly she announced, "Now, I take you for a quick moonlight look at where Martinů was born." In an instant, she was on her feet and out the door with me in her wake; Zdenka moved fast. Soon, the two of us stood in front of St James Church looking up at the bell tower, like the "ants" Martinů had commented on long ago. "We climb it together tomorrow", Zdenka said, adding "and you will meet someone who knew Martinů personally before he left to study in Prague. Her name is Maruška Pražnová and I am staying with her." Zdenka walked me back to the hotel, kissed me on both cheeks, and disappeared down the street. I took a deep breath and went into the Poličan.

The next morning, we returned to St James's and climbed those one hundred ninety-two steps to the tower flat, squeezing past huge church bells on our way to the top. The flat was furnished as it had been when the Martinůs were in residence. I was quite moved at being there. I kept thinking about Martinů's father lugging his son up and down that stairwell and of Martinů himself sitting by the window and looking out for hours on end. After Zdenka and I returned to the street, we took a short walk to the cottage where Maruška Pražnová lived. Maruška was in her early eighties, spoke only Czech, and straightaway led us into the garden where she proceeded to barbecue. She prepared sausages which we ate with chléb (bread) and washed down with beer. At one point Zdenka leaned in and whispered to me in English. "This is a luxury, a feast. Maruška is honoured to entertain Martinů's future biographer and wanted to do it up right. She really can't afford it. We must give her some money." Ordinarily, I wouldn't have called sausage and bread a luxury feast. Still, I was touched that the old lady had gone to such trouble and quickly slipped some crowns into Zdenka's waiting hand. I also ate with great gusto, adding lots of oohs and aahs to let my hostess know how much I was enjoying my meal. During our time with her, Maruška spoke about the Martinů family, what Bohuslav was like when he was young, what his parents and his sister were like, and how proud Polička was of its native son. That BBQ luncheon in the garden jumpstarted my research.

The next day we went to the Martinů Museum. Zdenka introduced me to the curator who showed me through the collection of photographs, manuscripts, and journals, and then gave me original scores to take to the hotel and study. *Original* scores, I couldn't believe it. I photographed them and still have those copies. Over the next couple of days Zdenka continued to escort me around the town. I talked to several village elders, notably František Popelka, who had a lot of personal insights. One way or another, all the town elders had interacted with the Martinůs. In the evenings, after dinner, I'd discuss everything I'd seen with Zdenka. On the third evening Zdenka heard me out and then said, "You know, darlink, I was planning to return to Prague tomorrow, but if it's okay with you, I could remain to help you further. Would it be okay?" I assured her it would be more than okay.

Somehow, Zdenka arranged for an extension of my visa and we stayed in Polićka for nearly a month. During that time Zdenka continued to make the Martinů rounds with me, which included several trips to the surrounding countryside. Wherever we went, Zdenka looked after me. She was very motherly, always concerned that I was getting enough to eat, enough rest, and not working too hard. After dinner one evening, she asked me if I knew of Leoš Janáček. I replied that although I was familiar with some of his music, I knew little about him. "Darlink, you will forgive me for speaking directly, but I have a favour to ask. You see, I was born in Brno, the town where Janáček lived and worked. He is one of our greatest composers and I think that you should do a book on him when you've finished with Martinů. I was hoping when you are done in Polička, do you think it could be possible for us to go to Brno together? I can take you to the Janáček Museum and you could see for yourself." I was immensely flattered that Zdenka thought enough of me to propose such a project and readily agreed. When my research in Polićka ended, we were off to Brno.

On the day we arrived, Zdenka purchased tickets to the Brno National Opera House where, for the first time, I saw a complete performance of *The Bartered Bride* whose overture was as familiar to me as "God Save the Queen". The colourful, traditional production with all Czech singers was simply marvellous, unforgettable. The fact that this masterpiece was not part of the standard repertoire in England was unfathomable. The next day we went to Janáček's home and, as had happened at the Martinů Museum, I had the run of the place. Allowed to finger the keys on the composer's piano, I was presented with various scores and letters which I pored over, Janáček was a composer of genius whose life and work, operas such as *Jenůfa*, *The Cunning Little Vixen*, *Kát'a Kabanová*, cried out for recognition in the West. On the train from Brno to Prague, I turned to Zdenka. "You were right, Janáček is special. When I finish with Martinů, I want to do a book on him."

Zdenka beamed and gave me a quick hug. And that's how it began. I, Brian Large, would bring Martinů, Janáček and their music to the attention of the entire world. Chutzpah really is the only word for it.

When I returned to London, I made another important decision. Why do this on my own? Why not find a sponsor? Why not approach a publisher? After all, I had the endorsement of the composer's widow as well as extensive material. Why not get a commitment? I asked John Warrack, a friend in the book world, if he could help me. He said it would be difficult, but he'd try. Difficult was putting it mildly, especially if you were in your early twenties and had absolutely no background in writing. Then again, that's when miracles are supposed to happen. Sure enough, John managed to get me an introduction to Colin Haycraft, the Chairman and chief editor at Gerald Duckworth & Company, publishers of, to name a few, Henry James, D.H. Lawrence, Evelyn Waugh, John Galsworthy, Anton Chekhov, and Gerald Duckworth's half-sister, Virginia Woolf. What a line-up! And to think that I might be joining them. Full of optimism I went to the Duckworth office on Henrietta Street where my miracle was promptly punctured.

"You want to write about Martin *who*?" demanded Mr Haycraft. "Look here, young man, there's simply no market for a book on a composer nobody's heard of. If you're so keen on Czech music, why don't you choose someone whose name is known. Find a viable subject and then come back and see us." Even though my Martinů project had run aground, I felt encouraged. I wanted to write and if all I needed to do was to find a "viable" subject, I'd find one. Dvořák immediately came to mind and just as quickly, was rejected. He was *the* most renowned Czech composer in the Western world and books about him in English were two a penny. I thought further and eventually came up with Bedřich Smetana. Thanks largely to *The Bartered Bride* overture he, too, was fairly well known in the West. But there were, as far as I could discover, no books about him in English. Smetana was just the ticket. I called Colin Haycraft. He liked my suggestion and told me to get cracking. I wrote Zdenka explaining that Martinů and Janáček had to wait while I tackled Smetana and asked if she would assist me. Once again, she agreed and sent me a list of people who would be helpful. Among the names was Erik Graf, Smetana's grandson. Zdenka arranged for me to meet with him in Vienna where I planned to go for a week of research. He kindly received me and generously allowed me to examine and photograph several of Smetana's letters which he'd inherited from his mother.

From the very beginning of this new venture, one thing concerned me. How would Charlotte Martinů react to this interruption? I kept putting off telling her, yet, at the same time, I didn't want her to hear about it from anyone else. Finally, I faced up and made the call, advising her I'd been necessarily sidetracked but assuring her that I hoped to make a two-book deal which would include her husband. Despite her disappointment, kind soul that she was, Madame Martinů expressed her complete confidence in me and wished me well. Buoyed, largely by my own enthusiasm, I prepared to return to Prague and begin a new chapter, rather, a new book in my writing career.

Looking back, I am struck by the way things fell into place. I'm still a bit astonished that I went about doing what I did so confidently without any knowledge of writing books or getting them published. Despite my audaciousness, of one thing I'm certain, if it hadn't been for Zdenka Podhajská, those books might never have happened. Everything that

I accomplished on my first trip to Czechoslovakia, and would achieve on future visits, came through her. I also had Charlotte Martinů to thank, and while I truly appreciated what that forbearing widow set in motion, the more I got to know Zdenka, the more entranced I became. A benevolent karma brought me in contact with a special person who profoundly affected the course of my life. Indeed, I am so indebted to her, I cannot go any further with my own story without sharing a bit of hers.

St James's Church, Polička, Czechoslovakia

Czech composer
Bohuslav Martinů
at work. The five-
member Martinů
family lived in
the bell tower of
St James Church
in Polička where
Bohuslav's father
worked as the tower
master and firekeep-
er. Bohuslav lived in
this aerie until the
age of eleven

5.

The Propeller Girl

Zdenka Podhajská was born on 27 August 1901 in Brno in the South Moravian Region of the Czech Republic. Her mother, Josefina Javůrková, an opera singer, had given up the stage when she married Alois Podhajský, a military officer. During that era, even the most admired and honoured performing artists were looked down upon by the middle and upper classes. Prominent men like Zdenka's father could not afford to have stage wives; before they took their vows, at her fiancé's request, Josefina retired. (That brand of bourgeois snobbery received a deserved comeuppance in a fable(d) incident involving the Metropolitan Opera's Marcella Sembrich, a renowned Polish soprano during the late 19th and early 20th centuries. Sembrich met with a society matron who wanted to engage the singer for a private soiree. The hostess agreed to the fee, a whopping $200 ($6000 in today's currency), pointedly advising Madame Sembrich that she could neither dine nor mingle with the guests. "In that case," replied the singer, "my fee is $25.")

During her active singing years, Josefina Javůrková had been a soloist in theatres in Brno and Vienna, where she sang leading roles in operas such as *Mignon*, *Cavalleria Rusticana*, *Fedora*, and *L'Africaine*. Many admired her and among her fans and friends were Johannes Brahms, Gustav Mahler, and Leoš Janáček. She also had a very close relationship with the Czech composer Vítězslav Novák. And

Zdenka Podhajská, my Czech angel, was known as the
"Propeller Girl" for her dynamic and striking performance
in a futuristic ballet of the same name

then she married Podhajský, a rapidly rising officer in the Austro-Hungarian Army. Indeed, Podhajský turned out to be the only Czech general to retain his rank throughout World War I. Later accepted into active service with the newly emerging Czech Army, he played a major role until his retirement. The Podhajskýs were comfortably well off rather than extremely wealthy and Zdenka and her younger brother Rudolf were raised in a decidedly cultured atmosphere. Their mother may have given up singing but she continued to stage performances at home. The *at home* or *salon* style of entertainment was very Viennese, very eastern European, and very fashionable. A hostess such as Josefina would invite friends and artistes to her home, provide libation and tidbits, after which musicians would perform. Dress was formal. Josefina wore gowns and flourished a large fan which famous guests were asked to sign. In her will, Zdenka left that fan to me and prominent among the signatures are Johannes Brahms, Leoš Janáček, Pietro Mascagni, and Josefina's former lover, Vítězslav Novák.

Highly educated, Zdenka graduated from the University of Vienna in 1920, then studied law at Masaryk University in Brno, and Philosophy at the Sorbonne in Paris. Along with her academic courses, she trained in classical ballet and, in the end, chose to make dancing, *modern* dancing, her life's work. In 1926, she joined Les Ballets Rythme et Couleur, the resident company at the Théâtre des Champs-Elyseés in Paris where she became close friends with another dancer, Lucia Joyce, the daughter of James Joyce. In every way, Zdenka Podhajská exemplified the modern woman. Her affinity for modern dance, for example, was a natural outcome of her interest in the burgeoning artistic and social movement, Futurism. On the artistic side, Futurism focused on technology, dynamism, motion, and rhythm. On the social and political side, Futurism, sad to say, was endorsed by Mussolini and subsequently linked to the rising Fascist movement. Zdenka subscribed only to artistic Futurism. In 1928, she joined the Marinetti/Prampolini company, a Futurist dance group which focused more on speed than dance; fast was good, faster better, and fastest best of all. Zdenka found instant fame as the Propeller Girl in an eponymous aviation ballet. Whirling around with dervish-like intensity, she was a sensation on and off the stage. Times had changed since her mother's day, performing artists were now welcomed into society and Zdenka became the toast of many towns all over Europe. She glowed in the spotlight. By the early thirties, Zdenka stopped performing and opened a dance studio in Paris. For five francs an hour, Bohuslav Martinů provided piano accompaniment in the studio and also cleaned her apartment. In return, Zdenka mended his clothes.

Zdenka might have spent the rest of her days in Paris had not the threat of war with Nazi Germany caused her to close her studio. That done, she returned to Prague to look after her parents. World War II began and when it ended, the Communists took over Czechoslovakia. The regime's rigid and relentless stringency affected everyone, especially expatriates like Zdenka. She desperately wanted to leave but couldn't. Why? Only citizens aged sixty-five and older were allowed to apply for emigration permits. Furthermore, those who did choose to leave at retirement age had to turn over all valuables to the state. For more than two decades the freewheeling Propeller Girl was stuck behind the Iron Curtain. Stuck, true, but active still. Just as she had opened a dance studio in Paris, Zdenka now opened one in the Colloredo-Mansfeld Palace, a Baroque residence near Prague's Charles Bridge. This time around,

Zdenka's clientele consisted exclusively of the wives of government officials, diplomats, and embassy staff members, the only women with the money or the time to spend on such activities. I became friendly with Jaroslav Mihule, Martinů's replacement as Zdenka's studio pianist and he described those classes to me. "Zdenka would stand in the middle of the studio shouting instructions at the top of her lungs as a thunderous herd of overweight, middle-aged ladies, encased in leotards, bounced around the room. I accompanied this frolic by playing the "Ride of the Valkyries" on the piano. It was hard to keep a straight-face."

Along with her classes, Zdenka, arranged social "at home" evenings in the Colloredo-Mansfield Palace where musicians and artists gathered to perform and to exchange ideas. Mihule recalled that the evenings always began with Zdenka slipping a thickly knit woollen sock over the telephone receiver to make it difficult for Big Brother to eavesdrop. Only Zdenka could pull off an intellectual and cultural assembly during a time of such political turmoil and only she could use those social evenings to cultivate connections that might prove helpful in her eventual relocation. She had decided that once she reached retirement age, she would make Vienna her new home. To ensure her future, Zdenka needed funds. Thus, in order to augment the pittance she received from teaching, she employed two money making enterprises, currency exchange and smuggling. I became involved in the latter, if only tangentially.

Zdenka was a few years away from the end of her enforced stay in Czechoslovakia when we met, consequently I became a willing, if nervous participant in the first of Zdenka's clandestine activities, money exchanging. My initiation came when I ran low on Czech crowns and asked Zdenka for the nearest exchange office. "Bank is around corner. What is rate today, Brian?" "Twenty crowns to the pound." "Give to me. I do better for you." I did what I was told, and thereby stumbled into a home industry run by Zdenka and her milliner friend, Ema. Wearing a bonnet lined with foreign bills, Zdenka visited Ema's shop. Once there, she proceeded to try on a succession of chapeaux which the milliner brought out, one by one, from a back room. During the process, currency was slipped in-and-out of linings. To my knowledge, Zdenka never bought a new hat. Rather, she'd leave the shop with her old one chock full of Czech notes. Incidentally, and not to be sneezed at, the Podhajská rate of exchange yielded one hundred crowns to the pound. As for Zdenka's smuggling enterprise, I knew of two schemes, the first of which did not involve me directly although I did play a leading role in the second.

Scheme One: Anka Kreisky, a close friend of Zdenka's, lived in Vienna where she had ties to a construction company specializing in theatrical scenery. Because it cost far less to build scenery in Prague, the sets were made there and then transported by trucks to Vienna. This was tricky as Czechoslovakia was communist run, and Austria was not. Anka maintained a small flat in Prague and moved freely in and out of Czechoslovakia. Because of her Czech residency as well as her strong political associations (one of her relatives was Austria's Foreign Minister and, later, its Chancellor) Anka was able to cut through bureaucratic barriers and helped establish the truck link joining Vienna and Prague. Along with the theatrical sets being transported, various pieces of Biedermeier furniture, none of which ever appeared in any stage productions, also could be found. In the past, those furnishings had adorned the Podhajský family's home. When the trucks reached Vienna, the sets were dropped off at theatres while the

Biedermeier pieces were squirreled away in a secluded warehouse. By declaring them to be part of a "theatrical consignment", Anka was able to export her friend's furniture.

Scheme Two: At the same time that Zdenka's furniture was rolling over the Austrian-Czech border, I was busy transporting much smaller items across the English Channel. Each time I visited Zdenka, there'd be a slight to medium-sized brown paper wrapped package waiting for me which I'd take to my London flat and put in the back of my clothes cupboard. The packages contained her valuables—jewellery, watches, and family heirlooms, including the occasional icon. It was a hell of a risk; had I been caught I'd have been arrested and jailed. But it was worth it because it was for her.

On my last sojourn to Prague, just before I returned to London, I went to say goodbye to Zdenka. We spent a quiet afternoon in her flat sipping tea and reminiscing. As I was leaving, she handed me a small package wrapped in the usual brown paper and uttered her typical caveats. "Darlink, don't open this. Don't lose this! Hide carefully. Keep safe for me! This is very important!" I thought I detected a heightened note of urgency but brushed it off, reminding myself that every package she gave me always included a flurry of importuning. I returned to London, put the parcel in the wardrobe, and got back to work. A month or so later, the telephone rang. I picked up the receiver and even before I brought it to my ear, I heard Zdenka crying out exultantly. "Darlink, it's me! I'm in Vienna! I'm out! I'm free! Now, bring the packages to me and all will be well. How soon can you get here?" Within a few days, I took off for Vienna carrying two large valises filled with the goods which I delivered to Anka's flat.

To establish residency in Vienna, Zdenka needed documents. She had none and thus was a woman without a country. Ah, but this was the moment for which she'd been preparing. The valuables would be sold, providing her with key money to get her own flat but to do that she needed Austrian citizenship. The decisive factor in obtaining that citizenship lodged in the last package I'd carried over the Channel. The packet contained her father's memoirs and included detailed observations of the Austro-Hungarian Army's military campaigns. Zdenka realized these documents would be of great interest. Armed with the memoirs of General Alois Podhajský, she went to the Museum of Military History where the records of the Habsburg Monarchy, from the sixteenth century to the end of World War I, are kept. She told them who her father was, waved the memoir in their faces, and proposed a deal—her father's memoirs, with its valuable military information, in exchange for her citizenship. The Museum officials discussed the proposal, and the deal was sealed. Zdenka Podhajská spent the rest of her long life in Vienna where, as an Austrian citizen, she received social security and health benefits, as well as a small pension and a passport.

Zdenka could not sit around and collect benefits, though. She had to stay active. After settling into a modest flat, she decided to start teaching again and immediately opened another dance studio. This time, instead of dance, she taught eurythmics and movement to an antediluvian clientele, some of whom had seen their teacher perform *The Propeller Girl* ballet with the Marinetti/Prampolini company. When her studio closed for the summer, Zdenka took off for Salzburg and its vaunted summer Festival. The minute she arrived, she'd go to the festival office, register as an extra and become, once again, a performer. Extras were paid well and kept very busy in Salzburg. The festival stage is enormous, in width rather than in depth, and the long proscenium line cried out for crowd scenes. During his long tenure as director, Herbert von Karajan answered that call. He revelled in presenting grand operas crammed with extras at the brim of the stage. In whatever production Zdenka appeared, she always managed to wriggle her way front and centre. Forty years on from her glory days as the Propeller Girl, Zdenka Podhajská still could find the spotlight.

For over twenty-five years Zdenka and I continued to see each other in Vienna, Salzburg, and London. During her visits to England, she met and grew close to my parents. They were most appreciative of her efforts on my behalf and a warm family spirit developed among the four of us. After my mother died, whenever I was in Vienna, I'd always visit Zdenka. My father occasionally accompanied me and when he did, we'd both go to see her. For a while I harboured a small hope that the two of them might get together and share their sunset years. It did not happen.

On her own, Zdenka lived a full, productive life but as she grew old, she uncharacteristically began to express regret at her single status. One afternoon, she and I chatted over tea at her flat. But she seemed distracted, fidgeting with her teacup, and looking around the room. I'd never seen her so jittery. At ninety she had yet to show any major age-related wear and tear. At last, she put down the teacup and looked me straight in the eye. "Darlink, I must talk to you. You may think I'm just a crazy old lady. Well, I'm not crazy, but I am old and I am troubled. Let's face it, I won't be here so much longer. I have things that I would like to pass on, and there's no one, no family. Only you, Brian. You are my family … like a son to me. I wonder, would you be offended or would your father be offended if there was a way for me to adopt you? I don't wish to take the place of your dear mother, no one could do that, I just want to look after you." Her words were so sincere and so loving, I had difficulty in responding. She had always been supportive and, except for my smuggling those packages, had asked for nothing in return. Yet here she was wanting to do more and, as always, for my benefit. I told her I had absolutely no problem with her request and that I would speak to my father. When I did, he had no objections, either. "She's a fine person, Brian, and she's done so much for you. If it's what she wants, if it will make her happy, and if it's something you want and will make you happy, you have my blessing. I know your mother would feel the same." I accepted Zdenka's munificent offer. She, in turn, said she would speak to her lawyers.

In late July of 1991, I was working at the Salzburg Festival when Zdenka contacted me again. Her "extra" days now over, I suggested that she come to Salzburg for a holiday, stay in my flat and attend a few festival performances. She said fine and that she would let me know when she'd be there, probably sometime in mid-August. On the morning of 4 August, an urgent phone call was transferred from the festival office to the recording booth. It was Anka Kreisky. Zdenka had suffered a stroke, was hospitalized, and wanted to see me. Immediately, I arranged to cover my absence from the festival and caught the next train to Vienna. Three hours later I arrived at the Westbahnhof station and took a taxi to the hospital. Anka met me in the lobby and brought me to Zdenka's room. Propped up in the bed, Zdenka tried to speak but could only mumble incoherently. She shook her head impatiently. A writing pad and pen were by her side; she took up the pen and began to write, sometimes in English, sometimes German, and sometimes Czech. She wrote things like *I am so glad to see you. Tell me about Salzburg? Where will you go next? What are your plans? How is your father?* We conversed for nearly half an hour, she writing and I answering aloud in whatever language she'd questioned me. Then, Zdenka visibly weakened and wrote *I am tired. I need sleep. I will see you tomorrow.* She put down the pen, reached out, clasped my hand in hers and closed her eyes. I gently extricated my hand, kissed hers, and left.

The phone was ringing as I walked into my hotel room. I picked it up. It was Anka. Zdenka was gone. It seemed impossible. I'd just been with her. I'd be seeing her the next day. Now she had died. Everything happened so quickly. Quickly, and yet, how like her to hang on until we were together one last time. I was comforted by the thought that Zdenka waited to say goodbye and then embraced death as she embraced life, full speed ahead. I never met a more talented, more intelligent, more resilient, more resourceful, more generous, more joyful person.

Summer ended. Zdenka's lawyers tended to her existing will. I received certain personal properties including her mother's fan. The adoption papers, however, had not been drawn up. I was not her legally adopted son. Zdenka had been unable to carry out her desired plan, but our bond needed no further strengthening.

In the decades since her death, Zdenka's identifying sobriquet, the Propeller Girl, was detached from its originator and adopted by models, performance artists, and the occasional ecdysiast. In 2002, although I seriously doubt that he knew of the original, Peter Stuart, an American singer-songwriter, wrote a song entitled, "Propeller Girl". For me, the lyrics capture part of Zdenka's whirlwind personality.

Propeller girl
You spin me 'round again
Every time you come around
Everything I know goes out the window

It all comes back to you
What you do, what you do.

Zdenka certainly did do a lot, not only for me but for all who were privileged to know her. I am so very gratified at this opportunity to bring the one and only Propeller Girl back where she belongs, centre stage. *Dekuji, moje česká matko. Díky, za všechno.* (Thank you, my Czech mother. Thank you for everything.)

As a dance teacher and performer, Zdenka played a key role in the spread and popularization of dances including the Cakewalk

Zdenka's mother, Josefina Javůková
Podhajská, performed at the Vienna
Court Opera. Her father was the
eminent Austro-Hungarian officer
and Czechoslovak Army General
Alois Podhajský

Zdenka as a child dancer

At the peak of her career

Zdenka discovered the art of dance in Vienna where she spent a significant part of her childhood and youth. Later, she lived in Brno, on the Côte d'Azur, in Paris, and in Prague. She returned to Vienna where she spent the rest of her long life.

A sketch of Zdenka by the noted Czech artist, Jan Zrzavý

89

6.
Czechmates

From 1961 to 1964, I continuously travelled to and from Prague. During those years, I relied on Zdenka to connect me with her endless circle of friends and acquaintances. I followed up on her leads and with her help and a lot of hard work, my projects moved forward. One major gain, I now could read Czech, which enabled me to directly research Czech sources along with French and German ones. Back then, English wasn't much help. Today is a different story, there's plenty of material on Czech music written in English.

At the beginning of my journeys to Prague I stayed with Zdenka. Her flat, however, was small and overcome with furnishings. What was comfortable for one was confining for two. Consequently, she arranged for me to rent a room in the home of her friends, Maria and Karel Svolinský. Karel, a member of the National Theatre, was an illustrious scenic designer and graphic artist; Maria was his first and third wife. They'd been married and divorced and during the break he married someone else. When he divorced his second wife, Maria came back to him. They remarried and lived happily ever after. The Svolinskýs were convivial people and Maria was a grand cook. I stayed with them whenever I went to Prague. To show my appreciation, I'd bring presents from London whenever I returned to Czechoslovakia. I did this for a few close friends. Blue jeans were the most coveted gifts, next came Beatles records, followed by silk stockings. One time I asked Maria Svolinská if she had a special request. Maria, a large woman who obsessed over every ounce she thought she'd put on, wasn't interested in jeans, the Fabulous Four, or hosiery, she had her eye on her own prize. "Please Brian, when you'll be in London, you'll get me *opasek*. Here is money, and also information for clerk." "What is *opasek*?" I asked. Giggling, Maria fetched the Czech-English dictionary, opened it, found her word and, still giggling, announced, *"Opasek* is girdle." She handed the book to me and I looked at the illustrated definition. I honestly didn't know what a girdle was until I was asked to purchase one and, while I didn't warm to the idea, I felt obliged to do as Maria requested. The mere notion of a twenty-four-year-old chap shopping for ladies' under-garments was daunting. I needed support. "Mum," I said to my mother one evening at dinner, "could you help me buy a girdle?" She looked at me quizzically. "What on earth are you talking about, Brian?" I explained and, bless her, she agreed not only to act as Maria Svolinská's very personal shopper but to do it on her own, thereby reliev-ing me of the burden. Maria was ecstatic when I brought her the goods. Tittering like a schoolgirl, she grabbed the package, ran into the bedroom, wriggled into the girdle and, with a gigantic negligée billowing around her like an open parachute, raced back into the living room. *"Krásá! Krásá!" (Beautiful! Beautiful!)* she shouted joyfully as, arms outstretched, she bounded towards me. The next thing I knew I was locked in her embrace. She danced me around the room crying, *"Hubička! Hubička!" (Kiss! Kiss!)* and smothered me with kisses. An appropriate reaction, perhaps, for a pair of jeans, or a Beatles record, or even a pair of silk stockings, but for a girdle? Incomprehensible.

The Svolinskýs hosted many social evenings with friends, two of whom, Josef Svoboda and Václav Kašlík, were regulars. Svoboda, as I've mentioned, was one of the creators of Laterna Magica and a genius lighting director with the National Theatre. Kašlík, a stage and television director, was a musician trained as a pianist and conductor. (Sound familiar?) He invited me to accompany him to the Barrandov Film Studios where he was directing a production of *Rusalka* for Czech television. Watching him at work was an education. Excited and intrigued by the world of cameras and lights surrounding me, I wanted to explore it further and offered to do anything, including coffee runs, just to participate in some way. As a result, I became a gopher of sorts. Duly impressed by what Kašlik, a musician working in opera for the media, was doing, I filed the information somewhere in the back of my mind.

During my time in Czechoslovakia, Zdenka's munificence allowed me to hobnob with the creative elite in music, theatre, art, and television. Without realizing, I was building the foundation for my future. By spring of 1964, I'd finished researching the Smetana book and had added final touches to the Martinů research. I worked in tandem on both hoping that the latter would ride the former's coattails into the presses. I'd also done some preliminary work on Janáček knowing full-well that he'd have to wait a while. And then the time came to return home for good. With Zdenka safe in Vienna there would be no need for me to commute between London and Prague. I said goodbye to my Czech friends not knowing when I would return, yet confident that it would happen soon. It did happen, but not "soon".

Back in London I began writing the Smetana book. By then, my hectic schedule offered less and less spare time.

Throughout my undergraduate years, I'd remained in my parents' home. Why not? I was still a student, my quarters were comfortable, my piano was there, and the rent (zero pounds) was unbeatable. But, once my academic degrees were under my belt and my writing projects on their way, I moved to a place of my own, a one-bedroom flat in South London. To support myself I followed the tried-and-true game plan for young musicians by giving concerts and, in my specific case, doing freelance choral conducting. Solo piano recitals weren't that easy to come by for fledgling musicians and the five-pound fee was barely profitable. You had to wear formal dress (white tie and tails!) when performing which, for most of us, meant renting a proper outfit from Moss Bros in Covent Garden—at a cost of two and a half pounds. Transportation had to be added in, too. The profit margin barely existed. Fortunately, I recalled a bit of practical advice from my erstwhile teacher, Dame Myra. "Once you're out there performing, Brian, it's a lot easier to sell yourself as part of a piano duo rather than as a soloist. People like to get more for their money. Two for the price of one is irresistible." Dame Myra's sage counsel in mind, I joined forces in duo piano ventures with Sven Weber, a former student at the Royal Academy. Sven was a first-rate pianist and a congenial colleague. We gave concerts in London as well as in the provinces and made a niche for ourselves. Dame Myra had been spot on, it's definitely easier to make it as a team. One concert stands out. Sven and I gave the first performances in England of Martinů's *Three Czech Dances for Two Pianos*. Sadly, shortly after that, Sven's left hand became paralyzed and the poor fellow had to stop playing. He asked Valerie Tryon, a fine artist to replace him, and the Large/Tryon duo fulfilled all the Large/Weber engagements.

Doing concert work is a good way to keep in practice and to put your name out there, however, it's rarely profitable enough to make a decent living. Realizing that I needed full time employment, I applied for a position as Head of Music for the Strand School in South London. To be honest, I never thought I'd get the job, but I did. The Strand, an eminent boys' grammar school founded in 1893, had an excellent choir and orchestra, and for the next couple of years I was in my element teaching music classes, conducting the choir and orchestra, giving piano lessons, playing concerts, and writing books. Music made my world go round. Still, my aspirations impelled me towards a higher goal. I wanted to be a university professor. I had the qualifications, a doctorate, teaching experience, and I was on my way to publishing not one but two, and hopefully, three music biographies. Somewhere inside my skull, I realized that being a published author would play an important role in getting me a university post. In short, while I was quite content at the Strand School, I was focused on the advanced halls of academe.

At last, the Smetana book was finished. I brought the manuscript to Colin Haycraft and as I handed over the result of my labours, cheekily reminded him that Martinů waited in the wings. Haycraft smiled, mumbled "we'll see, we'll see", took the manuscript, and told me that he'd be in touch. A few days later, he called to say that Duckworth would be pleased to publish my book. "Wonderful!" I crowed, and not wanting to let any opportunity go by, quickly slipped in another *aide-mémoire*. "Now will you consider the Martinů biography? Oh, and after that, I've got one on Janáček in mind." Haycraft laughed aloud. "Hold on, Mr Large, hold on, first things first. Let's see what happens. If the Smetana book does well, then we'll consider Martinů and anyone else you choose to write about." Music to my ears.

Smetana by Brian Large was published on 22 October 1970. The book was dedicated to my parents who were pleased as Punch. As for me, I was euphoric. For weeks, I could not pass a Waterstones, a WH Smith, a Dillons, a John Menzies or any of the bookshops that were so many once, without popping in. Nor can I adequately describe what a lift I got seeing my book on a store shelf—move over Henry James, D.H. Lawrence, and Virginia Woolf. Totally infatuated by my publication, I blush to admit that on quite a few occasions I had no qualms about picking up *Smetana* and moving him to a more advantageous selling spot. Somehow, I don't think that I'm the lone first-time author who has indulged in such shenanigans. The publication of *Smetana* was an incredibly important breakthrough for me. The brash young man with zero credentials who'd boldly proposed a book to a venerable publisher had proven himself. What's more, Duckworth kept their promise. They were, I was informed, looking forward to publishing my book on Bohuslav Martinů. I called Charlotte and Zdenka to tell them the good news. Both were elated. "Wonderful, darlink," Zdenka enthused, "next will be coming Janáček!"

Martinů by Brian Large was published on 1 May 1975. This book was dedicated to Stanley Spratt. Duckworth was satisfied enough with the sales to give me the go ahead on the third book. I planned not only to write Janáček's biography, but to include, as well, an informal history of Czech Opera. Naturally, I needed to do more research and immediately applied for a visa which, with no reason given, was denied. Talk about being taken aback, I was completely baffled. I asked a friend in the diplomatic corps to do a bit of snooping.

He obliged and informed me that I had become persona non grata in Czechoslovakia and was no longer welcome. "I wouldn't push it", he advised. "It could be dangerous if you returned." I found this hard to believe. After all the times I'd been there? What was going on? Had my smuggling days with Zdenka been revealed? The reason, I soon discovered, was utterly bizarre and a perfect example of the convoluted absurdity of the communist regime. Apparently, my book on Smetana had created a political brouhaha for a most preposterous reason. While fact-finding, I discovered that the composer, who died at the age of sixty, had been deaf for the last ten years of his life. Despite the devastating circumstances, Smetana, like Beethoven, wrote some of his most significant works during that period. His deafness, and how he dealt with it greatly interested me and I determined to find out more. In checking arcane medical records, I discovered that Smetana had contracted syphilis some twelve years before his death in 1884. Mercury, the prescribed treatment for syphilis in those days, produced damaging side effects, among them sensorineural hearing loss and impaired speech perception. Sure enough, after intensive treatment, Smetana's hearing eroded, and he soon became stone deaf. I wanted to be honest in my writing and quoted directly from medical records that Smetana's deafness was triggered by mercury poisoning and that his premature death was due to syphilis. After my book was published, as a courtesy (yes, and to let them know about the book), I sent a copy to the Smetana Museum in Prague and unwittingly set up my own banishment. The Museum looked at the book and immediately passed it on to the Ministry of Culture, which august body then denounced me. The gist of their tirade ran something like, Brian Large has defamed a great national artist; Smetana was pure, he did not have syphilis, he just went deaf all of a sudden. Ergo, Brian Large made up the whole thing and is a consummate liar. The result of this nonsense? I became an "undesirable", a status that ended both my quest to revisit Czechoslovakia and to memorialize Leoš Janáček.

All of this occurred long ago but, very recently, noteworthy details came to light. My dear friend Véronique Firkušny, daughter of the late Czech pianist, Rudolf Firkušny, put me in touch with Jaroslav Mihule, Zdenka's studio pianist with whom I'd become friendly in my early years in Prague. I hadn't seen or heard from Jaroslav in over fifty years. During that time, my former acquaintance had become a distinguished musicologist, university educator, and diplomat. Véronique met him on a trip to Prague and, by happenstance, learned of our earlier association. She urged me to contact him. In January of 2022, I sent an email reintroducing myself and, in hopes that he might have something to add, revealed that I was working on my memoirs. In response, Jaroslav emailed back a most enlightening account of what had transpired behind the Iron Curtain during *l'affaire Smetana*.

When Supraphon Music Publishers tried to publish a Czech translation of my book, the Politburo blocked it. Wrote Jaroslav,

The decisive sentence in one chapter was said to be the cause, and I quote from memory (fifty years later!)—"for it is so painful that one of the greatest spirits of nineteenth century Czech culture died of syphilis". That was too much for the hypocritical morality of semi-educated politicians. How come he's publicly associating Smetana with such an ugly thing! We can't print that!

This account corroborated what my diplomat friend had told me at the time I was barred from Czechoslovakia.

Jaroslav went on to write that the sixties held a promise of a possible democratic future and that my activity in his country was

> *… a breath of freedom, a break through the stale and painful fifties. You were a messenger from a better democratic world, the one that Zdenka Podhajská reminded us of in Prague with her every action and of which she was a kind of lonely survivor, shining through the darkness of totalitarianism.*

I was overwhelmed by his words. The fact that people, even in the worst of circumstances, can be inspired and uplifted by the truth is always encouraging. And his vindication of my work and his praise to Zdenka were particularly heartening. How satisfying to realize that one's actions can have such a positive effect on others. Still, the Janáček book never happened. My writing career began with Smetana and ended with Martinů.

Later, I did return to Czechoslovakia but as a member of a TV crew rather than a fledgling author. The BBC authorized filming of *The Music of Exile*, a Martinů documentary based on portions of my book and I assisted Anthony Wilkinson in the filming. I couldn't get a visa on my own but my big brother, BBC TV could. What a joyous time I had reuniting with friends in Prague and Polička. After the communists were overthrown, I often returned to Česká, the alternate name for what today is the Czech Republic. Most recently, I flew to Prague in September of 2021 to chair the Jury of the Golden Prague International Television Competition.

Over the years, I've received tangible acknowledgements for this unusual relationship between a man and a country not his own. Included among these tributes are a medal of honour from the Martinů Foundation, a Lifetime Achievement Award from Czech Television, and, perhaps most heartwarming, an honorary citizenship from Polička. My ties to the Czech Republic, forged in the worst of times, have remained strong. I am proud, and humbled, to know that I played a small role in helping to keep alive the great spirit of a great country. Yes, I was censured for telling the truth about Bedřich Smetana, but in the end, as the Czech national motto proclaims, *Pravda vítezí*! *(Truth prevails!)*

Radio Times (Incorporating World-Radio) April 16. 1964. Vol. 163: No. 2110.

APRIL 18—24

Radio Times

SIXPENCE   LONDON AND SOUTH-EAST

BBC
tv
Sound

BBC 1
BBC 2

BBC-2 opens this week

feingnum

7

The Beeb and I

By 1964, my life had settled into a routine, a pleasant one, but none the less, routine. I wrote books, taught at the Strand School, conducted choirs, gave piano lessons, and played solo and duo piano recitals. I was immersed in music which is exactly what I wanted. However, my sights had been raised. Much as I liked teaching at the Strand School, I remained on the lookout for a university post, the operative word being "patience". I continued my day-to-day activities even as I contemplated an upward move. And it came, though not in academia as I'd expected but, of all places, from my constant childhood companion, the British Broadcasting Corporation.

Occupied solely with defence efforts during World War II, the BBC, the world's leading presenter of radio and TV, returned to normal broadcasting on 7 June 1946. Operating with one channel, and despite the incursion of commercial TV in the mid-fifties, the BBC continued to dominate the radio and TV broadcasting waves. By the mid-sixties, enough interest, and enough money, had been generated to start a second channel, and BBC2 was scheduled to launch on 20 April 1964. Unfortunately, the gala opening night had to be cancelled when a fire at Battersea Power Station caused a blackout across West London. Thus, instead of the planned formal festivities, BBC2 unobtrusively slipped into being the following morning with an episode of *Play School*, a kiddie show. Together, BBC1 and BBC2 ruled the airwaves with the latter playing the role of intellectual little sister to big brother BBC1. Big Brother reigned supreme as a giant mainstream general entertainment and news venue while little sister transmitted to a loyal minority audience interested in the arts and history.

One morning while reading music reviews in *The Daily Telegraph*, an advertisement caught my eye. The advert stated that British Broadcasting Corporation was seeking a highly qualified musician or academic to join its staff to direct music programmes for their new channel, BBC2. I read the ad a few times, and each time it became clearer to me that I'd stumbled into my future. *The Daily Telegraph's* motto, "was, is, and will be", reprinted every day in its editorial pages, proved prophetic in my case. I had all the qualifications BBC2 desired. In the past, I'd been an academic, at present I was a performer, a working pedagogue with a doctorate, who had meticulously observed the workings of Czech television. "Was" and "is" were both in my grasp, and, thanks to the advertisement I had a clear vision of the "will be". In a flash, all thoughts of "Professor" Brian Large fled. The BBC called, and I would answer. This was not a slapdash decision. Music was my mission in life and here was an opportunity to present music, not simply as a teacher or as a performer or as a writer, but, rather, as part of a media monolith able to bring music to the widest possible audience. Straightaway, I wrote to the BBC requesting an interview. Shockingly, they turned me down. Crushed, but unwilling to take no for an answer, I swallowed my pride and wrote another letter. This time I included a brief résumé of my career to date, highlighting my experiences behind the Iron Curtain in Prague where I had seen Czech TV techniques at work. Dropping names with total abandon, especially Svoboda and Kašlík, powerhouse figures even in the West, I tied up everything by suggesting that the BBC might want to reconsider and grant me an interview. They did.

The BBCTV offices and studios were based in West London's Shepherd's Bush where, in October of 1964, I went for an interview with Antony Craxton, a well-known producer and director. Craxton came from a distinguished artistic family. His father, Harold, a composer and pianist, had accompanied Nellie Melba and John McCormack, and taught at the Royal Academy. His sister, Janet, was first oboe in the BBC Symphony Orchestra, and his brother, John, was an established painter. Tony Craxton worked in the BBC's Outside Broadcast Services and was especially

Producer
Anthony Craxton, 1973

renowned for documenting state events for the royal family beginning at a time when the convention dictated avoiding the intimacy of close-ups. Tony was the first to direct royal television broadcasts and eventually became the major producer for all royal ceremonial occasions, a big deal as the media thrived (thrives) on its coverage of the crown. Craxton's directorial skills guided major events from Princess Margaret's wedding to Prince Charles's Investiture as Prince of Wales.

At my interview, Craxton was cordial, thorough, and particularly interested in what I'd observed about cameras, lights, and lenses in Prague. Among other queries, he wanted to know how I would approach the job if it were offered, further, how would I use the medium to communicate. We talked for about three hours, shook hands, and said goodbye. A short while later, I received a second letter telling me that, along with a few others, I was being considered for the position. The letter ended with, "Would you return for a second interview?" Would I? Were they kidding?

Mr Craxton was not present at that second encounter rather, an official group of administrators from various departments posed questions testing my musical knowledge. For example, I was asked if I knew the composer of *The Swan of Tuonela*. I said I was familiar with Sibelius's score and spoke about it for a bit. "How would you direct *The Swan* in a concert at Albert Hall?" came the next query. I thought for a moment. Remembering the long and beautiful cor anglais solo, I suggested that, apart from showing the instrument and the player I would look for an attractive girl in the audience and build her emotional facial reactions into the shooting script. In time, this manner of filming would become a signature of my technique. (Twenty years later, when documenting Vladimir Horowitz's return to Moscow after a sixty-year absence, I spotted a middle-aged gentleman in the audience. His eyes half-closed, a trace of a smile on his lips, he sat there enraptured as tears slowly ran down his cheeks, a single close-up that told the whole story.) After a few more enquiries about my Czech television experiences and my current teaching experiences at the Strand School, the interview ended.

Three weeks later, I received another letter. This time I was asked to come and meet with Desmond Osland, a senior administrator for BBCTV. A genial fellow, Osland got right to the point. "Well Brian, we've interviewed you and we like you very much. You have excellent qualifications in music, and you're a performer so you know what it's like to perform. What's more, you saw how TV works when you were in Prague." I basked in his words as he continued. "All things considered we are prepared to offer you the post." (Bingo!) "But we want to make certain that we'll be happy with you and, equally important, that you'll be happy with us." I wanted to jump out of my chair and shout "Oh, I'll be happy!" but managed to control myself as he went on. "Let me ask you a question, Brian. How much are you earning in your current teaching job?" I told him. "Well, we are prepared to pay you three times as much as you're getting now." Struggling to maintain my composure I, again, resisted the urge to leap from my seat. "Here's how we're going to do it. We're going to offer you a trial, make-or-break, three-month contract. We'll give you two months to take everything in and during that time, you'll have the run of the studios to observe how things work from newscasts to dramas, from sports events to concerts. We'll show you how the BBC works and how BBC television functions. At the end of the two months, we'll give you a thousand-pound budget to create a television production of your own choosing. You'll be given the run of the studio and the use of all the facilities to choose and direct whatever you want. At the end of the third month, when your production is completed, we'll have a closed-circuit viewing. If we feel that what you've done is promising, you'll be given a full-time position. If we don't, we'll shake hands and say goodbye. Will you accept our offer?" Suddenly, the urge to leap from my chair had been replaced by a deeper concern that I'd fall out of it. Would I accept? You bet your life I would.

The minute I got home I called my parents who were overjoyed to hear the news. The BBC was the pinnacle, the absolute ne plus ultra and their son was going to be part of it. I had been given the opportunity of a lifetime. Neither of them paid the slightest heed to the possibility that I might not pass the final test. As far as Ruby and John Large were concerned, the appointment was signed, and soon to be sealed and delivered. Immodestly, I was pretty confident, myself. Everything felt right.

On 15 January 1965, I reported to work and was given a temporary office (cubicle), a desk, a chair, and a telephone. I had barely settled in when Antony Craxton dropped by. I got up, put out my hand and said, "Good to see you, Mr Craxton." "Call me Tony", he quickly responded. "I just wanted to welcome you and to tell you that if there's anything I can do to help or if you have any questions, don't hesitate to come and see me. And, by the way, I really wanted you for the job and am delighted that you accepted." I thought it was splendid of him to greet me in such a warm and encouraging manner. I couldn't have been happier.

8.
Back to School

In the 1960s, befitting a broadcasting behemoth, the BBC maintained its own in-house training facility for directors and producers. Along with ten other recruits from all over the Commonwealth, I participated in a four-week cram course covering the length and breadth of television broadcasting. Through lectures and demonstrations given by senior members of the production staff and technical experts, we trainees learned the ins and outs of television production. We were taught how to use pedestal cameras, crane cameras, handheld cameras, and camera mountings, as well how to manage the various lenses. We studied lighting techniques, graphic design, and costume and make-up design. We were shown how to shoot interviews, how to write spoken text/narration to newsreel footage, how to add music and sound to pre-shot material and how to edit filmed sequences such as car chases, men fighting, battle sequences, etc. ... Perhaps most important, we learned how to write a camera script with precise and meaningful instructions. If it sounds like a lot to learn in a month, I assure you it was.

Considering the advanced state of movie filming, technically speaking, television was positively primitive in the mid-1960s. Primitive is a harsh word yet what we were doing was comparable to a caveman doggedly swinging a club to a tennis player dexterously wielding a racket. A protocol existed, not a concept. For example, the established

A 1960s TV camera bulging
with turret lenses

method of televising concerts required four cameras, no more, no less: one on the left, one in the centre, one on the right, and one behind the orchestra. No matter what the music, the camera on the left would pan across and cut to the camera on the right. The camera on the right then would pan across the orchestra and cut back to the left, and thus they continued, back and forth, back and forth. Perhaps there'd be a frontal shot of the conductor from the fourth camera. Should a trumpet, say, have a solo, the director would shout into the microphone, "find me the trumpet!" But by the time the cameraman heard the cue, it usually was too late. I don't want to belittle what people were doing, let's just say it was early and, thankfully, things improved.

The television industry had inherited filming techniques and equipment directly from the film studios of the twenties and thirties, the difference being, TV programmes were live broadcasts. The only way to preserve them was through the kinescope process, a simplistic method in which a 16mm film camera placed in front of a TV monitor recorded programmes directly from the TV screen. The resulting film strip reproduced and reduced everything to a blurry, black-and-white, painful-to-watch replica. Those of us who lived through telerecording (kinescope) remember it as a blighted blessing. Programmes could be preserved but at the cost of artistry, not to mention clarity. A blessing came when Ampex, an American electronics company, invented the first magnetic video tape recorder to which TV signals were transmitted directly. I cut my teeth on the video tape recorder and while the final product was a vast improvement over telerecording, the editing process was crude and cumbrous. Holding a razor blade in his hand, the editor would kneel on the floor over the recording machine head. The director hovered above him watching the tape's progress on a monitor. Spying an edit point, the director would tap the editor on the head, and the editor would mark the cut point on the tape. The head bopping method did not guarantee precision, cuts were more approximate than exact. Like I said, crude. Editing continued to be rough going until Ampex introduced a linear video tape recorder and tapes could be edited electronically. By the end of the sixties, along with the introduction of colour, we had moved into the era of electronic digital editing. One drawback, however, still remained. Digitally edited tape, stored on huge reels, required an inordinate amount of storage space. Consequently, *space* became the operative word at the BBC. Forms were filled out to preserve a tape for six months or a year and then another set of forms would be filled out, and so on. Administrators regularly assessed the tapes. Reels marked "Of Historical or National Importance" allegedly were exempt from erasure. A drama starring Lawrence Olivier probably would survive; a church service, never. As time passed and because of the BBC's inevitable descent into bureaucracy, editorial judgement could be made by just about any senior administrator. The treasures that were lost because of this loose policy is beyond imagining. I can think of no better example of shelf-life carnage than a project with which I was directly involved.

I had been invited to direct the video of Benjamin Britten conducting his masterpiece, *Peter Grimes*, for what Britten announced would be the last time. Realizing the historical importance of this event, I immediately requested an additional camera placed on Britten for the entire taping. Everyone agreed it was a good idea. I filled out the necessary paper work to ensure that the tapes, especially the one featuring Britten conducting, would have maximum protection. The tapes were stored away. A few years later, while working on another project, I needed to refer to the Britten/*Grimes* recordings. When I went to the storage reels, I found every other tape connected to the programme except the one I was after. The specific Britten conducting tape had disappeared. Without much effort, I pieced the story together. Despite the attached paperwork attesting to the historic significance of Britten's conducting, some supervisor in search of storage space had deemed it extraneous and had it erased. The BBC grew lax in preserving its treasures and all in the name of more space. When digitalization took over, techniques became more organized and sophisticated and actual physical storage space no longer mattered.

The four-week BBC tutorial prepared me for the future. How fortunate I was to be part of that all-embracing training course. What I learned expanded and solidified my knowledge, stimulated my creative imagination, and provided a solid basis for my career.

9.
Close-ups

Nine days into my BBC residency, on 24 January 1965, Sir Winston Churchill suffered a stroke and died at the age of ninety. Six days later, although not a royal himself, Churchill would be accorded a funeral fit for a king. Royalty and dignitaries, both domestic and foreign, attended; two thousand five hundred soldiers and civilians took part in the procession, an estimated one million onlookers lined the streets, and the world watched via television as Sir Winston went to his reward. Who could imagine that at the same time he was laid to rest, the late great British Bulldog became an unwitting progenitor in my good fortune?

On the very day Winston Churchill died, the Queen issued a royal decree stating that his burial would reflect his importance in Britain's history, an unprecedented royal send-off for a commoner. Naturally, the BBC would televise the occasion and, of course, the coverage was placed in the hands of Antony Craxton, who received the official order of events. Churchill's body would lie in state for three full days in Westminster Hall, the funeral service would take place in St Paul's Cathedral, after which the coffin would be transported to the Tower of London and placed on a barge. The barge then would sail down the Thames to Waterloo Pier; from there, the coffin would be carried into Waterloo Station and transferred to the funeral train, and the train would carry the late Prime Minister to his final resting place. Churchill had many choices for his

Igor Stravinsky conducting the New Philharmonia
Orchestra in a programme of his music at the Royal
Festival Hall, London, 1965

burial site, including Westminster Abbey, but he'd opted for St Martin's Churchyard, Bladon, West Oxfordshire, his family's burial ground. From Westminster Hall to the funeral train's departure, the BBC would follow the coffin every step of the way. Pathé News also covered the funeral but this was a film company, their newsreels would be distributed around the world and viewed later on. BBCTV provided the main live output.

Once he knew the funeral cortege's complete route, Tony Craxton had to position his cameras in strategic, geographic locations throughout the city. The simple truth is, covering significant occurrences is all about positioning. From inside St Paul's to Waterloo Station, thirty-six cameras (one, or two, or clusters of three and four) were set up on the ground, on balconies, and on rooftops in exactly the right spots for maximum coverage. An event of such magnitude could not be managed from inside a studio control room. Consequently, the transmission equipment—monitors, microphones, and cables—was set up in banked rows inside St Paul's huge crypt, transforming the cavernous sepulchre into control headquarters. When everything was ready to go, I got lucky. Tony invited me to join the technicians in the crypt for both the rehearsal and the actual broadcast. Barely two weeks on the job and I'd be eyewitnessing a renowned director handle a monumental television transmission.

The day of the funeral I sat in the back of St Paul's vast undercroft and watched as Tony Craxton captured the moment, every aspect of which he'd planned and organized. Wearing a headset, microphone hanging round his neck, he sat in front of a wall of TV screens, watching, listening, and issuing orders. He knew exactly where each camera stood. He also knew precisely what shots he wanted and chose them quickly and brilliantly. For over four hours, Tony, cool as a cucumber, wielded total authority as he followed the cortège from location to location, cajoling the cameramen to do their best. "Camera 15, get closer. I want to see the Queen's reaction as the coffin is brought in. Come on, camera 20, you can get that shot of those two boys handing out cigars. Camera 31, grab the old man in uniform." Considering the magnitude of this broadcast, he had to have been a bit nervous yet he never raised his voice. A sense of calm suffused the crowded crypt for the entire transmission and it all emanated from the director. Gracious, and full of gratitude for the crew, he thanked each of the cameramen before moving on to the next segment. Tony Craxton set the tone which resulted in an iconic transmission as well as an object lesson in civility.

By all accounts, the most memorable and moving image of the day occurred in the Port of London. As the funeral barge floated by a row of cranes standing tall on the dock, one by one the cranes dropped their jibs as if bowing in tribute. According to the press, that gesture produced a lot of "lumps in a lot of throats". The scene can be viewed on YouTube and remains impressive. The backstory, however, is equally arresting. In an accompanying YouTube segment, a dockworker relates the true story of the bowing cranes, one which belies the accepted reverential version. With all due respect to his wartime leadership, many of the then working class didn't love Churchill who constantly battled with the trade unions. In fact, the regular crane operators refused to "bow" them and had to be replaced by operators who were paid exorbitant fees. The dockworker relating the tale disarmingly admitted that although he didn't much care for Churchill and had no respect whatsoever for the mercenaries operating the jibs, he, too, had been moved to tears at the sight of the saluting cranes.

While watching Tony Craxton at work that day, I learned the fundamentals of my trade and was given a masterclass in the art of video directing. One manifestation of his technique particularly impressed me. As he went about his tasks, waving his arms, pointing here, pointing there, pulling in everything, shaping it, and sending it out again, it struck me that Tony was "conducting". The director's chair was his podium and, in much the same manner as an orchestra leader, he brought all the elements together, choosing the best, and setting them forth. I liked what he did and following his lead became a "video conductor" myself.

After the Churchill hullabaloo died down, besides attending the BBC training sessions, I spent my time wandering around the studios gathering information and steeping myself in all aspects of television programming. During meals or tea breaks, I'd talk to directors, to members of the various crews—camera, lighting, scenery, costumes, make-up—to all participants who would explain how they functioned. I watched, talked, listened, and learned for eight weeks, at which point I was ready to begin. When asked, "So, Brian, what are you going to do for us?" my answer was swift. "An opera, I want to direct an opera." I knew what they were thinking. "Do an opera? This guy must be crazy." Look, I wasn't crazy. I knew I could do an opera for a thousand pounds, not a big one like *Ada* (sic), but a little one like Gian Carlo Menotti's *The Telephone*, a forty-minute piece with two characters, a soprano and a baritone. That's the one I chose and, oh, did I ever stretch that thousand pounds as far as it could go. An orchestra was out of the question, so I arranged the score myself for two pianos, hired a couple of terrific pianists, and paid them fifty pounds each. With nine hundred pounds left, I went to the Royal Academy in search of young singers who'd be willing to learn and perform for a hundred pounds each, not a lot of money for a lot of effort. Indeed, more a "favour" than a job. But, if they were willing to take a chance, I might be able to return the favour one day. Happily, I found a fine enthusiastic pair, Wendy Eathorne and Michael Rippon. The bankroll now stood at seven hundred pounds. Six hundred of that went for scenery and costumes and I used fifty pounds to hire an assistant, someone to type the scripts, prepare the camera cards and do whatever else was needed. I deliberately left fifty pounds unspent to show that I could accomplish everything and still come in under budget.

When all the components were assembled, the Brian Large production of *The Telephone* was assigned to Studio D in the legendary Lime Grove Studios. Originally built by the Gaumont Film Company in 1915, Lime Grove, the first building erected in England solely to produce films, poured out melodramas, thrillers, and comedies starring the likes of Margaret Lockwood, James Mason, Patricia Roc, and Stewart Granger. Not to be overlooked, Alfred Hitchcock fashioned *The Lady Vanishes* in that hallowed space. The BBC took over Lime Grove Studios in 1949. Sixteen years later, the Corporation still used them even as construction continued on a new BBC TV centre in West London. Given the run of Studio D, I devised the staging, directed the singers and, in the end, produced a black-and-white television show completely under budget.

Never actually broadcast, *The Telephone* was shown on closed circuit to a select group of BBC executives. I later learned that when the presentation ended, Tony Craxton stood up and said, "Give that man the job." The morning after the "world" premier I was called in, complimented on my work, and offered a lifetime contract. The BBC did things like that; they don't any more. Apologizing for my immodesty, I think I was unusual. If not, I surely was in the right place at the right time. I signed the contract and never looked back.

When I told my father and mother that the BBC wanted me to stay on, they were euphoric. Their "lazy little brat" had made it to the top. Employed by one of the country's most illustrious organizations for the rest of my working life, I would be generously pensioned at my retirement. Who could ask for anything more? On that cheery note was launched a long and productive association between the BBC and me, one that also enabled me to do something special for my parents.

The destruction of our Lambeth home during the Blitz had left its mark on the Larges. I had been forced to live with my grandfather, then sent away to the countryside to be with an ancient couple until my parents and I were reunited in tumbledown quarters in a one-horse town. My parents, accomplished artists, accepted their present surroundings and put all their efforts into my future. What's more, they never complained about anything, including our haphazard living arrangement. Conscious of their sacrifices during my childhood and adolescence, I fantasized that someday I would put a roof over their heads, their own roof, not a rented one. The opportunity arrived when my father retired. He and my mother wanted to move somewhere on England's south coast but the cost was prohibitive. My gainful employment with the BBC made it possible for me to purchase them a seaside cottage in Brighton. In one fell swoop, I turned my childhood fantasy and my parents' retirement dream into a reality.

My potential having been recognized because of *The Telephone*, I was officially hired by the BBC Outside Broadcast Unit and promptly tossed into the deep end of the directorial pool. For a while I crawled around in an assortment of utilitarian service tasks, none of which were particularly inspiring and most of which had nothing to do with music. *The Most Beautiful Grandmother*, an early reality show, was my first assignment followed by another competition show, *Who's Wearing the Silliest Socks?* Need I say more? I bounced from one to the other and then was assigned to cover a live Roman Catholic Mass. I wasn't a Catholic and knew nothing about the Mass; I had to do some research. The BBC maintained a department for everything and anything and each department had a head so I dropped in on the head of Religious Broadcasting to get the lowdown. Over a cup of tea, I was steeped in the essentials of the Catholic Mass. I learned that the priest genuflecting before the altar, a movement symbolizing everyone bowing as one, was the key shot. Or, as the department head put it, "That's what people are looking for and, every time it happens, the cameras must focus on it." Fortified with religious insights and facts, on a Sunday morning I rose at six and within an hour or so was positioning cameras inside a lovely little country church. "This is my first Catholic Mass", I confessed to the young priest. "Would you be good enough to tell me what you're going to do and when you're going to do it?" The priest obliged and, leading me around the altar, literally walked me through his routine. "Here's where I'll be, and then I'll do this and bow, and then I'll do that and bow, and then I'll speak in front of the altar and bow, and give the sacraments and the blessing and bow, and that's it." I scribbled a few notes and soon thereafter the congregants arrived. The organ rumbled and the Mass began. We got lovely shots of the church interior and the choir pouring their hearts into the hymns, and of the congregation following along in the prayer books and hymnals. As for the priest, well, he raced around the church apse making all the genuflections that he'd outlined but at breakneck speed, stopping for a millisecond, and promptly dashing off again. I couldn't keep up with him. The result?—not a single bow made it to the screen. The following day, I was put on the block. "How could you do such a terrible job? You missed the essence of the Mass. This is appalling." "I'm sorry, I'm so sorry. I did my best. But I told you, I'm not a Catholic. Anyway, I was trained as a musician and this isn't music." "What are you talking about? Hymns are music." They tore me apart. But the good news was, I never again had to cover a Catholic Mass.

That's not to say that I didn't continue to receive assignments that were far afield of my interests. Tedious as some of them were, I ploughed through them all. Further along in my career, it fully dawned on me that those early light-headed shows had been invaluable. *The Beautiful Grandmothers*, *The Silly Socks*, even the misbegotten Mass, all of them forced me to think like a director and the more I thought like one, the more I acted like one.

Gradually, along with the run-of-the mill presentations, I was granted additional programmes that were right up my street, particularly a series of talk shows with musicians including pianist Denis Matthews, musicologist Deryck Cooke, and conductor Eugene Ormandy. Those programmes went beyond pointing a camera at a venerable senior citizen or at a pair of ridiculous socks. I had to record the intellectual musings of learned men of music and it was challenging. A director is both a recorder and a reporter and, to bring everything together, must have a concept in mind. It's no good saying, oh, I wonder what I should do with that? You must be ahead of the game.

In July of 1965, thanks to Tony Craxton, I took a giant step forward in my career. Tony decided to push the hatchling out of the nest and promptly stepped away from a Proms concert putting me in his place. The Proms were, are, and no doubt always will be, inexorably linked to the BBC. Founded in 1898 by Sir Henry Woods and held for eight weeks at the end of summer, The Henry Woods Promenade Concerts, affectionately and exclusively referred to as the Proms, is an endearing and enduring series of concerts held in London's Royal Albert Hall. While the music is classical, the atmosphere is relaxed. Casually dressed audiences are allowed, even encouraged, to walk about or promenade. "Prommers" (short for promenaders) are seated on the floor in an open arena in front of the orchestra, and pop up and down at will. Directing a Proms concert was a plum and my directorial debut was made even more special because Sir Malcolm Sargent, the Proms' chief conductor, was on the podium.

On the morning of the concert, I did all the procedurals—fussed over the camera positions, then held a camera, lighting, and audio rehearsal. That evening the programme was transmitted live. I thought everything went well and became a bit smug about my work. The next morning, following BBC routine, a critique took place. The opinions, a collection of faint praise, featured phrases like, "It was fine, it was good but it could be better." "A few cock-ups, but passable." "It's a work in progress and the way to make it better is to have more practice." More practice? That's what you want? Bring it on! And they did. I was given another concert, this time with Yehudi Menuhin playing the Beethoven Violin Concerto. After that, criticism mellowed. "Nice job, Brian", "Nice going", "Good work". I basked in the praise but, at the same time, I received no indication that I stood at the threshold of something big. Thus, when told that my third major assignment would be a live telecast of eighty-two-year-old Igor Stravinsky conducting his *Firebird Suite* with the New Philharmonia Orchestra, my response was a plaintive, "Why me?"—as if I needed to be given a reason for such an honour. The answer was swift and to the point. "We want you because you're a musician and we need someone who knows the score, figuratively and literally." I was agog. Who could believe my first opportunity to work with a composer conducting his own music would be with Igor Stravinsky! What's more, the concert would be done in the Royal Festival Hall, my childhood stomping ground, the "chicken coop". Further, it would be Stravinsky's last London appearance on the podium, a historical event. Because I knew the *Firebird Suite* backwards and forwards, I, indeed, was ahead of the game. Still, I pored over the score repeatedly and by the time I'd finished, I knew it backwards and forwards, and sideways, too. Fairly bursting with excitement, I arrived at the first rehearsal where I was introduced to, arguably, the greatest composer of the twentieth century.

Igor Stravinsky, a giant in the world of music but, in person, barely five feet three inches tall, was known to be sensitive about his height. Still, I wasn't prepared for how diminutive he appeared in person. No bigger than a minute, his whole being was dominated by a pair of eyeglasses perched on the end of his nose. (Marilyn Horne, who was very close to the composer, told me that in the days before progressive lenses, Stravinsky, while working, wore three pairs of glasses at the same time; one on top of his bald pate, one over his eyes, and the last hanging below his nose. He'd flip the glasses around to see close, normal, and distant.) The orchestra manager introduced me to the maestro, and as we shook hands, I desperately sought for appropriate words. What do you say at a time like this? I finally managed to squeak, "It's such an honour to meet you, sir." "Well, of course it is", chuckled Stravinsky as he turned and hobbled off on his cane. He needed the support yet, even tottering along, he seemed to bestride the world. Tiny, frail, brilliant, acerbic, but with a twinkle in his eye and an inner core of steel. Igor Stravinsky was indomitable.

Introductions over, the rehearsal began. An assistant discretely helped the maestro into a chair facing the orchestra. On the stand in front of him lay an open score which he used at the performance as well. He did not conduct from memory. Two cameras were placed at the back of the auditorium and on the right and left sides of the hall, standard procedure. A camera also was set up behind the musicians to capture the maestro "head on". Head-on shots allow viewers to see the conductor just as the musicians see him and usually are interspersed with multiple visuals of the orchestra. When directing a concert, you try to bring in the viewing audience by selecting the images that best reflect the music. On the simplest level, if the brass is dominating a section, then show the brass, or if a particular instrumentalist has a solo, then show the soloist. It's basic and makes sense but easily can become predictable. You must factor in not only the appropriate shot, but how long to hold it. The shooting must be fluid. It's part of the director's job to select the best possible images and choose how long to run them.

Stravinsky raised his arms and began to conduct. Completely mesmerized, I watched him on the head-on monitor. I could not take my eyes off him. He did not use a baton and his arm and hand movements—a steady one, two, three beat—were contained, nothing flamboyant. His composure, his steady gaze, the delicacy of his hands, the graceful sweep of his arms, all were under control, and yet beneath the calm exterior one felt the core passion. At one point I noticed that in preparation for page turns, Stravinsky would swipe the fingers of his left hand on his lips then flip the page with his moistened fingers. What an unabashedly disarming gesture, one I simply had to capture. The head-on camera needed to be on the conductor for a good stretch to fully realize his performance. At the same time, I kept saying to myself, too much of a good thing is too much of a good thing. You can overexpose people. It was a gamble but I knew the music and I was certain that Stravinsky's face would register everything. Now, I had to select the perfect musical spot to begin the lengthy coverage. About ten minutes before the conclusion of the *Firebird Suite*, Kastcheï, an evil magician, goes into a rhythmic dance that slowly builds to the explosive finale. I was convinced that Stravinsky would be at his peak during this passage and that those final ten minutes would have the ultimate dynamic impact. I made an instantaneous decision to reserve the sustained head-on shot for the end. During the actual broadcast, when the magician's dance began, I locked in the head shot of Stravinsky and it's stunning. Everything's there, the steady beat, the maestro's intense gaze, his fingers touching his lips as fleeting shadows of emotion play across his face. In one extraordinary moment, Stravinsky actually miscued the first horn's entry. Fortunately, the player brushed off the cue and came in correctly. Realizing his own error, Stravinsky, a grin dancing on his lips, mumbled a "thank you" to the first horn. Honestly, as many times as I've viewed it, the scene remains spellbinding. Vera Stravinsky, her husband's constant companion, told me it was one of the most impressive videos of her husband that she'd ever seen. (You can see for yourself on a YouTube excerpt, "Stravinsky Conducts the *Firebird*", Royal Festival Hall, 1965.) That concert marked the only time that I ever videoed Stravinsky, indeed, along with the rehearsals, this BBC2 event was the only time I was in his presence. I was blessed to be in the right place at the right time.

Stravinsky's broadcast dominated the music reviews and I received my first press notices. One critic wrote that he hoped the same innovative shots would be used in future programmes. I like to believe that I obliged that request throughout my entire career. Another bonus, a DVD was released which contained a Royal Ballet dance version of *The Firebird* coupled with the Stravinsky-led performance at the Royal Festival Hall. I remember thinking, "Two *Firebirds* for the price of one." The Stravinsky episode over, I went back to my regular routine but not for long; shortly thereafter came another lucky break.

10.
American Idol

In 1966, Leonard Bernstein, well known in England as the composer of *West Side Story* but not fully acknowledged as an orchestra conductor, wanted to rectify that situation and make his mark on UK podiums. To expedite matters, he allied himself with Ernest Fleishman, managing director of the London Symphony Orchestra, and Humphrey Burton, head of BBCTV's Music and Arts division. The result was a string of LSO concerts beginning with a live performance of Mahler's *Eighth Symphony* followed by a separate presentation of three symphonies (Sibelius's *Fifth Symphony*, Stravinsky's *The Rite of Spring*, and Shostakovich's *Fifth*) lumped under the collective title, "Symphonic Twilight". Bernstein's title for this project reflected his theory that the end of the symphonic era was upon us. Not only would Bernstein conduct the concerts, he also would speak directly to camera, explaining why he termed the series "Twilight" and commenting on his ideas. Named as the video director, I flew to Vienna where Bernstein was conducting *Falstaff* at the State Opera House and recording the Verdi masterpiece for Sony in the Sofiensäle concert hall.

I arrived in Vienna and went directly from the airport to Sofiensäle where I was taken to Bernstein's dressing room. Meeting Leonard Bernstein one immediately fell under his spell. An extremely handsome man and ridiculously charismatic, he could, and did, charm the birds right out of the trees. After an enthusiastic exchange of greetings,

Leonard Bernstein during
a mid-1960s rehearsal

Bernstein cut short the conversation. "Look, this really isn't the place for us to talk things over. And we can't do it tonight because I'm conducting at the State Opera, so why don't we get together tomorrow afternoon." In the next breath, he added, "Come to think of it, would you like to see *Falstaff*? You can sit in my box." Overwhelmed by his spontaneous generosity, I quickly accepted. "Great," he said, "meet me at the stage door a half-hour before the opera begins, and I'll give you your ticket." He left the dressing room and went back to the recording. On my way out, I slipped into the auditorium to watch Bernstein at work. His enthusiasm, not to mention his rapport with the musicians, impressed me.

After the rehearsal I checked into my hotel room, took a refreshing nap, and then went to the Staatsoper stage door. Bernstein arrived and handed over a ticket saying, "We'll meet up afterwards. Come back and see me." It was about 6:30; the opera began at seven, so I took the opportunity to take a look around the theatre and happily, if briefly, reacquaint myself with the Vienna State Opera House. Following which I went to the Maestro's box, took my seat, turned to the attractive lady seated beside me, and tendered a "good evening". She returned my greeting and began to converse in English. "Have you seen Mr Bernstein conduct before", she asked. "No", I answered. "Well, you are in for a treat." Nodding my head, I smiled.

The house filled, the lights lowered, Bernstein entered the pit, whereupon my companion went completely bonkers. Squeaking and squirming in her chair, she began clapping and cheering wildly. Bernstein stepped up to the podium, stood there, facing the audience and accepting the unbridled applause. He looked directly at the lady next to me, tilted his head in an obvious gesture of recognition, then turned and addressed the open score in front of him. A rose had been placed on the page. Bernstein picked up the flower, turned, and again looked up at my neighbour. Planting a kiss on the rose petals, he raised his arm, pointed the flower towards her, and turned back to the orchestra. Lifting the rose, he brought it down on the first note of *Falstaff*. In the next second, he quickly swapped the flower for his baton and continued conducting.

All during this interlude, writhing as if possessed, the lady next to me clung to her seat. Suddenly, she leaned over and loudly whispered in my ear, "Gott, das ist ein Mensch!" (God, what a man!) The first act ended. My neighbour turned to me saying, "Isn't he amazing?" "Indeed, he is", I responded. "I know about conductors", she replied, matter-of-factly. I'm sure you do was my thought; I said nothing. She looked at me intently. "I mean it; I know all about conductors. My husband was a conductor." "Really?" "Yes, I am Anita, the former wife of Herbert von Karajan. He was very good but not like Bernstein. Bernstein is absolutely magnetic. He hypnotizes the orchestra; he hypnotizes the audience, and he hypnotizes me. Most conductors don't do that kind of thing. I've never seen a conductor exactly like this man." At the time, I thought perhaps the ex-Madame von Karajan had gone a bit overboard. Still, she wasn't wrong about Leonard Bernstein's compelling effect. Indeed, he proved to be one of the most captivating human beings I ever met. One thing's for sure, I never saw another conductor give a downbeat with a rose.

The opera ended and after joining in the ovation, the former Mrs von Karajan, sans comment, flew out of the door and disappeared into the hallway. I made my way to Bernstein's dressing room and entered a scene reminiscent of the stateroom melee in the Marx Brothers' film

A Night at the Opera. Worshippers kept popping in to pay homage and it seemed that not a one popped out. It got to be pretty crowded. Prominent among the celebrants, the former Mrs von Karajan hovered over the seated Bernstein. Elbowing my way through the crowd I reached him and offered my heartfelt congratulations. Bernstein threw his arms around me, gave me a huge bear hug. (Bernstein definitely was the number one distributor of bear hugs in the music world. Full of life, music, and fun, the ebullient Mstislav Rostropovich was a close second). As I gasped to catch my breath, Bernstein insisted that I call him Lenny, and arranged to meet me the next day. With a quick nod to Mrs von Karajan who, by then, had wrapped herself around the conductor's chair, I took my leave. All these years and I've never forgotten that initial encounter with Lenny. I know I'm repeating myself, but he was irresistible.

The following afternoon we got together at his hotel and set up plans for the Mahler *Eighth* and the Symphonic Twilight. The former would be a single performance at the Royal Albert Hall. The latter would occupy two separate evenings; two symphonies would be shot in Fairfield Hall in Croydon and the third in the Royal Festival Hall. Lenny used the word "twilight" because he hypothesized that this was the end of the symphonic era after which symphonies no longer would be written. I didn't agree with his premise and I got the feeling that Lenny wasn't convinced of it, either. For me, symphonic twilight was more gimmick than logic, a convenient rubric under which he could lump together the three symphonies. Despite Lenny's dire prediction, composers, including Shostakovich, Sibelius, and even Bernstein himself, continued to write symphonies. Anyway, who really cared? My job was to record whatever theory Leonard Bernstein espoused.

After the *Falstaff*, rehearsals began for the televised live performance of Mahler's *Eighth* with Lenny, the London Symphony Orchestra, eight soloists, the Leeds Festival Chorus, the Orpington Chorale, the Highgate Boys Choir, and the Finchley Childrens Music Group. Called *The Symphony of a Thousand*, Mahler's *Eighth* is not often performed simply because the forces required are enormous. When we gathered for the first choral rehearsal it immediately became apparent that the Leeds Festival Chorus members, whose usual repertoire embraced the likes of Handel's *Messiah* and Mozart's *Requiem*, were out of their comfort zone. Not only was the chorus taxed by Mahler's complex chorale writing, there weren't enough of them to produce the robust, forceful sound the conductor wanted. Lenny hit the roof and began hurling insults at anything and anyone. "I need more singers, I must have a 'round' sound", he railed at the top of his lungs. Management quickly put out a call to various choral societies and began rounding up alternates to swell the ranks. It became a bit of a scramble because like the Leeds singers, the new choristers while at home with Handel and Mozart, were at sea when it came to Mahler. Last minute sessions in how to handle the exacting score were given until the chorus proved able to provide the punch and depth the conductor demanded. Once that happened, Lenny again became his enthusiastic, inspiring self and willed his musicians and singers into shape.

My main task during the rehearsals of the Mahler and the Symphonic Twilight, was to figure out how to capture the hyperbolic antics of the conductor. Nearing fifty, Leonard Bernstein remained vigorous, athletic, dramatic, and dynamic. On the podium, he became a study in motion, not just his arms but his entire body got into the act—leaping, crouching, twisting, turning, swaying, and high jumping. High jumping became a hallmark of his conducting. Every time a musical climax appeared in the score, he'd spring into the air to acknowledge its presence, just in case the musicians missed it. Climaxes abounded and Lenny bounded. During those early London sessions, I was adapting to his modus operandi, learning how to adjust to his geography, and geography is the word for it. He covered a lot of territory, leaning left, leaning right, backwards, forwards, arms above his head, then below his knees. Everything seemed choreographed and almost too complicated for the camera. And, hellishly frustrating for me. "Don't just do something, stand there!" I yearned to cry out. I did manage to get the camera close for the slow movements and extracted a few headshots here and there. And what a noble head lay on those gyrating shoulders, like some Roman carving of a classical bust—lofty brow, piercing eyes, prominent but well-shaped nose, generous mouth, and firm chin. Truly, this was a handsome man. And boy, did he know it.

After one rehearsal, we looked at some of the video tapes together and Lenny gushed with enthusiastic praise. "What a great musician you are, Brian. All these shots so well placed. Oh, it's so musical, the woodwinds, perfect here. Oh, and the strings there. And the brass. Good, good, good. Yes! Oh, you absolutely understand the musical structure." I may even have been blushing when he paused from his lavish compliments to add, "But, you know Brian, … somehow, I think it might be a little more interesting to look at me rather than the violins, or the horns, or the brass. See!" he crowed, placing his index finger on the viewing screen, "… just look at this moment, look at my eyes, they're so expressive." Instantly, everything became clear to me. Not only was Lenny conducting the orchestra, he was conducting me and calling the shots, not every single shot, but almost every other one. The video would be a document with him, of him, and for him. I learned a lot about my craft while working with Leonard Bernstein.

I often am asked what is the most difficult art form to capture, is it drama, opera, ballet, a recital, an orchestra concert? Quite honestly, I don't think anything's too difficult to document. Everything is possible and doable as long as you know what you're trying to say. Whatever art form you're taping, you're telling a story and you have to know how to translate the material into visual terms. Going back to Bernstein. Say you're recording Lenny conducting Sibelius's *Fifth Symphony*. You've got two ways to approach it and when you decide which way you want to go, you cut your cloth accordingly. Do you want to tell the story of Bernstein's idiosyncratic, flamboyant, conducting technique? Or, do you want to tell the story of Sibelius's *Fifth Symphony*. Which comes first, the chicken or the egg, the composer or the conductor? In this instance, the obvious way to attract an audience is to present Lenny conducting Sibelius. ("Oh, Leonard Bernstein's conducting. Who did you say was the composer?") But if you have a nobody conducting, then you take the other route. You emphasize Finland's greatest composer, Jean Sibelius's mighty *Fifth Symphony* with its magnificent "swan hymn" finale inspired by the sight of sixteen swans flying in formation overhead. "One of my greatest experiences!" wrote the composer. "Lord God, that beauty!" This way, Jean Sibelius is the bell ringer. However, just as some people are above the law, some conductors are above the composer. Knowing who or what to emphasize is essential.

I dare say, Bernstein could take on any composer and lead the way. As for his activities on the podium, many disliked his style but even those who deplored his perpetual motions had to respect his musical integrity. An acrobat, a tumbler, a jumping-jack, yes, he was all that, but his authenticity, his commitment, and his genius could not be denied. He himself said, "I can't live one day without hearing music, playing it, studying it, or thinking about it." He believed in the music and he believed in his way of translating it to the public. Put it this way, Leonard Bernstein was hundred per cent sincere but his working method was highly personal. You either got him or you didn't. Most, got him.

On 17 April 1966, a packed Royal Albert Hall, which included the presence of the Queen and members of the royal family, saw and heard Leonard Bernstein conduct Mahler's *Eighth Symphony* on the grandest scale imaginable. The audience responded with unrestrained enthusiasm. Later in the year, we taped the Symphonic Twilight trio which also met with audience approval. Recorded in black and white, the results were an exercise in chiaroscuro, sort of Video Noir. I'm very proud of these documents. They not only provide an enduring testament to Bernstein's art but display, equally, the dramatic effects of which television filming was capable. As a result of these concerts and others to follow, Leonard Bernstein became as much a sensation in the UK and on the continent as he was in the States, maybe even more so.

In the coming years I was with Lenny on quite a few projects including performances of Ravel's *G Major Concerto* with Lenny as pianist and conductor, as well as concerts featuring Bach's *Magnificat*, Stravinsky's *Mass*, and the European premiere in Vienna of Bernstein's own *Mass*. Lenny's *Mass* had bombed at its world premiere in Washington, D.C. in 1971. He wasn't about to accept that judgement on his piece, however, and gave his blessings to a student production at Yale University. This time, the *Mass* was acclaimed and Lenny arranged to export the production, lock, stock, and barrel, including 150 student performers and musicians, to Vienna in 1973. Conducted by John Mauceri, a Yale faculty member, the *Mass* received an unqualified thumbs up. In my opinion it is a fabulous piece of music-theatre well deserving of success, and I appreciated the opportunity to get it down on tape.

After the Vienna experience, I didn't work with Lenny that much. To tell the truth I didn't want to, mainly because he became increasingly difficult. I am not revealing anything that already isn't well-known when I say that Bernstein, the man, had a real fall from grace and descended into alcoholism and drug use. The charm curdled. All too often, he became nasty and abusive and while I could take being screamed at myself, I couldn't be a witness to his mistreatment of others. I did direct a performance of his *Second Symphony, The Age of Anxiety.* (The unusual title came from a W.H. Auden poem.) André Previn conducted and Leonard Pennario played the solo piano part. Lenny wasn't personally involved so conflict between us didn't arise. Still, I'd reached the stage where it just wasn't pleasant to work with him. I couldn't do it any more and made up my mind that I would no longer be available. *The Age of Anxiety* marked the end of our working partnership. I always admired his musicianship, though, and I did keep up with his professional appearances.

On 11 March 1990, I attended a performance of Bruckner's *Ninth Symphony* that Lenny gave with the Vienna Philharmonic at Carnegie Hall. I went with Mirella Freni and Jack Mastroianni, both of whom you'll hear more about later. I wanted to attend the performance but I did not want to go backstage. Mirella, however, did, and after the performance she and Jack insisted that I go with them to his dressing room. We were let in by Lenny's manager, Harry Kraut. Bernstein sat slumped in a chair, soaking wet, clearly exhausted. He looked up and caught sight of me. "It's Brian!" he shouted. "Oh my god, it's Brian. Come here, come here." He motioned for me to approach him. I crossed the room, knelt in front of him and leaned over. He wrapped his arms around me as he'd done after the *Falstaff* in Vienna, but without the trademark bear hug. He simply didn't have the strength. Planting a kiss on my cheek, he dropped his arms and leaned back in his chair. "Where did you go, Brian. Where have you been? Oh, wait, I remember, you went to Australia." "I've never been to Australia", I answered. "Well, where are you then?" "Right here, Lenny. I live two blocks away from you." "But you went to Australia." "No, no," I answered, "I live here." He turned to Harry Kraut. "Harry, Harry," he called out, "why did you tell me Brian went to Australia?" Kraut looked perplexed and shrugged his shoulders. I'm pretty sure Lenny spontaneously made up the Australian bit simply to explain why he'd lost contact and then tried to put the burden on his manager. We began to reminisce and then he reached out his arms and embraced me again. "Good to see you Brian, good to see you", he mumbled in my ear. "Same here", I responded, and I meant it. Mirella and Jack said their hellos and goodbyes and the three of us left. I felt incredibly sad. Lenny seemed so depleted. I never saw him again.

The Bruckner *Ninth* was Leonard Bernstein's last appearance at Carnegie Hall, the very stage where he'd burst upon the musical scene in November of 1943 when he replaced an ailing Bruno Walter and made his spectacular conducting debut with the New York Philharmonic. Pianist, conductor, composer, educator, Leonard Bernstein had it all. I'd been bowled over by his talent from the very first and I'm gratified that I was able to work with him in his incandescent heydays. And I am ever grateful that Mirella and Jack dragged me backstage where I was able to make my peace with him.

Partying and working with Lenny Bernstein

11

Upbeats

After the Mahler *Eighth* and the Symphonic Twilight with Bernstein, I was scheduled to direct the sweetest plum of them all—the Last Night of the Proms. Adding to my delight, Sir Malcolm Sargent, who'd been on the podium for my debut concert, was the scheduled conductor. I greatly admired and respected Sargent, the first major music figure with whom I worked closely; in fact, we'd become friends. Sir Malcolm was an elegant, impeccably groomed man with a shiny dark mane of Brylcreem-blackened hair. His sartorial splendour always on display, he was known in the business as "Flash Harry", an old expression for someone who's a bit over the top in dress and action. Ironically, Sir Malcolm Sargent, the ultimate Toff, had been born within the sound of Bow Bells which, traditionally, made him a Cockney.

The following year, 1967, for the second time in a row, I was given the Last Night of the Proms and, once again, Malcolm Sargent was scheduled to conduct. However, a few days before the concert a statement was released advising prommers that the conductor had withdrawn. I was disappointed as I had looked forward to working with him. The morning of the final Prom concert, Sir Malcolm's secretary called and asked if I would come to the Maestro's flat that afternoon for a brief visit. Non-plussed by the request I nevertheless said I'd drop by. Sir Malcolm lived in the Albert Mansions right next to Albert Hall, an easy

Sir Malcolm Sargent leads the BBC Symphony Orchestra and the Prommers
in the National Anthem. Last Night of the Proms, September 1952,
Royal Albert Hall; Cockney or Toff, a true gentleman   143

stop. When I arrived, I was taken to the drawing room. Sir Malcolm, slumped in a large wing chair, looked grey and drawn. He thanked me for coming and after a quick exchange, got to the point. "I won't take up your time, Brian, but I really do need to speak to you. I so wanted to conduct tonight, but I cannot. However, I am going to come out and say a few words. I'd like to be shown on the television screen while I'm speaking but, as you can see, I'm not looking quite myself. And so, I'm going to ask you, in your kindness, not to show me in close-up." I guaranteed him that I would do as he asked. He thanked me and I left. I was moved by his request, and shaken by his appearance.

That evening at Albert Hall, Sir Malcolm, accompanied by two attendants and a nurse, arrived on a stretcher and immediately was taken down to the conductor's room. The concert about to begin, he was carried up to the artist's entrance behind the orchestra. The attendants helped him to his feet and, pushing them aside, he strode through the door onto the stage. In measured steps, and to wholehearted applause, he walked past the seated musicians until he reached the podium. Standing beside it he said his few words, thanking everyone for being there, and telling them how disappointed he was that he could not conduct that evening. He concluded by promising that he'd be back next year. That gallant man then turned and began his exit. The audience erupted in shouts and cheers and gave him a standing ovation as he slowly left the stage. A painful, albeit courageous, leave-taking for the Proms' stalwart leader. For my part, I did as I had promised and within a few days received a barely legible hand-written note from him which read: *Dear Brian, Thank you so much for your sensitive and discreet coverage of my appearance.* Shortly thereafter, Sir Malcolm Sargent, a gentleman to the end, died of cancer.

At the time I began directing the Proms, although there were various guest conductors, Sir Malcolm, along with three others, Sir John Barbirolli, the Italian/English conductor of the Hallé Orchestra, Basil Cameron, leader of the London Philharmonic Orchestra, and Sir John Pritchard, long associated with Glyndebourne, did the bulk of the work. Their names may not resonate as much today but those four were among the principal British conductors of the era. And, of course, I was doing my directorial "conducting" along with them. Because of the relaxed atmosphere anything could happen at the Proms which meant you had to be super alert in your reactions and camera work. What fabulous training, the perfect way to learn how not to make mistakes and how to relay live events which capture the electricity of the moment. For ten years the Proms became part of my BBC summers. Each programme had its own distinctive spark, but some stood out.

Customarily, the Proms honoured eminent composers on big birthdays. I directed two of those concerts, Sir Arthur Bliss's 75th and Sir William Walton's 70th. Sir Arthur was Master of the Queen's Music, a prestigious position involving a lot of ceremonial work. The Master has to whip up fanfares and marches for Royal occasions of which there are many. The post was supposed to have gone to Walton but to Walton's alleged relief—he didn't fancy being responsible for all that spur-of-the-moment composing—the position went instead to Bliss. Sir Arthur was a lovely old boy who sported a bulky moustache which made him look like a walrus. I went to his home in St John's Wood to discuss his birthday programme and was served tea by his lady wife, a quite charming American woman. The afternoon couldn't have been more English with Lady Bliss pouring and Sir Arthur harrumphing his birthday choices.

Later, I met with Sir William to plan his special celebration. Both gentlemen led the orchestra on their respective evenings. Neither were "natural" conductors. They each knew how to wave the stick and that was about it. But it didn't matter, these were important events, ideal occasions to document. And what a charge I got capturing those fabled English composers presenting their own works.

Although it wasn't a Prom concert, another BBC musical transmission must be mentioned. Years before I came on the scene, Sir Adrian Boult had experienced a long and fruitful association with the BBC. Standing over six feet tall, Boult commanded the podium, the epitome of a great classical conductor. In 1930, he was hired to lead and train the BBC Symphony Orchestra and act as the corporation's musical director. For the next two decades he served in this capacity and, during his tenure, turned the BBC Symphony Orchestra into a major international ensemble. In my student days I attended his master classes and much admired the discipline and handwork of his immaculate technique. He did incredible work, especially with British composers such as Edward Elgar, Vaughan Williams, and Frederick Delius. For twenty years Adrian Boult reigned supreme at the BBC, and then he turned sixty-five. Lightning struck. He'd reached the company's retirement age and, following protocol, had to be pensioned off. Sir Adrian, however, refused to go docilely into that goodbye; he demanded that the age rule be dropped for him. The corporation declined, forcing the conductor to resign rather than be fired. At the peak of his artistic and musical career Sir Adrian Boult was cast aside. He was furious. In his mind, the BBC had used him all those years only to reward him with exile. His hatred for the company, and everything to do with it, was palpable. He stated publicly that he would never again have anything to do with the British Broadcasting Corporation. The wily maestro was down but not out. Instead of retiring, Sir Adrian became chief conductor of the London Philharmonic and his stellar career with them continued way beyond his BBC banishment. At the age of seventy-nine he still flourished and I desperately wanted to capture him on tape. Unfortunately, I happened to be employed by his arch enemy.

I'd about given up hope of documenting Sir Adrian when I read a rave review of a Boult concert in *The Daily Telegraph*. The glowing notice renewed my interest. I simply had to video Boult at work and the very best place for that would be a BBC studio. However, I did not belong to the BBC Television Music Department; I worked in the Television Outside Broadcasts Department, another of its multitudinous divisions. In order to utilize a studio, I needed to be inventive. BBC studios were available for indoor events covering a full range of programmes. If, however, BBC2 wanted to present an opera or a ballet, say from Covent Garden or Glyndebourne, they had to be produced in their respective venues and serviced by BBC's Outside Broadcasting Unit. Most significantly, all such events had to be coordinated from a mobile control room, usually a truck parked in the vicinity of the event. Inside the truck, eight or ten camera monitors were set up above a control panel. The video director sat in front of the panel, selecting his camera shots. The director's choices then went to the main monitor and from there were transmitted to the viewing audience. On the left side of the director sat the lighting engineer controlling monitors to ensure that the transmissions were of the highest visual quality. On the right side of the director, behind a glass screen, a sound engineer sat at the audio desk, controlling the sound balance. When I was at the helm, I thought of myself and my two associates as a transmission (un)holy trinity, director in the centre, lighting to his left, and audio on his right. Altogether, I spent at least eighty per cent of my directing life in the hot seat of cramped mobile control rooms all over the world.

Sparked by *The Daily Telegraph* review, I began to muse about various ways to achieve my goal of recording Sir Adrian. In a serendipitous instant, I came up with a plan to bring Boult back. Why not invite him to record in a BBC studio, not with the BBC's orchestra, but with his own ensemble, the London Philharmonic? In other words, just use the BBC's facilities to put a roof over his head. What better way to cock a snook at his detested former employers? I called his secretary and, without going into details, declared that I wished to record Sir Adrian in concert and asked if he would meet with me. Sir Adrian proved amenable, inviting me to lunch with him at the restaurant atop Jones & Higgins Department Store. We met, and I told him that I thought that the BBC had disrespected him, adding that he'd really shown them up by continuing his brilliant career with the London Philharmonic and ending with "I want to document you for posterity." I explained that recording inside a BBC studio would produce optimal results. Hearing the words "BBC" and "studio", Sir Adrian momentarily looked askance but I rushed ahead. "I'm not suggesting that you conduct the BBC Orchestra, Sir Adrian, rather I propose that you conduct the LPO orchestra. And, you can choose whatever music you want." Sir Adrian briefly mulled the situation. Realizing that using the BBC's studio while snubbing their orchestra (the one he created) would be a moment to savour, he accepted my proposal. Half the battle. I then spoke to BBC2's administrators. Musicians can be temperamental; corporations don't take things personally. The upshot? Sir Adrian Boult returned to the BBC in a programme of English music. Everything went so well, he consented to return for a series of similar studio concerts. I had brought the lion back into the den.

Putting together the programme with Adrian Boult proved to be an invigorating and inspiring experience. Indeed, we were so enthusiastic about our cooperative effort, we decided to collaborate on future productions; specifically, Edward Elgar's *The Dream of Gerontius*. Having conducted the piece many times, some in the presence of its composer, Sir Adrian felt that the work should be documented on television. I sensed that he understood that this accomplishment not only would pay appropriate homage to a masterpiece, but also would serve as a testament to his own legacy. I immediately took the idea to BBC2's comptroller, David Attenborough. Attenborough had assumed his position in March of 1965 and went on to establish a programme schedule distinguished by its emphasis on the fine arts. Yet even as he brought superior cultural presentations onto the screen, Attenborough juggled the viewer's perspective by throwing in oddball experimental comedy and sports programmes—think *Monty Python* and *Snooker*. David Attenborough, a brilliant educator and performer, also happened to be a programming genius. At the time he was appointed, BBC radio already had an established commitment to contemporary classical music. The question now became, how would television handle the situation? The answer arrived when Attenborough appointed John Culshaw to head the BBC's Music and Arts Division in 1967. Mostly self-educated musically, Culshaw was a trailblazer in the history of recorded classical music. At age twenty-two, he went to work writing album liner notes for

Decca eventually becoming a producer. After a stretch at Capitol Records, he returned to Decca where he was put in charge of classical recordings. In those days most LPs (Long Playing records) were recorded from concert halls, opera houses, and theatres. Culshaw revolutionized the recording industry by pioneering the use of stereophonic techniques to create studio recordings that were alive with sound. His greatest success was overseeing the first studio recording of Wagner's *Ring*, a milestone in recording history and one that figured prominently in my own musical education. Head over heels about all music, including contemporary, Culshaw produced a series of recordings of Benjamin Britten's music with Britten himself involved as conductor, composer, or pianist. Called "a priceless heritage for posterity" by *The Times*, the recordings became legendary. Once in his new position Culshaw wasted no time in bringing Benjamin Britten into the television fold. The collaboration between the composer and the BBC proved to be a rare artistic phenomenon, a perfect marriage of the cultural and the commercial which fully realized both the BBC's highbrow aspirations and Britten's virtuoso achievements. All told, between David Attenborough and John Culshaw, BBC2 had a lock on artistic excellence.

When Culshaw took over the Arts and Music Department, he was taken aback to discover that my employer, Outside Broadcasts, did not fall under his purview, Culshaw immediately began negotiating. Before you could say David Attenborough, I was transferred from Outside Broadcasting to Music and Arts. Culshaw, my rescuer and new boss, soon became my promoter and friend. His belief in me as a director and as a musician led to untold opportunities, the first of which would be the video recording of *The Dream of Gerontius*. I did not have to sell *Gerontius* to

John Culshaw. He was eager to do it, not only because he admired the work, but because of a new development in television broadcasting—colour. Britain had lagged in the breakthrough technology until late in 1968. But, by the beginning of 1969 everything we shot had to "fully exploit the brilliance of colour". The picture wasn't all rosy, though, there were casualties. The transference from black and white required technical staff members to take eye tests. Anyone found to be colour blind could no longer work on productions. Those technicians who didn't pass the test were offered positions in other divisions where their condition would have no effect on their performance. In those days, the BBC looked after its own.

When I presented *The Dream of Gerontius* to Culshaw, I'd already investigated incorporating the colour aspect. To exploit colour to its fullest, I wanted to tape inside Canterbury Cathedral and utilize the magnificent stained-glass windows. The idea of music and art blending within the glimmering breadth of a great cathedral appealed to Culshaw, who quickly gave *The Dream of Gerontius* the go-ahead. We had three outstanding soloists, Janet Baker, John Shirley Quirk, and Peter Pears, along with the orchestra and choir of the London Philharmonic under the direction of Sir Adrian Boult. As an added attraction, I felt comfortable giving the piece a dramatic tweak and semi-staged the work. The broadcast was a whopping success for Sir Adrian, the singers, the orchestra, the choir, the Cathedral, and for me, too. The shots of the Cathedral's architectural details and those of the participating soloists and musicians blended in a brilliant fusion of sight and sound. Sir Adrian, thrilled with the recording, showed his appreciation by presenting me with a score of Elgar's overture *In the South*, autographed by the composer.

The elegant Sir Adrian Boult wielding
his long baton, 1969

Sir Malcolm Sargent in rehearsal with the
Liverpool Philharmonic Orchestra,
Philharmonic Hall in Liverpool, January 1946

12.

A Shining Hour

On 20 August 1968, led by the Soviet Union, Warsaw Pact troops from Poland, Bulgaria, and Hungary invaded Czechoslovakia. The reason? … to halt Western reforms that Alexander Dubček, the First Secretary of the Czechoslovakian Communist Party Central Committee, recently had brought forth. In effect, lightning had struck twice. Thirty years before, in 1938, Neville Chamberlain, the UK prime minister, declared "peace in our time" and the western world sacrificed Czechoslovakia to Hitler and his Nazis. When World War II ended, the Russians replaced the Nazis. The repression of the Czech people continued until Dubček's liberalization policies, known as the Prague Spring, brought inspiration and hope. Alas, winter came early that August evening. Tanks rolled into Prague as Soviet troops occupied the beleaguered country. Unbelievably, the Soviets launched their attack at the very same time the touring USSR State Symphony Orchestra, with conductor Yevgeny Svetlanov and soloist Mikhail Rostropovich were appearing in a Proms concert at the Royal Albert Hall. Protestors gathered in the streets outside, and voiced their shock and horror. Inside the Hall, I sat next to Zdenka Podhajská, who had come to visit my family. The experience is seared in my memory. Sitting there, listening to glorious music played brilliantly, one did not know how to express appreciation while at the same time, acknowledging the heinous crime being perpetrated. To applaud or not to applaud, really

The brilliant English cellist
Jacqueline du Pré, circa 1970

was the question. I could hear the crowds outside calling for freedom and inside, certain members of the audience did the same. The programme began with the Overture to *Russlan and Ludmilla*, followed by the Dvořak *Cello Concerto* and closed with Shostakovich's *Symphony No. 10*. During the Overture, members of the audience cried out, "Cancel the concert!" Various pockets of protest remained active throughout the evening. A weird controlled chaos existed. I cannot remember for sure but the newspapers reported that Rostropovich played with tears streaming down his cheeks. In the days that followed, the free world desperately searched for ways to show solidarity with the Czech nation. I felt this outrageous incursion deeply. My love for the Czech people knew no bounds; they had nurtured me when I lived among them, they were my family. I desperately wanted to do something to honour my friends and to assure them that the western world stood by them. Fortunately, others felt the same.

Five days after the invasion, another concert was hastily arranged and performed at the Royal Albert Hall in order to raise relief funds for the Czech people. Once again, Dvořak's *Cello Concerto* took centre stage, this time with Daniel Barenboim conducting the London Symphony Orchestra and his wife Jacqueline du Pré as soloist. In a rare gesture of solidarity, ITV and the BBC agreed to join forces and share the transmission expenses. The former paid the orchestral fees and the BBC provided the technical resources. In another diplomatic gesture, it was agreed that I should share directorial chores with Humphrey Burton, then on staff at ITV. Humphrey chose to cover the first movement of the Dvořak, leaving me in charge of the Andante and Finale. The performance, a highly charged emotional affair, was made all the more dramatic when, in the impassioned opening moments of the Finale, a string

Holding hands
with Jacqueline
du Pré

snapped on du Pre's cello and the music came to a sudden halt. She immediately leaned towards the audience and asked to be excused to restring her cello. The audience applauded as du Pré stood up and, cello in hand, gracefully made her way through the orchestra and out the stage left door. Barenboim stepped down from the podium and began chatting with a couple of string players as the on-air broadcasters provided kill-time informational tidbits for television viewers. One of them announced that this was the second time that du Pré had had a string break during a performance of the Dvořak. I kept the cameras focused on the orchestra and in less than five minutes, her cello whole again, Jacqueline du Pré reappeared, sat down, did a few fine tunings, and once more began the last movement.

The performance that afternoon was electrifying, supercharged, and you could feel the tension in the air. For me, it was live TV at its most inspiring, capturing the moment, and fully illustrating the power of music to soothe and inspire. I am inordinately proud to have been associated with this historic event which was especially meaningful to me because of my love for the Czech Republic and its citizens. An extraordinary concert, indeed, and I invite you to enjoy it on good old YouTube.

13

The Melody Lingers on

Under John Culshaw's auspices, I met the pre-eminent musicians of the day. Indeed, my career was fully launched and advanced because of my affiliation with two of them, the conductor Georg Solti, and the composer/conductor Benjamin Britten. Let's begin with the former.

In 1938, when Nazi inspired anti-Jewish laws were enacted in Hungary, Georg Solti, an opera and orchestral conductor, saw the handwriting on the wall and left Budapest for London. After conducting a season of Russian ballets at Covent Garden, he went to Switzerland where he found refuge during World War II. When the war ended, he was appointed musical director of the Munich-based Bavarian State Opera and from there he moved on to Oper Frankfurt. In 1961, he returned to London and was appointed musical director of the Covent Garden Opera Company. During his ten-year tenure, Solti raised the standards so high the company was granted the title, "Royal Opera House, Covent Garden". Throughout his directorship Solti, in collaboration with John Culshaw, produced a goldmine of recordings. With 31 Grammys to his name, more than any other recording artist, classical or popular, Georg Solti remained the top Grammy Award winner of all time right up to 6 February 2023. That evening, the R&B mega star Beyoncé received her 31st and 32nd Grammys. The occasion was both astounding and disheartening. Astounding because Solti died in 1997 and his record had endured for a quarter of a century; disheartening because

the likelihood of a classical artist ever again attaining anything anywhere near that goal is naught. Classical music
has been reduced to a footnote by the Grammys. So much
so that when one host, Billy Crystal, mentioned that he'd
met Vladimir Horowitz at a Grammy Award many years
earlier, he quickly quipped, "Horowitz? Google him."
Withal, Georg Solti's record remains a miracle and no
small credit for his achievements could and should be
ascribed to John Culshaw.

I became a beneficiary of the prodigious Culshaw/Solti
alliance when John assigned me to a concert with Solti
conducting the London Symphony Orchestra in Mahler's
Ninth. Aside from my long-ago introduction to that composer via Stanley Spratt, I didn't know Mahler. I didn't
know Solti, either. Obviously, I had some learning to do
and I went right to the source by ringing up Solti's secretary at the Royal Opera House. Explaining that I was a
television director with the BBC and looking forward to
recording the conductor's performance at the Royal Festival Hall, I suggested that it might be a good idea for us
to get to know each other so that we could work together
harmoniously. Would Mr Solti agree to meet with me?
The next day, the secretary called back to say that Mr Solti
"would be delighted to see me". I went to the Royal Opera
House where I was ushered into his office. Solti was extremely gracious, very pleasant. A slight problem was his
thick Hungarian accent, occasionally you had to strain to
understand him. Confessing that I knew little if anything
about Mahler and that I'd never directed any of his works
before, I told Solti I was looking to him for guidance. How
would he like me to document the performance? Cordial
and helpful, he talked to me at length. Thanks to his counsel, I was well prepared when it came time to record the

symphony. After the taping Solti asked to view the result, and I ran the tape for him in a screening room. As he watched he began mumbling under his breath, "I don't believe it, I don't believe it" and kept repeating that phrase throughout the viewing. I was shaking in my boots. Oh my God, what doesn't he believe? What have I done wrong? Finally, I couldn't hold back. "Excuse me, Mr Solti," I stammered, "is there something the matter?" He turned to look at me, his eyes blazing. "It's beautiful," he cried, "so beautiful. I've never seen anything like this before. Beautiful. We must talk." And talk we did. We sat down together and Solti opened the conversation. "Let me ask you a couple of questions, young man. First, do you speak German?" "Yes." He smiled and continued. "Second, by any chance, do you play Bridge?" "No, I don't", I replied, a bit bemused. Solti shook his head. "Ah, my dear young man, I hate to say it, but I must tell you, that was a bad career answer." I had no idea what the man was talking about when I suddenly recalled that Solti was a Bridge fanatic and often played with cronies during rehearsal breaks. I'd also heard that he didn't like to lose. Sizing up the situation, I thought fast, and gambled. "Well, Maestro, I'm sorry to disappoint you. I don't play Bridge myself but I've heard that you're an excellent Bridge player. I've also heard that you like to win and have been known to ... ah, finagle here and there." Solti's eyebrows arched as he fixed his gaze on me. I looked straight back at him. He broke the silence with a hearty laugh, clapped his hand on my back, and said, "You know something young man, now you've said the right thing." He reached out and shook my hand. "Let me explain what I'm talking about. I'm doing a special concert honouring my teacher Béla Bartók and I'll be conducting his *Concerto for Orchestra* for ZDF (the second German television channel). Since you speak German, and even though you don't play Bridge, may I recommend you to be the director?" Permission instantly was granted. Thanks to my ability to speak German, Solti's mania for Bridge, along with his sense of humour, and to John Culshaw for putting us together, in April of 1969 I took my first independent step from the BBC and made my freelance directorial debut for ZDF. That programme also signalled the beginning of a lifelong alliance with the inimitable Georg Solti.

Getting together with Benjamin Britten, the other half of John Culshaw's initial gift to me, proved to be polar-opposite from my encounter with the gregarious Solti. In fact, it very nearly didn't take place. That we eventually met was all due to *The Dream of Gerontius*. As I've noted, *The Dream* was well reviewed and received which was heartening to me as it was a good example of my basic technique—the continuous linking of the visual and the musical. A few days after the transmission, John Culshaw called me into his office and following some chit-chat, got to the point. "Brian, it's my opinion that *Gerontius* should lead us to similar projects. I'm thinking we could do a series of oratorios. Why not an *Elijah*, or a *Messiah*, for that matter? Anyway, that's the future, for now we've got a perfect follow-up. Benjamin Britten is going to conduct Bach's *Christmas Oratorio* in Long Melford Church and I'd like you to direct. What do you think?" "I don't have to think", I laughed, "I'd love to do it." "Wonderful", said John. "And, by the way, I want you to work directly with Ben." "Wow", I blurted out. I couldn't help myself. The idea of working with Benjamin Britten was mindboggling. Culshaw concluded the conversation with, "Here's his secretary's phone number. Ring her up, introduce yourself, and tell her I told you to make an appointment with Ben." Thus far the pattern was like the Solti meeting. Call the secretary and then see the maestro. I rang up Britten's secretary who said she would get the message to him and get back to me. I waited to hear from her. I continued to wait. Days passed. Why wasn't she calling? A week passed; the concert date was getting closer. Finally, I took matters in hand and descended on John Culshaw. "I'm a bit concerned because Mr Britten is not responding." "Don't worry, I'll get him to call you", reassured John. I never received a call from Benjamin Britten. Rather, John contacted me. "Well, Brian, I spoke to Ben and, well, you don't know him but he's a very shy person and he doesn't know you and, well, he doesn't feel that he's able to work with people he doesn't know." Okay, John's trying to get Britten to call me so he can get to know me so we can work together but Britten doesn't want to work with me because he doesn't know me. Here's a How-De-Do. "I'm awfully sorry," John continued, "but Ben's made up his mind to work with a stage director rather than a television director. Ben's comfortable with him and there's nothing more I can do." What could I say? I thanked John for trying and thought that was that. And then, Edward Elgar came to the rescue.

Britten's conducting of Bach's *Christmas Oratorio* had been presented during the Christmas season in a traditional manner which many found less inspiring than the trend-setting *Dream*. Apparently, the *Oratorio's* conductor was one of those. Months later, out of nowhere, Benjamin Britten's secretary called and asked if I would come to the composer's home in Aldeburgh to meet with him. All I could think was how the hell did this happen? I quickly said yes, arranged the date and time, said goodbye, hung up, and immediately called John Culshaw. "Did you say anything to Benjamin Britten", I asked after telling him about the call. "No, I didn't," he answered, "though I can guess what happened. Ben and Peter must have seen

Gerontius and Ben must have been impressed. I'll bet anything Peter recommended that you and Ben get together." John was right on the money. Britten did watch the programme along with Peter Pears, his life companion. Peter, who enjoyed working with me, took the opportunity to suggest that Britten get in touch with me. And that is how Elgar's *The Dream of Gerontius* paved the way to my meeting with Benjamin Britten.

14.
Rule Britten-nia!

As I drove up the Suffolk coast of East Anglia to Britten's home in Aldeburgh, I was mentally pinching myself. Soon, I'd be in the presence of the man generally acknowledged to be Britain's greatest contemporary composer, an opinion I shared then and still do. Indeed, in July 1967, Britten was created *Baron Britten, of Aldeburgh in the County of Suffolk*, the first British musician to be elevated to the peerage. As mentioned, Britten had long been a particular idol of mine. The prospect of meeting him sent my mind a-tumble on that coastal drive. East Anglia, a brutal part of England, was Britten territory. He was born in Lowestoft a forty-five-minute drive up the coast from Aldeburgh and though he could have lived anywhere, he chose to return to his roots. The rugged country along the North Sea drew him; it was in his blood. Aldeburgh means "old fort" which Aldeburgh had been in Tudor times. There, shipbuilders plied their trade and built, among other renowned vessels, Sir Francis Drake's *Golden Hind*. Aldeburgh's glory days were long past when, in 1947, Britten and Peter Pears arrived and moved into a seafront cottage. A decade later, they exchanged homes with Mary Potter, an artist friend, and settled into a rundown seventeenth-century farmhouse on the outskirts of town. The house was completely remodelled and dubbed The Red House. For two decades, the two men lived and worked there. After Britten died, Pears stayed on for another nine years until his own death. Today, The Red House, a handsome building with

Benjamin Britten with one of his
favoured dachshunds, 1953

beautiful grounds and gardens, is a major heritage site, a combination of a personal and archival museum as well as the headquarters of the Britten-Pears Foundation.

On that far-off afternoon, I arrived at my destination and drove up to a closed gate hung with many notices in many languages all of which translated: *Beware the Dog*. Allegedly, the sign in Russian had been painted by cellist Mstislav Rostropovich, a frequent visitor. Assuming that the dog had been notified of my impending visit, but still wary, I quickly got out of the car, opened the gate, got back into the car, drove through, got out of the car, shut the gate, and leaped back into the driver's seat, all the while terrified that some huge, snarling cur would come barrelling towards me. Later, I would be introduced formally to the fearsome Cerberus guarding The Red House, an adorable, affectionate dachshund named Gilda. Leaving my car in the garage as instructed, I walked up to the house and knocked on the door. The door opened and Benjamin Britten stood before me. "Hello. I'm Ben Britten and it's so nice to meet you." He shook my hand, invited me in, and led me to the library, where tea awaited. We sat down, sipped, and talked. Never mentioning that he'd rejected my participation in the *Christmas Oratorio*, Britten told me how much he'd enjoyed a concert I'd recorded of the Brahms *Double Concerto* with his good friends David Oistrakh, Mstislav Rostropovich, and Kirill Kondrashin. For a while the conversation centred on my accomplishments, which struck me as completely mad. Then, Britten paused in his paeons and got down to business. "Do you know the score of my *Burning Fiery Furnace*?" While I knew that piece was one of three church parables Britten had set to music, I had to admit I was not familiar with it. Without saying a word, he stood up, went to the piano, picked up a vocal score from the music rack, and handed me a copy of *The Burning Fiery Furnace*. "John Culshaw and I are planning to do a TV version. It's going to be performed by players from the English Chamber Orchestra at the local church in Orford. I'll be conducting, and Peter Pears will sing the role of Nebuchadnezzar. I would like you to work with me on it." I sputtered the obvious reply. The arrangement set, our meeting ended. Britten saw me to the door, shook my hand once again, said goodbye, and disappeared back into the house. I walked to the garage, got into my car, gently placed *The Burning Fiery Furnace* on the seat beside me and, with my head in the clouds, headed home.

That first meeting with Benjamin Britten presaged a long and consequential working relationship. I say working relationship rather than friendship because, although I respected him greatly and I know he thought well of me, that's the way I classified our affiliation. Indeed, my association with him followed a pattern established early in my career. Professionally speaking, with major exceptions here and there, I found it wiser to put some distance between me and the artists with whom I worked. Directors deal with technical details and talent, and while the former usually can be resolved, the latter can be problematic. Simply put, performing artists are very different from you and me. You can kiss the ground they walk on yet if things aren't going their way, they can turn on you at the drop of a hat. I'm not blaming them; they're artists and entitled to temperament. However, when temperament erupts into tumult, authority matters, and that bit of self-imposed detachment allowed me to best handle many tense situations. Then too, as regards Benjamin Britten, I may have remained reserved because I didn't want to get burnt. The fact that he could burn you was common knowledge. Charles Mackerras told me that Britten notoriously dropped colleagues and friends who he thought had affronted him. Those discarded became known as Ben's "corpses", and they were legion. (Ironically, Charles himself offended Ben and for a while joined the outcast ranks. Eventually, they patched it up and Charles was reanimated.) Britten did have defenders. Janet Baker, for instance, felt he was entitled to take what he wanted and move on. As she put it, "He did not want to hurt anyone but the task in hand was more important than anything or anybody." Somehow or other, I managed to stay in Ben's favour and we worked together quite amicably.

During his lifetime and since his death, much has been said and written about Benjamin Britten. Not by me. Save for conversations with close and knowing colleagues, I shied away from sharing my impressions of him. Back then, it would have been gossip. Now, it's history. Most of the players are long gone and I hope that my honest personal observations might add to the portrait of a great artist.

Benjamin Britten was the son of a dentist and a slightly over-bearing, music-loving mother who doted on him. (To her son's embarrassment, Edith Britten was wont to pepper her conversations with references to the Four Bs, Bach, Beethoven, Brahms, and ... Britten.) From my point of view, Benjamin Britten was a mixture of greatness and smallness in his relationships, and always a bit of an outsider. Shy, intensely private, full of suppressed emotions, he was constantly in control of himself in public situations. Like the East Anglian climate he hailed from, he could be serene and stormy. He had a fine sense of humour but along with that also evinced a streak of pettiness. If something or someone upset him, he would blow his top. Moreover, he bore grudges, hence the "corpses". At the same time, I never heard him utter a vain word. He had an astonishing mind but was never boastful, always modest. He had incredible energy as a performer and as a composer, and he wrote with purpose. That purpose was for his music to be performed and, equally important, to be understood. Unlike contemporaries such as Stockhausen, some of whose scores you have to be a rocket scientist to figure out, Ben wanted his music to be accessible to everyone. As for his method of composing, he'd become obsessed with an idea and work things out by taking long walks along the beach. Walking, he told me, gave him inspiration. Benjamin Britten created music in his head while on his feet, then went home and set it down on paper. I also observed him as a conductor; he was very clear in his beat, nothing fancy, no frills, straightforward, and always true to the composer's wishes. A phenomenally instinctive pianist, he gave the world premiere of his one and only piano concerto at a Promenade Concert. I watched him play on many occasions, always a profoundly moving experience. Technically there was nothing he couldn't do. Sometimes I'd look at his hands and marvel that such incredible music could just spring out of those fingers. Ben's health always presented a problem. Following a childhood bout with pneumonia he'd suffered innumerable ailments. To keep himself in shape he swam and walked religiously. He was, as well, a passionate tennis player and a good one. Like Solti with his Bridge games, he liked to win though he did not go to Solti's lengths to do so. Everyone knew about Ben's passion for fast cars, perhaps his one obvious indulgence. A ride with Ben at the wheel was a heartstopper. He drove as fast as the law allowed, maybe a bit more, to which my stomach could have attested. Aside from these diversions, he lived a relatively simple life. A local lady, Mrs Hudson (shades of Holmes and Watson!) did for him and Peter Pears. She looked after The Red House and cooked for them. The place always was neat and the food always delectable. "Let's have those leftovers", Ben would enthuse. Small wonder as Mrs Hudson's tidbits were just as tasty on the following day, especially cold beef with pickles. Occasionally, Ben went out for dinner to one of the local hotels but most of the time, he was content to be at home. Basically, he lived a simple and fruitful life. As far as his relationship with Pears, it was a strong and good one. They got along well together, sharing many interests. Both were pacifists and conscientious objectors during World War II. Peter Pears, a gentleman at heart, could be tetchy at times; then again, he was a tenor. Overall, he provided a good steadying force. If ever I had a problem with Ben, a difference of opinion perhaps, or an inability to make clear what I wanted, and I simply couldn't get through to him, I'd go to Peter. He'd address the issue, bring it to Ben, and the problem would disappear. It didn't work in reverse, though. On the rare occasion that a dilemma arose with Peter, Ben would step aside rather than in.

Composer, conductor, pianist, Benjamin Britten had enormous vitality and virtuosity. Curiosity was another motivating force; Ben wanted to know about everything. For a long time, he'd been trying to get away from the traditional forms of operatic conversation to find a new way of expressing himself. He found his answer during a visit to Japan where he became fascinated by Noh and Kabuki theatre. Participants in Noh are more storytellers than actors and use visual appearance and movement to tell their tale rather than enacting it. Applying the Noh aesthetic, he took three parables and composed *The Prodigal Son, Curlew River,* and *The Burning Fiery Furnace.* The last brought us together.

Recording *The Burning Fiery Furnace* at the Orford Parish Church presented a challenge. I didn't want a conventional beginning inside the church with all the participants in a row, I wanted something different, something that would build rather than just be. I found the appropriate atmospheric touch by opening the programme with a procession of torch bearing monks intoning Gregorian chants as they walked into the churchyard, then entered the church. A calm serenity set the mood perfectly. (Once again, you don't have to take my word for it, it's available on YouTube.) Ben liked the production enormously. In fact, he was so impressed that he contacted John Culshaw and asked if the BBC would be interested in documenting more of his works using the Snape Maltings as the setting. The BBC leaped at the opportunity. The composer and the corporation became working partners for the next five years and I became a part of this creative power block.

Back in 1948, Benjamin Britten established a summer music festival in Aldeburgh. All events took place in Jubilee Hall, a 240-seat theatre built to celebrate Queen Victoria's Golden Jubilee. The Aldeburgh Festival flourished and became an international draw. Britten himself wrote small operas, such as *Let's Make an Opera, Noah's Flood,* and *A Midsummer Night's Dream,* especially for the festival. But, with no room to swing a cat and no possibility of expansion, the little theatre simply couldn't keep up with the burgeoning crowds. Accordingly, two decades in, Ben Britten waved his baton and, *presto chango,* with the backing of affluent and influential friends, and a strong fund-raising drive, the festival was transferred, lock, stock, and barrel, to an abandoned malt-vinegar milling complex in the nearby village of Snape. Soon, a restored and renovated malthouse reemerged as the 810-seat Snape Maltings Concert Hall. Unlike its petite predecessor, the new hall could accommodate a symphony orchestra and chorus on its stage, and, wonder of wonders, there were actual dressing rooms.

In June of 1967, I directed the BBC relay of the twentieth Aldeburgh Festival's Gala Opening in the new Snape
Maltings Concert Hall. Gala it surely was, as was any
event which Queen Elizabeth II and Prince Philip attended. Their presence attested to The Festival's (and Ben's)
importance as well as putting Snape in the forefront of
Britain's musical sites. No question, the Queen's appearance gave the Gala Opening a majestic boost.

Whether in the Suffolk marshlands or in Piccadilly
Circus, everywhere the Royals went, the press was sure
to go. Worth noting, the royal family never just happened
to drop in on an event, every aspect of every visit was mi-
nutely choreographed through a series of agreements with
the Buckingham Palace Press Office. Nowadays, things
are more relaxed, "Royal Walkabouts" and the like, but in
the 1960s and 1970s, protocol ruled. During a prescribed
visit to the press office, you explained precisely how you
wanted to report the occasion. A formality that you had
to go through every single time and each time the same
procedural dos and don'ts were trotted out. Basically, it
boiled down to camera etiquette. To wit: you could show
the Royals as they entered the Royal Box, you could show
them during the playing of the National Anthem, you
could show them acknowledging the applause from the
audience, and you could show them settling into their
seats as the houselights lowered. But the minute the performance began the cameras turned away and during the
actual concert, none of them could point in the Royal
direction. The show over, cameras again picked up the
waving and smiling Royals as they exited. Why the ban
on continuous coverage? Except for Prince Charles, the
Royals were not noted music lovers, any of them might
have nodded off. Heaven forbid that such an image be
transmitted.

Ecstatic at the way the Snape Maltings Concert Hall turned out, especially its brilliant acoustics, Ben approached John Culshaw with an idea. He wanted the BBC to turn his new auditorium into a television recording studio and use it to document his most renowned opera, *Peter Grimes*. As a further enticement Ben added, "I'll be on the podium; probably the last time I'll conduct my first opera." Culshaw immediately contacted David Attenborough who, posthaste, put the project on the BBC's fast track. John was named executive producer and I was asked to serve as director. By this time, I was pretty near the top of my game, the go-to director for musical events. Others may have surpassed me in fields such as current affairs and documentaries but when it came to concerts, operas, and the like, my name, like Abou ben Adhem's, led all the rest. Eagerly, we went to work on *Peter Grimes*.

Production and filming, a nightmare of planning and organization, took place during the last half of January and the first three weeks of February 1969, the height of the winter snows. From London's BBCTV centre we imported equipment and personnel: cameras, lights, audio components, costumers, make-up artists, and technicians. An army of singers, musicians, and crew members descended upon the snug village of Snape. The local citizenry welcomed the invasion with open arms; they housed us, fed us, and ferried us to-and-fro; *Peter Grimes* became a community effort. Turning a concert hall in the middle of the Suffolk marshes into a TV studio was our first challenge. Straightaway, we had all 800 plus seats removed, leaving a long tunnel-like space, nicknamed the "shoe-box". To accommodate the set, the soloists, and a sixty-member chorus, plus the cameras, the designer, David Myerscough-Jones, extended the stage into the audience section. At the opposite end of the shoebox, we built, on various levels, a large seating area for all seventy-five members of the London Symphony Orchestra along with a small mountain of acoustical equipment with cables running to the outside control room in the Maltings courtyard. At the other end of the shoebox, Britten would conduct from the elevated position which gave him a bird's eye view of the stage action. For him to coordinate with the soloists and chorus, a TV camera stayed on Britten for the duration of the recording, relaying his image to monitors concealed in the scenery. Scattered about the set, a cadre of music assistants and sub-conductors kept a close eye on the monitors, then cued the soloists. Without doubt, this huge undertaking cost an astronomical amount of money but such was the power of the BBC and Benjamin Britten, it had to happen. The impressive cast headed by Peter Pears, recreating the title role of the tortured fisherman, featured well-known Britten soloists including Heather Harper as Ellen Orford, Grimes's fiancée. Also on hand was soprano Joan Cross. Back in 1945, Joan Cross had created the role of Ellen. An outstanding figure in British opera both as a singer and as an administrator, Joan Cross happened to be one of Britten's earliest and staunchest supporters. Ben adored her and, as previously noted, if he liked and trusted you, he could be extremely loyal. Still, should you cross him, he'd go right for the jugular. Not a chance of that happening to the rock-solid bond between him and his beloved "Joanie". The roots of their friendship went deep.

At the end of World War II, opera did not top the list of matters that had to be attended to post haste. Joan Cross thought otherwise. She believed that opera was essential but that it had to change with the times. Enough of the old boys, let's hear from the new composers. She grabbed opera by the seat of the pants and pulled it back up by putting her money on Benjamin Britten. Ben had run up against a wall of opposition. He couldn't get Covent Garden Opera to present *Peter Grimes*, his first opera; other houses turned it down as well. Only Joan Cross, then director and chief administrator of the Sadler's Wells Opera, wanted to give *Peter Grimes* its world premiere and she had to face opposition to do so. Certain members of the company judged the work not good enough; they, and others, further questioned Joan's motives when she took the lead female role for herself. Disgruntled company members accused her of presenting Britten's opera simply to put herself in it. Whatever her motivation, she created a brilliant Ellen Orford and went on to originate roles in other Britten operas. Although she continued to sing past her prime, Joan Cross still made an indelible impression in whatever part she performed. What's more, her faith in *Peter Grimes* was thoroughly vindicated. Britten's opera, now a universally acknowledged masterpiece, pushed Sadler's Wells into the headlines and became the company's first box office hit after the war. Following her retirement, Joan moved to Aldeburgh, no doubt to be near her friend, Ben. Once ensconced, she held court at one or another of the local pubs, reminiscing at length with anyone who cared to listen. Many cared. Smoking like a chimney, swearing like a sailor, and knee-deep in admirers, Joan carried on for nearly two decades. Ben was determined to involve her in the Snape Maltings production of *Peter Grimes*. "Joanie knows more about that opera than anyone", he informed me. The next thing I knew, Ben asked Joan to stage the opera. I never figured out whether Ben wanted me to help her or her to help me but he was right, she knew that opera inside out and passed on that knowledge. That she knew nothing about television or filming was irrelevant, she completely won me over. I fell in love with that feisty lady and we became fast friends as well as colleagues.

Everything seemed to fall into place during the recording sessions. A notable occasion for me came when Ben found out about my upcoming thirty-second birthday. He and Peter promptly chose to host a party at The Red House. What a delightful event, especially when the hosts and Joan Cross led the singing of "Happy Birthday". As a gift, Ben and Peter presented me with a drawing of the original design of Act One from the Sadler's Wells premiere of *Peter Grimes*. That sketch holds a special place among my souvenirs. The BBC2 transmission of *Peter Grimes* was a resounding success, and solidified my relationship with Benjamin Britten. The rallying cry now became "what next?" For that we had to look backwards.

In 1966, the BBC offered Ben a commission for a television opera. Though not the first time a broadcast network had done so, Menotti's *Amahl and the Night Visitors*, commissioned by America's National Broadcasting Company, had premiered in 1951, this was the BBC's initial directive. Surprisingly, Ben was not sold on the idea. The ten-thousand-pound commission, peanuts, even for those days, hardly provided an incentive. Money aside, television was new to him and remained a bit of a mystery. At the same time, Ben found the prospect of using television techniques intriguing. Earlier in his career, he'd composed soundtracks for British documentary films and remained fascinated by the process of putting music to film. Still, Ben hesitated. It took John Culshaw to convince him. John pointed out that, although written for the small screen, the opera would be a major work which could be performed in large opera houses. *The Three Parables*, Ben's most recent operas, were written for small ensembles, and John knew Ben was eager to return to full scale opera. Regarding the complexities of television, John also encouraged him. "No need to worry,

Ben, Brian will be there." The determining factor came when John reminded him that television would bring his music to thousands of viewers. Thus assured, Ben accepted the commission. That done, he needed a librettist and a subject. A decade prior, he had worked well with the Welsh poet Myfanwy Piper on an adaptation of *The Turn of the Screw*, a Henry James ghost story. Ben contacted her and Piper came aboard. As for the subject, Ben believed that the supernatural best lent itself to television and looked again to Henry James. This time he chose *Owen Wingrave*, an even darker tale than *The Turn of the Screw*. The future set, Ben turned back to the present and the upcoming Aldeburgh Festival.

The highlight of the 1969 Aldeburgh season would be Colin Graham's production of Mozart's *Idomeneo* with Ben on the podium. Except for his own works, *Idomeneo* was the only other opera that Benjamin Britten ever conducted. No Verdi, Puccini, Bellini, Rossini, Donizetti, Strauss, Wagner, not even another Mozart. Why did he avoid the entire operatic canon? I haven't a clue. I only know that *Idomeneo* was his favourite Mozart opera. He really loved that piece. Once the festival ended, the plan was to record *Idomeneo* à la *Peter Grimes* in Snape Maltings Concert Hall.

The 1969 Aldeburgh Festival opened with an orchestral concert on 7 June; not long after the programme ended, even as the opening night party proceeded at full swing, an electric fault ignited a fire on the roof of the concert hall. Within minutes the entire building was ablaze, and within hours the Snape Maltings Concert Hall went down in flames. Ostensibly, the 1969 Aldeburgh Festival began and ended on the same evening, however, a few concert performances of *Idomeneo* were given in local churches. Heartsick at the collapse of the festival, Ben was equally depressed that *Idomeneo* would not be televised. He refused to let it go and appealed for help to the BBC. They suggested producing *Idomeneo* in their Shepherd's Bush studios, a plan Ben would not consider; he wanted the same shoebox set up as he'd had for *Peter Grimes*. Enter Joan Cross. She proposed using the former Troxy Cinema in East London which, after the war, had become the permanent home of the London Opera Company. Ben embraced the idea and *Idomeneo* was transferred to the Centre. Seats were removed, new sets were installed resulting in a slightly modified and even bigger shoebox than had been created for *Grimes*. While the cast remained the same the production was restaged. In September of 1970, *Idomeneo* gracefully made the transition from Snape to East London in a much-praised television version which, as you already might have guessed, is available on YouTube.

Meanwhile, back in Snape, reconstruction had started and, amazingly, within the year the Snape Maltings Concert Hall was rebuilt, rededicated, and reopened. The BBC, ever at the ready when it came to Benjamin Britten, televised the gala (re)opening in July 1970. Once again, the Queen and Prince Philip attended and, once again, I was asked to direct. Fittingly, the programme contained excerpts from *Gloriana*, the opera about Elizabeth I, that Ben had composed for Elizabeth II's coronation in 1953. And so, the Aldeburgh Festival returned with a flourish and true to his word, Benjamin Britten began working on *Owen Wingrave*, the BBC2's commissioned opera.

Composing for a media that both puzzled and intrigued him challenged Ben. Reputedly, he "hated" television and the fact that he did not own a television set purportedly provided evidence of his disdain. Personally, I never heard him cast any slurs. He may have been mystified by the technical workings which were different from film making but if anything, he wanted to understand them not scorn them. As mentioned, in seeking a subject, he deliberately chose another Henry James ghost story because he believed that, musically and dramatically, the supernatural best suited the television media. Although I already had directed Ben's *The Burning Fiery Furnace* and *Peter Grimes*, *Owen Wingrave* was different. The other operas were faits accomplis when I took over; this time I'd be on hand as "advisor" to the composer during the actual creative process. Mind blowing! It got even better when the BBC informed me that they wanted my "above and beyond" participation. "We're of the opinion that the best way for you to help is to be on Ben's doorstep. Would you be willing to move to Aldeburgh while he's working?" Willing? It makes me laugh to think of all the times I was asked to do something that I was dying to do.

John Culshaw and Benjamin Britten.
Culshaw masterminded the Britten/BBC
collaboration

The Snape Maltings Concert Hall,
a malt warehouse, transformed
into a music paradise

15.

In a Kingdom by the Sea

The BBC rented a tiny shoreline cottage, installed a piano, set up a telephone line, and I moved in. My sole function was to be available for Ben. Other than that, I was free to work on projects of my own. He might simply wish to chat on the phone, in which case I would listen, or he might call and ask me to come to The Red House and confer with him. To be in on the creative process excited me, though I must admit, because of the time of year, it was a weird existence. A typical seaside resort, Aldeburgh shone brightly during the summer months. October through May, however, bitterly cold temperatures with heavy low-hanging clouds, rough seas, and biting winds prevailed. Also, Aldeburgh had but one cinema and a couple of small hotels, empty for the most part. As for dining, I can't recall any restaurants open other than in one of the hotels. Most days, I'd go down to the beach, buy fish directly from the fishermen, purchase veggies from the greengrocer, go home, and cook. I spent a good deal of time waiting for the phone to ring, all alone by the telephone, as Irving Berlin put it. Whenever he felt the need, Ben would call and either we'd chat on the phone or he'd invite me over. If the latter, I'd immediately get into my car and drive to The Red House. The vicious dog alerts on the gate no longer troubled me, little danger lurked in the loveable dachshund now in residence. Each time I arrived she scrambled all over me licking my face with complete abandon. Ben and I spent our time together in the library where he'd sit at the piano and talk about this scene or that

character. Occasionally, he'd play something he'd just composed and, to my delight, sing along in his croaky voice.
What an experience being side by side with a composer
creating an opera. I couldn't get over it. I'm not a very religious person but I thanked God every day for this gift. Ben
was on Cloud 9 working on a large-scale opera for the first
time in many years. The score called for an orchestra of fifty
players, with a large percussion contingent of various gongs
and a xylophone, perfect for the eerie effects he was after.

Owen Wingrave is a pacifist piece. All his life, Ben had
avoided any form of violence or bloodshed. In 1939, he and
Peter emigrated to the United States to avoid being called
up for service in World War II. Midway through the conflict, rather than sit out the war in safety and comfort, they
returned to England. As conscientious objectors they were
exempt from military service. Back home, Peter needed to
work and subsequently found a position with the Sadler's
Wells Opera Touring Company. Their London home out
of commission, the troupe travelled around, particularly
in the north country where bombings were rare. Peter hit
it off with the administrator of the troupe and introduced
her to his partner. And that is how Benjamin Britten, the
composer, and Joan Cross, the administrator/singer, found
each other. Kismet.

Owen Wingrave is the story of a military family that traditionally sent the eldest son into service. Owen, a pacifist,
wants none of it. Accused of cowardice by his family and
his girlfriend, he tries to prove his bravery by spending
the night in a remote room of his home. During that time,
he's confronted by the ghosts of his ancestors and dies of
fear, not cowardice. Sinister and frightening, James's woe-
ful story is intensified by, arguably, the darkest music Ben
Britten ever composed. From the beginning, Ben knew

exactly where he was going and who was going with him. He envisioned *Owen Wingrave* as an opera for eight singers. Before he wrote a note, he chose artists whom he knew and liked and whose voices he admired: Peter Pears, Heather Harper, Jennifer Vyvyan, John Shirley Quirk, Benjamin Luxon, Sylvia Fisher, Nigel Douglas, and Janet Baker. Then, he fashioned their roles specifically accommodating each singer's fach, an incredible feat.

One afternoon, on a particularly blustery day, I got the call from Ben, hopped in the car, arrived at The Red House and, as usual, was ushered into the library. This time, however, Ben didn't go to the piano; he wanted to talk about the television production, especially the camera's placement and function. He knew what you could do on film. But television had its own methods. Over the usual cup of tea, Ben clued me in. "I asked you here because I need to write some interlude music to get from one scene to another and I want some insights into the scene changing procedure." "You don't need to write any interlude music", I responded. "If you want to go from one scene to another, we'll just fade into it by superimposing one image over the other." (The technical term is "cross fading".) "Yes, but I still need to write interlude music." "Ben, there's really no interlude for you to write music for, the change of scene is instantaneous in TV." "But I feel like writing interludes." "Well, if you want to write them, go ahead. But why do it if you don't need it?" "You don't get it, Brian", answered Ben with a knowing smile. "I have to write interlude music because eventually *Owen Wingrave* will be produced on the stage of an opera house where you need music for scene changes, so why not do it now?" Quite satisfied with himself, Ben actually giggled as he explained his two birds with one stone rationale.

Owen Wingrave begins with a prelude introducing the Wingrave family from its origins in 1536 to the present day. The designer, David Myerscough-Jones created a progression of nine family portraits which ends by introducing us to the real-life Owen. Ben precisely marked my score where each portrait should appear on the screen as the music plays. In a way, he was creating a camera script for me to follow. He did the same for the first interlude which links Coyle's Military Academy to Owen's first soliloquy in the park. Originally, Ben had talked about incorporating archival film footage of the Horse Guard Regiment parading and fighting in battle. Realizing that would create, stylistically, a visual conflict, he asked us to find another solution. We proposed two montages, the first a sequence of military flags triumphantly blowing in the wind to suggest the glory of war. For the second, after Owen's final soliloquy the flags were replaced by tattered and blood-stained flags to underline the horror and destruction of war. Again, Ben marked my score where each flag should appear. The third interlude announces Owen's return to Paramore, the family home. Stylistically, we couldn't use footage of an existing manor house, so we resorted to early film makers' technique by building a huge model of a manor house and garden, the details of which were so precise, viewers couldn't detect that it was a fake. The Ballade which opens Act II retells the history of Paramore, the haunted house, and it was this sequence that most intrigued Britten and moved him to create music distinctively inspired. Out of the camera's range, a narrator (sung by Peter Pears) and boys choir recounts the history of the house as two young boys enact the story. To underpin the supernatural, Ben agreed that we shoot the scene in slow motion, using sepia and soft-focused monochromatic tones. The resulting effect is not only arresting but one of the most original parts of the score.

Ben, a worrier, fretted over every element. For example, he wanted the atmosphere to be as threatening as possible. The stage director, Colin Graham, and I tried hard to capture the creepy atmosphere of a haunted house. We spent hours discussing ways to make the production as frightening as possible, from the mise en scène to the cross fading of the ghostly comings and goings. Although Ben never actually told me, I'm certain that *Owen Wingrave* was meant to be an indictment of the recent war in Vietnam. (Not thoroughly examined at the opera's inception, the parallel to Vietnam is now accepted as a probable underlying theme.) Because *Owen Wingrave* was a major work on pacifism, a subject close to his heart, he was nervous about it and often questioned the opera's value. I don't think he relaxed for a moment during the rehearsals. That is, until 22 November when Ben would turn sixty. To mark the occasion, production was paused as a giant size birthday cake in the shape of The Maltings was wheeled onto the *Wingrave* set. Too stressed and too weak to conduct any of the rehearsals, his assistant Stewart Bedford had been responsible for the musical preparation, Ben summoned all his strength and, while the cast and crews sang "Happy Birthday", cut the cake. The occasion, a beautiful moment, broke the tension which had accompanied rehearsals up to then. The birthday celebration, alas, proved to be a momentary cessation; anxiety returned and would continue to hover in the air to the final day of shooting. On that day, Benjamin Britten stepped in and conducted his opera for the first and only time.

Owen Wingrave premiered on 16 May 1971 and scored a great success. Admired by viewers and critics alike, the results exceeded John Culshaw's predictions. Apart from BBC2 viewers, thousands watched on twelve international networks serving Belgium, Denmark, Yugoslavia, the Netherlands, Norway, France, Austria, Sweden, Ireland, Switzerland, Germany, and the USA. No composer in history ever had such a premiere. Paradoxically, although he wrote the opera for TV, Ben still didn't own a television set. Most likely he never would have had not Decca presented him with one on his sixtieth birthday in November of 1973. Whether he ever turned it on or not is another story.

In our conversations during *Owen Wingrave*'s preparation, Ben occasionally talked about his next project, turning Luchino Visconti's film of Thomas Mann's novella, *Death in Venice*, into an opera. From what he told me, I got the feeling that he wanted to incorporate his own life story into Mann's tale of an artist whose creative juices were drying up, a situation Ben feared he was facing. I sensed that he wanted to confront his own creative demons through his music. Once *Owen Wingrave* was recorded, Ben turned to *Death in Venice*. Sadly, his efforts were hampered by his ever-failing health. He struggled to finish the score and by the time he completed the opera, his physical being had greatly declined. Sensitive to his friend's weakening condition, John Culshaw did not feel comfortable approaching him about documenting the premiere. He waited for Ben to rally but that never happened. Thus, Benjamin Britten's last opera opened the Aldeburgh Festival in June of 1973 without BBC2's presence.

In constant pain and unable to function the way he wanted, Ben elected to have heart surgery and during the procedure, suffered a stroke. He survived, but as an invalid. Often confined to a wheelchair with his right hand severely affected, Ben could barely hold a pencil. Composing became an arduous task. He literally had lost the will to work when, miraculously, through a touching intervention that only recently has been revealed, Benjamin Britten was inspired to compose again by no less a personage than Queen Elizabeth II. Twenty years before, he had been commissioned to compose an opera to celebrate her coronation; in the ensuing years they maintained a warm, if distant, relationship. Having learned of his present desperate straits, in a generous act of thoughtfulness, the Queen commissioned him again, this time privately and personally. In January 1975, she wrote a letter in her own hand which begins, "Dear Ben". The informal salutation was unusual, moreover, letters customarily were sent by a lady-in-waiting on behalf of the Monarch. Precedent already shattered, the contents held even more surprises. Elizabeth wrote that she had a request to make, not as a queen but as a daughter. Would he write some music for her mother's upcoming 75th birthday? The letter ended "Please try." He accepted the offer by return mail. In honour of the Queen Mother's Scottish roots, he suggested songs for voice and harp based on poems by Robert Burns. Elizabeth quickly answered saying she thought the songs would be perfect and Ben eagerly took up his composing pencil. He and the Queen exchanged further letters, his making suggestions and hers encouraging him in his choices.

On her 75th birthday, the Queen Mother received her daughter's present, the manuscript of Ben's songs. At once she wrote a three-page thank you in her own hand. In the letter, she told Ben that Lady Fermoy, her lady-in-waiting and grandmother of Diana Spencer, the future Princess of Wales, picked out the harp music on an old upright thus providing the Queen Mother a welcome opportunity to hear her gift. She added that she looked forward to a future, formal presentation with him in attendance. The letter ended, "I honestly don't think that anything in my life has given me greater pleasure than your birthday gift." True to her promise of a proper presentation, Ben, in a wheelchair, would attend an intimate gathering of the Queen Mother, the Queen, Princess Margaret, Lady Fermoy, and Britten's nurse to hear Peter Pears sing the birthday songs accompanied by harpist Osian Ellis. Inspired and encouraged by the two Queens, Ben continued working and managed to complete a couple of powerful late works, the *Third String Quartet*, and *Phaedra*, a cantata written for Janet Baker. A life that easily could have ended in misery had been revitalized by the two Elizabeths.

Edward Benjamin Britten, Baron Britten, of Aldeburgh in the County of Suffolk, died at the age of sixty-three on 4 December 1976. To this day, I feel such gratitude to have known him. What an honour to spend time with Ben and to have participated in documenting three of his operatic masterworks, *The Burning Fiery Furnace*, *Peter Grimes*, and *Owen Wingrave*. Each had its own special splendour and yet *The Burning Fiery Furnace* remains closest to my heart; I think that's because it marked the beginning of a working relationship which, over the years, turned into a beautiful friendship.

LEFT:
Benjamin Luxon as Owen Wingrave, Dame Janet Baker as Kate Julian in the televised production of Britten's *Owen Wingrave* in 1971

OPPOSITE PAGE FROM TOP:
Ben Britten and I on the set of *Owen Wingrave*

Ben and I during rehearsals for *Owen Wingrave*. Peter Pears, who created the role of Sir Philip Wingrave, stopped by for a chat

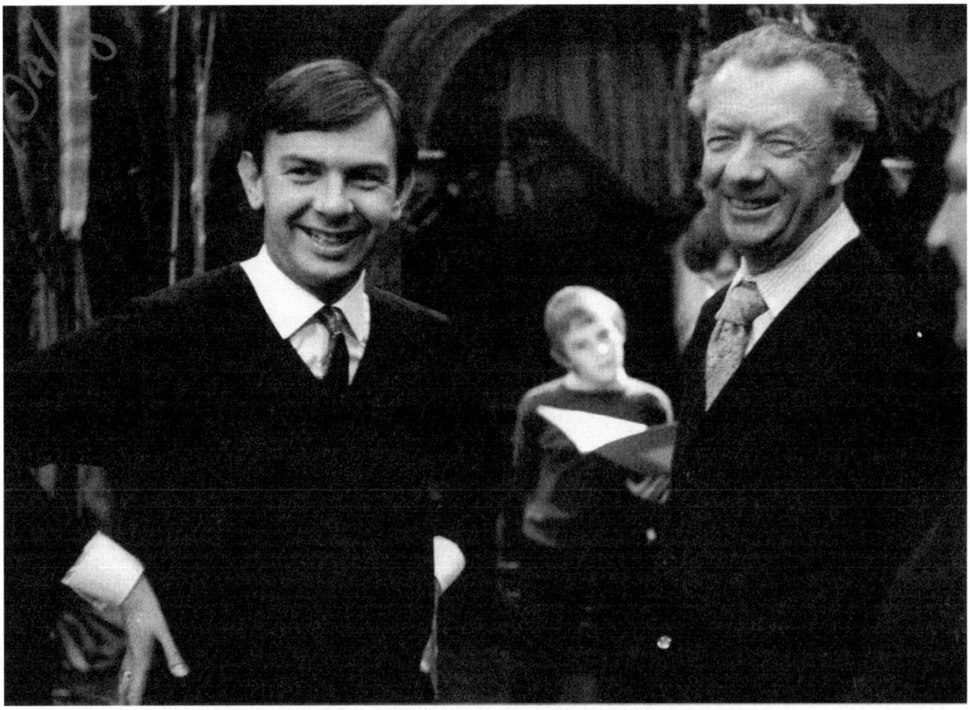

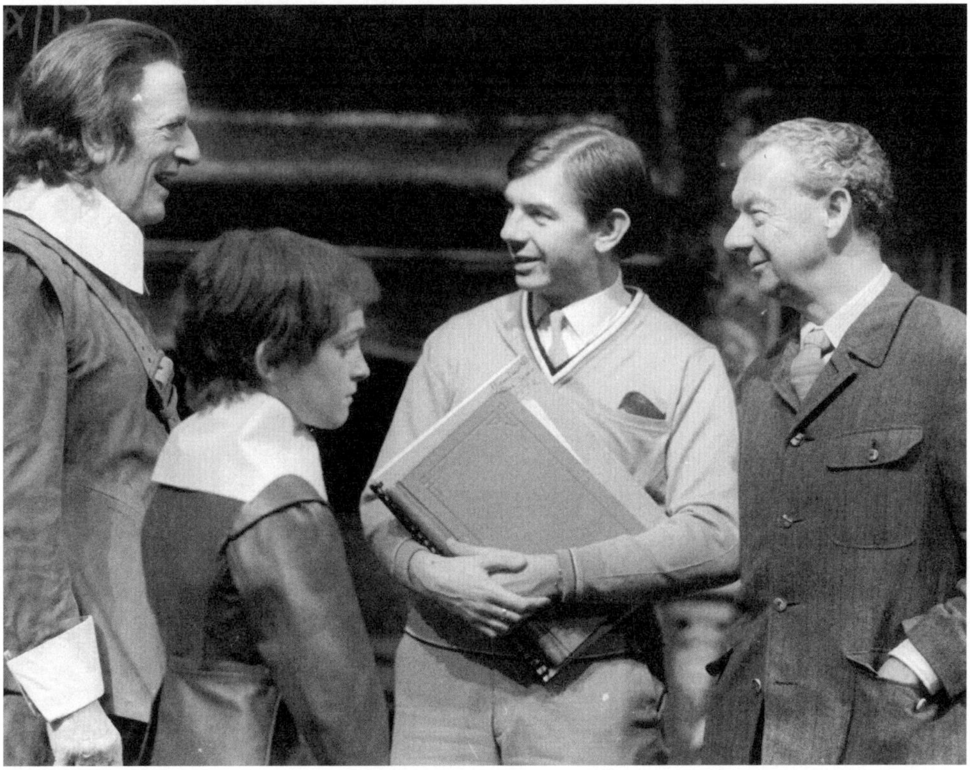

II

ACT

Me in the late sixties during a BBC broadcast

16.
Adventures with Auntie

Incorporated in 1922, the state-owned British Broadcasting Corporation Ltd. grew into the world's largest public sector media company. For decades, in both radio and television "Auntie", aka "The Beeb", did very well indeed, that is, until the Television Act of 1954 opened the way to commercial broadcasting and competition. ITV, the first commercial network aired in September of 1955 and, before long, others leapt into the airwaves making it increasingly difficult for Auntie to hold pride of place. By the time David Attenborough took over as BBC2 comptroller in 1964, the ongoing battle of the TV Broadcasters had settled in.

On the other side of the airwaves, the three BBC radio stations, the Home Service, the Light Programme, and the Third Programme, held sway. Of the trio, the Third Programme, at first heard only in the evenings, highlighted cultural programmes and demonstrated a standing commitment to contemporary music as well as the standard orthodox repertoire. BBC2 truly joined the modern-day classical music trend when David Attenborough named John Culshaw to head the Music and Arts Division. Head over heels about all music, John, a staunch Wagnerite, also greatly admired the music of Benjamin Britten. He already had produced a series of Britten's works for Decca Records with Ben himself as conductor, composer, and pianist. Designated "a priceless heritage for posterity" by *The Times*, the recordings were an unprecedented success. After his BBC appointment, Culshaw wasted no time in bringing Benjamin Britten more prominently into the TV fold and their salubrious collaboration thrived.

BBCTV continued to produce outstanding programmes as part of its routine lineup but the relentless onslaught of commercial television increasingly challenged Auntie's grip on the airwaves. Perforce, major changes began to take place within the company itself. Beset by the Sisyphean task of balancing administrative duties and his creative impulses, David Attenborough finally threw up his hands, threw off the managerial chains, and left his chancellorship to spend full time writing and producing programmes as a freelancer. Simultaneously, Ben Britten's failing health prevented him from continued participation with the BBC; and the vaunted composer/corporation partnership faded away. For me, the coup de grace came when the BBC chose not to renew John Culshaw's contract. John left in December of 1975. Ratings and revenue ruled and cultural lineups took a nosedive. Speaking candidly, from a personal perspective John Culshaw had not been completely at home in the television medium. While he had an incredible aural imagination and recognized and encouraged visual artistry, his own visual ability was limited; he simply didn't "see" in the precise way he "heard". For example, John once directed Benjamin Britten and Peter Pears in a video of Schubert's *Die Winterreise*. Peter sang brilliantly and Ben played fabulously but the camera remained fixed on the former who stood stock-still as various wintery scenes flashed behind him. Now and again, Peter would reach up and clutch his collar or finger the buttons of his coat. The result? A static seventy minutes of glorious music but with nothing much to look at … and there definitely had been something to look at, namely, Ben's spellbinding performance at the piano. I couldn't believe that John never envisioned moving his camera off the still figure of Pears for shots of Ben's bravura pyrotechnics. In my book this was proof positive that, by nature, John wasn't a visual person. But he definitely was a visionary. His imagination and exceptional ability to deal with people made things happen and it's thanks to him that we have records of extraordinary musical events. When times became unsettled the BBC brushed aside John's achievements and let him go. Undaunted, he began a few years of whirlwind independent activity that took him all over the world. Tragically, he contracted a rare form of hepatitis and died at the age of 56, leaving behind an exemplary record of accomplishments and a host of grateful associates, myself included. John Culshaw's influence on my career and my life is beyond measure.

Attrition continued at the BBC. Antony Craxton, my other in-house advocate, reached retirement age and prepared to leave the scene. John Culshaw was an ear man, Tony Craxton was an eye man, a master of the visual. From the very beginning of my BBC tenure, Tony had been my champion. After giving me my first big break with the Proms, he never stopped bestowing projects. His last beau geste was a particular delight. In 1977, Tony covered the Queen's Silver Jubilee, his 200th programme involving the royal family, which included a state procession from Buckingham Palace to Westminster Abbey for a service of Thanksgiving, followed by an evening of live opera and ballet from the Royal Opera House, Covent Garden. Tony, who easily could have done the entire programme himself, turned over the evening's festivities to me. I had to deal with the procession of sixteen Royals coming from Buckingham Palace to the Royal Opera House where they were greeted by John Tooley, the general director, and

Lord Drogheda, the Chairman of the Board. Her Majesty and the other Royals then ascended the grand staircase into the auditorium where they took their places in the smothered-with-floral-arrangements royal box. What an experience to participate in the Silver Jubilee. (Who could have imagined that the future would hold two more such celebrations? God saved the Queen for a trifecta of Silver, Gold, and Platinum Jubilees!) Tony Craxton's largesse literally set me up for many years of various broadcasts involving the Royals. Oddly, while he was ever beside me as advisor and friend, we never actually worked together.

Aided and encouraged by John and Tony, each of whom made it clear that their support was based on my abilities, I moved forward, gratefully and happily, if not entirely smoothly. Some colleagues were peevish because I received more top assignments; others accepted my good fortune with a *che sera, sera* attitude. Whatever the individual response, I functioned alongside all of them and everything went well, except in one instance. Sherlock Holmes had Moriarty, Jean Valjean had Javert, Popeye had Bluto, and I had my own nemesis within the BBC ranks. I tried to deal with it by taking the highroad and for a good long time succeeded. Inevitably, we clashed. As part of company policy, department heads periodically called members of the staff together to review programmes transmitted during previous weeks. Each director would cite his contribution(s), state his purpose, throw in a platitude or two, and end with "I hope I captured the essence of the story." Other staffers then politely offered critiques. When it came my turn, a barrage of what I felt to be unwarranted criticism was hurled at me. Which is not to say that I believed everything I did merited praise, far from it. Critiquing is important but less so if there are mitigating circumstances. This fellow had a bone to pick which had nothing to do with the quality of my work. I put up with his denigrating dismissals until it became apparent the meetings were worthless. Consequently, I stopped going. Deprived of conference pot shots, my antagonist next threw his energies into openly competing with me by rashly taking on multiple projects. Predictably, he became swamped and that's when I received a phone call. "Brian," says he, "I'm in a hell of a spot. I have a concert in two days and I don't have time to prepare the camera script. I'll pay you 250 pounds if you'll do it for me." I thought a minute and responded, "I don't want your 250 pounds because that wouldn't come anywhere near my fee. But I'd be willing to take over the assignment." "Oh no, you don't," he blustered, "it's my contracted engagement!" "Fine," I retorted, "then do the f**king script yourself!" and I slammed down the receiver. Not my finest moment but a satisfying one. I reacted strongly because behaviour of this sort not only affected me but others. All that being said, generally speaking, I had no major beefs with my colleagues. In fact, one of them, Tony Palmer, I found quite entertaining if a tad overwhelming.

Had you searched from the Antarctic to the Arctic, you could not have found a more polarized pair than Brian Large and Tony Palmer. I was quiet, methodical, and intense as I went about my labours. Loud, colourful, and off-the-wall, Tony worked at a frenetic pace, screaming into the telephone while bouncing around our office. Yes, "our" office. For some unfathomable reason Tony Palmer and I had been assigned a share space in the East Tower of the BBC TV Centre. That two such opposites could not function in such close quarters quickly became apparent. However, we had to find a way to get things done and to get along—and we did. From 9 a.m. to lunchtime, Tony occupied the office whilst I did what I had to do elsewhere. Come one o'clock, Tony exited the premises and I had sole occupancy until six. To this day, I haven't a clue as to where Tony operated in the afternoon but the schedule suited both of us. Best of all, being relieved of the constant burden of his overpowering presence allowed me to thoroughly appreciate him. Tony really was a character, a genial sort who went on to achieve acclaim turning out films on, among others, William Walton, Gustav Holst, Margot Fonteyn, and Maria Callas. He also tackled pop subjects such as the Beatles, Jimi Hendrix, Frank Zappa, and Cream. I particularly admire his monumental 9-hour dramatization of Richard Wagner's life. He persuaded Richard Burton to play the lead, did all the shooting in the correct locations, and I still can't figure out where he got the financial backing. All I know is, I loved watching it and still sneak an occasional peek.

Throughout the sixties and seventies, my BBC projects were strictly musically oriented—Proms, recitals, concerts, and operas as well as a series of music-inspired interview/talk shows featuring an array of prominent conductors, performers, musicologists, and critics. In our discussions about repertoire and interpretation, I found out what made these artists tick and, in the process, became a more informed musician and, I hope, a better director. Although archival copies may have been made, to my knowledge, few of these live programmes have survived. Some remain etched in my memory and I'm compelled to share with you a handful of lost historical treasures beginning with a series of masterclasses given by Paul Tortelier, the brilliant French cellist and composer.

I learned early on that run-of-the-mill pedagogy is as dull as dishwater. That's why masterclasses, with their implicit promise of the exceptional, always captivated me. I attended many of them and discovered that despite the superlative appellation, a masterclass only fulfilled its designation when conducted by a true master such as Paul Tortelier. Tortelier was a brilliant teacher (Jacqueline du Pré studied with him) and a charismatic human being. His classes stood out because he was able to demonstrate the difference between what he could do with the bow and the instrument with what his students were doing. At the same time, he inspired them not to imitate, but to apply his observations where necessary and then strut their own stuff. That kind of encouragement is not always present in masterclasses. Teachers can be too eager to demonstrate their own (perhaps fading) talent rather than elicit the best from their learners. Or, they can be so harsh in their criticism, students are reduced to tears. Oh, the humanity of Tortelier's teaching was infectious. The class members were completely captivated and their improvement obvious and all because their teacher brought joy to those sessions. Of all the masterclasses in any discipline I attended or videoed, Paul Tortelier's never were bested.

The second programme in my limited parade of video highlights, featured conductor Eugene Ormandy and musicologist Deryck Cooke discussing the long and complicated history of Gustav Mahler's *Tenth Symphony*. At the time of the composer's death, the *Tenth* had been largely completed in a continuous draft form but not fully orchestrated. Thus, a few prominent musicologists and musicians, including Bruno Walter, deemed the work not performable. Correspondingly, the composer's widow, Alma, steadfastly refused to let anyone touch her late husband's sketches. And so, despite several scattershot performances of bits and pieces, Mahler's *Tenth* remained on the shelf for nearly half a century. Then, of his own accord, Deryck Cooke, who'd spent decades studying Mahler's music and was thoroughly immersed in the composer's style, took it upon himself to complete the *Tenth*. He polished one movement (there are five and I can't remember which one he chose), had it recorded, and sent the tape to Alma Mahler. The widow, now an octogenarian, had eased the constraints on her husband's work. She listened to the tape, she loved it, and gave Cooke permission to complete the symphony. Thus, at the Proms concert on 13 August 1964, Berthold Goldschmidt conducted the world première of Deryck Cooke's revised and completed version of Mahler's *Tenth Symphony*. Later, Ormandy and the Philadelphia Orchestra recorded the Cooke version. Cooke and Ormandy appeared together on BBC2 to elaborate on Mahler's final work. Hearing them bring their thoughts together while harmoniously playing off each other was pure heaven. The Cooke/Ormandy Mahler broadcast hooked me and I've been a quiet Mahlerite, as opposed to a vociferous Wagnerite, ever since.

Have you ever heard (of) Liszt's *Hexaméron*? Don't despair, few have. It's a prodigious piece for piano and orchestra created when Princess Cristina Trivulzio Belgiojoso, a charismatic Italian noblewoman and journalist, imagined a piano/orchestral suite comprised of variations from six different composers writing on a single theme. The Princess then passed on her idea to her friend, Franz Liszt. Liszt, in turn, selected a theme, "The March of the Puritans" from Bellini's *I Puritani*, and invited five other composers, including Frédéric Chopin, to join him. Liszt wrote his own variation and then composed an introduction, connecting sections, and a finale for the orchestra. He collected the other five variations and the extraordinary work premiered in March of 1839 with Liszt at the piano. Though well received at the time, over the centuries the *Hexaméron* dropped out of sight. In the 1970s, the American conductor Michael Tilson Thomas came across the work, immediately wanted to present it, and arranged to conduct the London Symphony Orchestra at the Royal Albert Hall in the *Liszt et al.* epic ... with a twist. In lieu of a single soloist and a single piano, Tilson Thomas chose to present six pianists at six pianos, a stunning challenge for both the musicians and the stage crew. When advised of the pumped-up piano situation the BBC immediately assigned the project to me. I never had heard of the Liszt opus and while excited to be part of the bravura concert, was somewhat sceptical about a half dozen grand pianos huddled together on the Royal Albert Hall stage. I met with Maestro Tilson Thomas to discuss the situation and within minutes we were at loggerheads. I'd given some thought to the visual aspect; Tilson Thomas hadn't, he just wanted the pianos set up in front of the orchestra like gigantic pretty maids all in a row. I allowed that that would present a Wall of Jericho to the audience and a major headache for me. I made a few suggestions, none of which appealed to the maestro. He dug in his heels. I'd about given up when, at last, I advanced a workable compromise. I proposed that the pianos be spread out in a fan shape rather than side by side, which would leave more space for the cameras and present a slightly less formidable barrier to the audience. Tilson Thomas cocked his head, thought for a bit, and, agreed. Everything went smoothly and the concert was a hit. Why wouldn't it be? Just the sight of six grands on stage was mind blowing. Tilson Thomas gamely filled the role of ringmaster and, given the circumstances, I was delighted to be a part of this somewhat wacky musical circus. Tilson Thomas enjoyed himself so much that decades later, to celebrate his 70th birthday, on 15 January 2015, he led the San Francisco Symphony in a performance of the *Hexaméron*. (The pianists included himself along with Emanuel Ax, Jeremy Denk, Marc-André Hamelin, Jean-Yves Thibaudet, and Yuja Wang.) Whether the pianos were lined up or fanned out, I couldn't tell you; I only know that once again the Hexaméron+6, made headlines. To my knowledge, no video of that incarnation exists, either. Such a pity.

Last, but in many ways "most", I want to call attention to possibly the biggest international challenge I ever pulled off. It happened in December of 1977 and the premise was to unite the world in a live satellite broadcast of six different vocal groups from the four corners of the globe singing Christmas Carols. The celebrants included a steel band on a beach in Jamaica; a boys' choir gathered around a Christmas Tree in Bad Tölz, Bavaria, Germany; a children's choir in a French chateau; a boys' choir in Westminster Abbey; a daredevil group of sixteen Māori tribesmen in canoes, paddling and carolling up a New Zealand river; a children's chorus singing in a South Carolina shopping mall, and culminating with an in-situ selection by the choir of the Church of the Nativity in Bethlehem. I visited all the locations except for New Zealand where a resident BBC agent set up everything. The success of the programme depended on perfect timing and the fact that I was dealing with four different time zones made that task especially difficult. Even so, everything went off like clockwork. If I must say so myself, and I must because I'm one of the few who even recalls the broadcast, "Star Over Bethlehem" captured a universal holiday spirit, one of the first television shows to put the whole world in the viewers' hands. And here ends my personal favourites.

Me getting accustomed to a new camera
during the switch to colour

Although I directed some three hundred plus programmes for the BBC, of the many musical events for
which I was responsible, the four I've mentioned were
particularly meaningful to me. The fact that posterity has
been denied them still stings.

17.

Feet of Clay

A singing colossus, Jon Vickers stood over six feet and had the build and swagger of a *heldentenor*, which indeed he was; he also had an irascible nature and working with him could be difficult. A devout churchgoer, Vickers easily took affront at any suspected criticism concerning his religious beliefs, and was equally sensitive about his singing abilities and his physical being. However, his talent was such that opera companies put up with his sporadic belligerence because of his mesmerizing performances. Without question, he held his place among the greatest tenors of his time. I greatly admired his Tristan, Otello, and Fidelio and really wanted to work with him but it never happened. I did come close, though, but not in the way I'd hoped.

In 1957, while performing Aeneas in *The Trojans* at Covent Garden, Jon Vickers agreed to sing the role of Herod in a live, English-language version of *Salome* for BBCTV. The production starred the celebrated German soprano, Helga Pilarczyk, with Walter Goehr, also a German, conducting the London Symphony Orchestra. Rehearsals began and it became apparent that despite his oft-repeated boast that he could learn any opera by heart in less than a week, Vickers was unprepared. Rehearsals continued as Vickers went through the motions but did not sing. Concerned, Goehr offered to take him aside and coach him, whereupon the tenor blew his top and screamed at the hapless conductor. "How dare you tell me what to do? I would never dream of

Jon Vickers as Peter Grimes at the Royal Opera House, Covent Garden, 1981. Where does the role end and the singer begin? Hard to tell with Vickers, he lived the part telling a conductor how to conduct!" The situation smoldered as Vickers continued to play catch-up with the music; a ticking time bomb, for sure.

One afternoon, Lionel Salter, head of music for BBCTV at that time, brought administrative staff members on set to watch a rehearsal. One of the staffers caught sight of the tenor costumed in a short tunic and unthinkingly blurted out, "Vickers is bow-legged." The tenor overheard him, became enraged, and walked off the set. Soon after, his agent informed the BBC that Mr Vickers had withdrawn from the production. The BBC flew in a last-minute replacement from Germany who, unfortunately, only knew the role of Herod in German. Consequently, while the rest of the cast sang in English, except for a few key phrases such as "Dance for me, Salome" and "Kill this woman", he sang *auf Deutsch*. The press picked up the story prompting headlines questioning why Vickers had jumped ship. The situation worsened when some papers additionally reported that Vickers had vocal problems and needed surgery. None of which was true. To add to the commotion, Helga Pilarczyk's husband, quoted in *The Times*, claimed that Vickers had come to rehearsals without knowing his part. Vickers hit the roof. Declaring that opera companies would cancel his contracts because of the damaging reportage, he threatened to sue *The Times* for defamation of character and BBCTV for loss of engagements and monies. Not surprisingly, the suits didn't go anywhere and were dropped. At which point, Jon Vickers formally announced that he'd never again sing for BBCTV. He kept his word.

In 1969, about to appear as Radames in *Aida* at the Royal Opera House, Vickers learned that BBC2 would be televising the production. Indeed, this would be the first full-length, live, colour transmission from Covent Garden, a noteworthy event for sure. Not for Vickers, who immediately withdrew. Talk about cutting off your nose to spite your face. But that was Jon Vickers. No one carried a grudge longer. More proof? In 1978, the Royal Opera House asked him to appear as Ramerrez in a new production of Puccini's *The Girl of the Golden West*. Again, he turned them down because BBCTV was involved. The vendetta continued and Vickers's misguided antagonism caused him to miss out on some choice roles over the years. To all intents and purposes, it truly seemed that Jon Vickers never again would appear on BBCTV.

Hope springs eternal in the corporate vest, especially when it comes to superstars. In 1981, when Vickers was scheduled to appear as Grimes at Covent Garden, his manager, John Coast, at long last, persuaded the tenor to let BBCTV tape a performance. To start things off smoothly, John Coast arranged a meeting with Vickers, himself, and the TV director—me! Eagerly, I walked into Coast's office and was introduced to Vickers, who took one look at me and shouted, "You! What the hell are you doing here? You're the one who called me bow-legged back in '57. How dare you approach me." My mouth fell open. "B-b-but, Mr Vickers," I stammered, "you've got me confused with someone else. I was a student at the Royal Academy of Music in 1957." I continued to make it clear that he'd made a mistake but he paid no attention. A mad scene followed in which Vickers continued to rage against BBCTV, *The Times* of London, and me, until, crazed with fury, he leaped from his chair and tried to grasp me around the throat. Luckily, John Coast grabbed him from behind and pulled him back into the chair. "Take it easy, take it easy", he admonished the ranting singer. John motioned for me to leave the office and without another word, I exited. After I left, John calmed down the tenor and actually got him to agree to the recording of *Peter Grimes*. Yes, he'd do it, Vickers said, but only on two conditions, this hateful person (me) could not direct nor could he come anywhere near Jon Vickers, ever again.

And so, Jon Vickers's magnificent Peter Grimes was documented, a gift for posterity and a heartbreaker for me. I wanted very much to work with the man. Tragically, Vickers's odd behaviour continued to worsen. In the end, he would be diagnosed with Alzheimer's.

Another example of Vickers's intense fusion with his characters. Tristan at the Royal Opera House, Covent Garden, 1982

18.
The Pilgrimage

From the beginning of my tenure at the BBC, I kept busy directing music projects, under John Culshaw's aegis. At the same time, our friendship flourished because of our mutual love of music, particularly operas, and especially Wagner. At this point, I feel I should clarify my feelings about, arguably, the world's most controversial musical genius. My passion is solely for the music, not the man. The musician was a god, the man a beast, a raging ego-maniac whose iniquities, ranging from cruel exploitations and vile betrayals to noxious antisemitism, are unforgivably damnable. For many, when Adolf Hitler appropriated Wagner's music to glorify the Nazi cause, the music and Nazism merged forever. Emotionally and intellectually, I was very aware of the situation. I couldn't bear the man and yet I couldn't bear to give up his music. Fortunately, Leonard Bernstein resolved my conundrum. Allegedly questioned as to how he, as a Jew, felt about Wagner, the conductor answered, "I hate him. I hate him. I hate him. On my knees, I hate him!" Like Bernstein, I worship the music and loathe the man. Having made this point clear, I'll return to John Culshaw and our shared fanaticism for the abominable/magnificent Richard Wagner.

To my way of thinking, John and I were members of what George Bernard Shaw termed an "inner ring of superior persons" aka "Perfect Wagnerites". Admittedly, John was far more perfect than I. To wit, in 1951 while I, a fourteen-year-old, was picking out leitmotifs from the *Ring* on the piano, thirty-seven-year-old John Culshaw was attending the re-opening of the Wagner Festival in Bayreuth where he formed an alliance with the founder's grandsons, Wieland and Wolfgang. During that visit, John received permission to record the first complete *Parsifal* live on the Festspielhaus stage, a historic documentation. Two years later, John returned to do the same with *Lohengrin*. Overall, the Wagner brothers planned to record their grandfather's entire Bayreuth canon, which includes the above-mentioned plus *Tannhäuser*, *The Flying Dutchman*, *Tristan and Isolde*, *The Meistersingers of Nuremberg*, and the *Ring Tetralogy*. Exhilarated by the *Parsifal* and *Lohengrin* experiences, John had his eye on the *Ring*. However, he didn't want to do it in Bayreuth where the brothers were in complete control. Rather, he wanted to use a studio which would allow him to take charge of everything and create his own production, from casting to recording. Accordingly, he crafted the iconic Decca *Ring* with Solti and the Vienna Philharmonic and "knocked out" the Wagner Bros. Appropriately miffed, Wieland and Wolfgang stepped away and the rift between them and John endured for many years. Not until 1969 did John return to the festival to try and rebuild bridges. And that's where I enter the picture. One fine morning, John called me into his office. "How would you like to come with me to Bayreuth?" he asked, as if that were a question. And so it was, at thirty-two years of age, I made my first pilgrimage to Wagner's shrine, another charmed occurrence that forever altered my life.

21 July 1969, the same day the American astronaut Neil Armstrong walked on the moon, I was over the moon, transported to another level of awareness as I sat in Bayreuth's Festspielhaus watching a dress rehearsal of *The Flying*

Dutchman. The Festspielhaus, a brick encased building with a wooden walled auditorium, is unique among music theatres of the world. Wagner, himself, "adapted" the hall's design from architect Gottfried Semper's plan for an unrealized project. Permission to do so was never asked, therefore never granted, the principle being, "Whatever Wagner wanted, Wagner got." Conventional opera houses feature tiers of seating in a horseshoe-shaped auditorium. The seats in the Festspielhaus are arranged in a slightly modified fan shape, a single steep wedge and boxes on the back wall, not the sides, thus every seat has an equal view of the stage. Much is made of the theatre's incredible acoustics created by the wooden building materials in the no-frills auditorium and its distinctive shroud-covered orchestra pit. Because the orchestra is not visible, the music seems to emanate from everywhere. No matter which opera is presented or what singers are performing, the audience is bathed in the free-floating, all-enveloping empyrean sound of music. The covered pit also creates a double proscenium which gives the illusion that the stage is further away and thus creates, as Wagner stated, a "mystic gulf" between the audience and the stage. Seated in that legendary building on that fateful Monday in July of 1969, I knew, somehow, somewhere, sometime, Richard Wagner's music would play an important role in my life.

On that first visit to Bayreuth, John also had invited David Myerscough-Jones, set designer of The Maltings' *Peter Grimes* and another passionate Wagnerite, to accompany us. We three had flown to Nuremberg, rented a car and proceeded to our destination. We arrived during the dress rehearsal period when the Festspielhaus was open to the public. A new production of *The Flying Dutchman*, and revivals of *Die Meistersinger, Parsifal,* and the *Ring* were scheduled that summer. Indeed, this would be the last opportunity to see Wieland Wagner's complete *Ring*. He'd died in 1966, at which point Wolfgang had taken sole charge of the festival. When John introduced David and me to Wolfgang and his son and daughter, Gottfried and Eva, I felt somewhat intimidated in the presence of all those Wagners. Bear in mind, members of that family also were descendants of Richard Wagner's wife, Cosima, the daughter of Franz Liszt. Liszt and Wagner—who wouldn't be intimidated? Wolfgang and his family, however, were unpretentious and friendly although one odd thing struck me. Wolfgang spoke a heavy Franconian dialect, which, although German, is almost impossible to understand. I spoke German to him, which he understood, but when he answered me, I had to scramble to make out what he was saying. Whatever the reason, listening to Wolfgang wasn't easy.

Bayreuth ran like a music factory and David and I took full advantage of everything offered. We were given access to all the rehearsals and to the canteen where we met that summer's resident artists, singers Birgit Nilsson, Leonie Rysanek, Gwyneth Jones, and Norman Bailey; conductors, Silvio Varviso and Lorin Maazel; and stage director August Everding. (In the years to come, I would work very closely with Nilsson, Jones, Bailey, and Maazel.) While David and I soaked up the Bayreuth air, John spent his time discussing various projects with Herr Wagner. John was especially keen to connect with Anja Silja. Silja had debuted at the festival in 1960 and appeared there regularly for the next seven years. During her Bayreuth days, something untoward occurred; specifically, Wieland Wagner left his wife, Gertrud, and entered a close relationship with the twenty-years-his-junior singer. During their liaison, he created productions for Silja in Bayreuth, Wiesbaden, Weimar, and Stuttgart. One of those productions, a sensational *Salome,* rocketed Silja into international stardom. Up to that time, the Salome du jour had been Ljuba Welitsch, a voluptuous red-haired Bulgarian, whose frequent appearances in that exacting role had taken its toll on her voice. Barely out of her teens, Anja Silja represented a younger generation of singers and became *the* Salome for contemporary audiences. Wieland's no holds barred production was shocking. Shocking in the sense that it hid nothing, and shocking in the way it dealt with John the Baptist's relationship to Salome, and most shocking when, at the end of the "Dance of the Seven Veils", Silja stood stark naked on the stage. (Mind you, this was the early 1960s. Nowadays, naked Salomes are practically de rigueur.) John Culshaw hoped to convince Anja Silja to do a video of Wieland's eye-popping *Salome,* a project he already had mentioned to Georg Solti. John planned to do it the same way we'd done *Peter Grimes* in The Maltings, that is to turn a concert hall into a television studio; this time, the Sofiensäle concert hall in Vienna. Solti was willing, Decca was willing, Anja Silja was not. She flat-out refused. "That production was created for me by Wieland. He is dead and it cannot be recreated. No assistant can revive his works. *Salome* ...", she thundered on, "is a sacred work. I'll never do it again!" Although John politely pointed out that Peter Lehmann, a former assistant, was reviving Wieland's *Ring* on the Bayreuth stage at that very moment, Silja stood firm. And that was that. One project downed, John moved on to the next, getting his friend Georg Solti into the Bayreuth conducting ranks. He took every opportunity to encourage Wolfgang to hire the Hungarian maestro. It did happen, but not until 1982, by which time John had died.

While Wolfgang Wagner and John Culshaw held their meetings, David Myerscough-Jones and I continued to knock about on our own. The Bayreuth atmosphere sizzled. Going to the rehearsals, wandering around the grounds and taking the air, the freshest air you can imagine (the Festspielhaus sits high on a hill outside the town), and having lengthy discussions about the productions with anyone willing to talk, and everyone was willing. Bratwurst was another highlight. During the hour-long intermissions, we gobbled them up and downed them with beer. (Another way of looking at my career: I went from frankfurters in Battersea Park, to sausages in Prague to bratwurst in Bayreuth and finally, hot dogs in New York.) Time came for John to return to London, however, since David and I had no imminent commitments, we decided to stay on as long as we could. Our living arrangements, not to mention all the bratwursts and beers, had become too expensive for our dwindling funds. Accordingly, we checked out of the hotel and into our car which we parked near the Festspielhaus. One evening, I'd sprawl on the back seat while David folded himself into the front; the next night we'd swap places. Our vehicular residence was damned uncomfortable but worth it just to awaken early in the mornings and see the sun rising over the Festspielhaus in a spectacular display of dawn's early light. Once up, we'd drive down to the railway station to do our ablutions, have a cup of coffee, and then spend another splendid day full of music. I was not only over the moon, I was in seventh heaven until, all too soon, the money ran out.

My last evening in Bayreuth I attended a performance of *Tristan and Isolde* with Wolfgang Windgassen and Birgit Nilsson. Aware that I was running out of money, Wolfgang Wagner arranged for me to view the opera from a lighting tower some thirty feet above the stage. Zeus-like, or Wotan-like, I could look down from my perch and see the entire stage from the front where the action took place, to the back, which was hidden from the audience's view. I watched the first act spellbound as the music wafted up to my aerie in the rafters. Near the end of the first scene in Act II, Isolde waits for her lover to join her. Nilsson sang, gloriously, of her love for Tristan. Then, in a bravura exit, she flung open her arms, turned, ran upstage, and entered the backstage area. The minute she was out of the audience's sight, she dropped her arms and swiped the back of her right hand across her mouth. Next, she pressed her hands on her stomach, and let out a huge belch. Her shoulders slumped forward as she plodded over to the back wall and, leaning against it, slid down to the floor. The musical interlude continued as I gazed down to see what would happen next. Nilsson reached out her arm and from behind a fake boulder, brought forth a bottle of beer. She twisted off the cap, raised the bottle to her lips, and downed the contents in three long swigs. Swiping the back of her hand across her mouth once again, she recapped the bottle and returned it to its resting place behind the boulder. She sat still for a few moments, then slowly got to her feet. Putting her hands on her hips, she threw back her head, and let out a second belch that I, and perhaps the stage crew, heard but, fortunately, the audience did not. Nilsson re-entered the opera. As she passed from the backstage into the spotlight, she tossed her head, threw her arms skyward, and rushed to meet her lover. In a matter of minutes, I'd witnessed the sublime descend to the ridiculous only to rise once again to the sublime. And then, the opera ended. *"Mild und leise, wie er lächelt"* (*How softly and gently he smiles*). Isolde sang her farewell to Tristan, a moving and profound parting for them, and for me as well.

The next day I gathered my few belongings, exchanged addresses with my new acquaintances, said my goodbyes, and, along with David, returned to London. But Bayreuth had taken possession of me, I couldn't get back to earth. I walked around in a daze reliving the sights and sounds of the past few weeks:

Was it a vision, or a waking dream?
Fled is that music:—Do I wake or sleep?

LEFT:
Götz Friedrich and I behind the scenes of the Bayreuth *Lohengrin*

OPPOSITE PAGE FROM TOP:
With Wolfgang Wagner at Bayreuth, 1980. Look at the score and you'll see we're talking *Meistersinger*, 1980

Götz Friedrich, Peter Hofmann, and I recording *Lohengrin* at the Festspielhaus Bayreuth, 1982

221

19

Busy in the Beeb

Following my too brief fling with Bayreuth, I eased back into the bosom of the BBC and continued working on music-centred programmes. I enjoyed doing what I did although, admittedly, assignments were more often standard rather than stimulating. I wanted to go beyond the strictly musical regime. I ached to direct my own opera productions, not simply record the work of other directors. I'd acquired that taste of honey when I prepared *The Telephone* for my BBC "audition". I don't remember saying anything directly but I probably dropped hints, and John Culshaw picked them up. At one of our occasional luncheons, he posed yet another of those rhetorical questions, the answer to which would never be in doubt. "How would you like to work with The Royal Ballet, Brian?" Shortly thereafter, I could be found knee-deep in cameras and cables at the Royal Opera House, Covent Garden. Individual artists had performed in the BBC studios but the opportunity to film dance programmes at the opera house itself challenged me and gave a real boost to my spirit.

Eagerly, I entered another phase of my career beginning with *Sleeping Beauty* and on to another repertoire highlight, *Cinderella*. Then came a plum, Kenneth MacMillan's new work, *Elite Syncopations*, a delightful concoction of Scott Joplin rags, slow drags, and cakewalks. Among the principal dancers, Monica Mason, an attractive artist of skill and charm, stood out. When her dancing career ended, Mason became the company's

"When shall we three meet again?"
Norman Bailey, Nicolai Ghiaurov,
and I recording the BBC2 *Macbeth*

principal repetiteur and, eventually, its artistic director. Along the way, she was made a Dame Commander of the Order of the British Empire. Although I never saw her after our brief *Elite Syncopations* encounter, Dame Monica remains an exemplar of the illustrious performing artists who waltzed in and out of my life leaving me with so many gratifying remembrances.

The world of dance intrigued me since my earliest encounters with the Royal Ballet. In the years to come, I met and recorded many outstanding dancers, among them Erik Bruhn, Mikhail Baryshnikov, Alicia Markova, Natalia Makarova, and Margot Fonteyn. While I never had the opportunity to document Fonteyn in a complete ballet, I did have the privilege of recording her solo performance to Edward Elgar's haunting *Salut d'amour* during the Metropolitan Opera's blockbuster 100th Anniversary celebration on 13 May 1984. Fonteyn's longtime colleague and friend, Frederick Ashton, had choreographed the piece for her and, in a gallant demonstration of camaraderie, came out of the shadows at the end, danced a few steps with her, then escorted her into the wings. In those last seconds before her exit, Fonteyn, a radiant smile warming her face, looked up and caught the light. I still get a lump in my throat when I watch that exquisite moment.

Working with the Royal Ballet added zest to my schedule but I hungered to direct my own operas. Within a year or so, my craving ended thanks to John Culshaw. We ran into each other in a BBC corridor and after exchanging hellos, John began talking. "You know, Brian. I've given it a lot of thought ..." I had no idea what "it" was, so I just kept quiet as he continued, "... we've done so many wonderful projects together I think it's time for the music department to run the whole show. It's a lot to take on but it's worth a try and I'd like you to be involved. Would you be interested?" (Sometimes I wondered, was John pulling my leg when he asked all those "would you like to?" questions). John was as good as his word. Together, we proposed a series of operas and, without much ado, my dream project began to take shape.

From 1973 to 1980, I directed six studio operas, each a stepping stone in my career. In the process, I mastered the BBC's two-studio opera technique, the one studio containing the chorus and orchestra, the other enclosing the setting, decoration, and performers. At the time I started the series, studio opera was classified as "drama" and as such, was serviced by the BBC drama group. Prominent in the department was Cedric Messina, a larger-than-life personality who'd been responsible for the celebrated *Billy Budd* telecast as well as the complete Shakespeare canon, quite an achievement. Too often, however, Messina's productions fell below the mark; he was not a "detail person". BBC executive Susan Willis wrote, "That we have the televised Shakespeare series at all is entirely due to Messina; that we have the series we have and not perhaps a better, more exciting one is also in large part due to Messina." Despite his spotty record, Cedric Messina made things happen and before John could put me in the driver's seat for the opera series, he had to get Messina's approval. Messina wasn't enthusiastic about my directing the upcoming studio opera; he saw me as a threat. Thanks to some good old-fashioned diplomacy on John's part, Messina finally agreed to yield the director's chair though he would not give up his title as producer. *Traviata* went into production and Messina invited me to lunch where he proceeded to make my position clear. "You'll direct, and I'll produce. If *Traviata* is a success, I'll take the credit. If it fails, you will take the blame." That said, he proceeded to pay the bill while I, having no recourse other than to accept his lopsided terms, took up the challenge. Tough as it was to listen to Cedric's ultimatum, he did, at least, pay for the luncheon. He couldn't discourage me, though. I determined to make *Traviata* a success no matter who got the credit.

When my work with the BBC studio operas series began, it touched me that *Traviata*, the opera with which my mother had hoped to wean me from Wagner, would be the opener. By this time, I'd grown increasingly fond of Verdi's work and wanted to do right by it. The role of Violetta is a jewel in the operatic crown, requiring a phenomenal singer and actress. I had discovered one such performer at the Royal Opera House in 1960, when Romanian-born Virginia Zeani took over for an ailing Joan Sutherland. Zeani gave a beautifully sung, heart-rending performance which I never forgot. Indeed, she became my template for Violetta. For our BBC broadcast I chose Elizabeth Harwood, a young British singer with the voice and face of an angel, and directed her as I had seen Zeani perform. Norman Bailey whom I'd met in Bayreuth and one of Britain's finest bass-baritones, splendidly sang the role of Germont, père. Joan Cross had prepared a more than adequate English translation and, overall, *Traviata* was sumptuous and satisfying. I earned my directing wings with that lovely programme, the first opera production I could call my own. The next season, we didn't have much money and thus had to do a more modest presentation of Gian Carlo Menotti's *Amahl and the Night Visitors*. One significant bonus, I invited the composer to become involved and he agreed. What's more, he suggested that we meet in person to discuss the production and forthwith invited me to visit his Edinburgh home.

Five years previously, I had driven up the coast to Alde-burgh to see Ben Britten; now I was flying to Scotland to meet another composer. What would he be like? Menotti's chauffeur picked me up at the airport in a Rolls Royce limousine. We drove to Yesterhouse, an eighteenth-cen-tury mansion formerly the residence of the Marquis of Tewkesbury. The composer warmly welcomed me. My luggage, a battered overnight case, was transported to my room by one of God-only-knows how many servants, and Menotti and I took tea in an elegant drawing room. Fol-lowing which, we strolled around the estate's magnificent manicured gardens. I then retired to my room to dress for dinner. That evening Menotti hosted a formal, candle-lit mini-banquet. Apart from myself, the guests were local dignitaries all of whom were appropriately clad in dinner attire while I faded into my business suit and tie. Menotti, resplendent in a traditional patterned tartan kilt, could not have been more charming and led the conversation until we were summoned to the dining room by the wheezy dron-ing of a kilted bagpiper. Flowers were everywhere and the wine flowed and laughter filled the air. What a show. The next morning, we got down to business. Menotti poured over the studio designs and costume sketches I'd brought with me and shared his thoughts on how the camera could best capture the right atmosphere. Since 1951 when NBC had premiered *Amahl* in the States, Gian Carlo had seen many TV adaptions and generously gave me tips on what to look for and what to avoid. He urged me not to make *Amahl* too sentimental, adding, "I want it to move peo-ple. I want it to be special, not cloying." At our parting, though there was no contractual bind, Menotti promised to come to the BBC studios in London for the rehearsals. He was as good as his word and showed up for the final taping. He sat next to me in the control room during the performance and then went onto the studio floor to greet the cast and thank the camera crew. On Christmas Eve, he watched the transmission at Yesterhouse. Within minutes of the closing credits fade out, he phoned to thank me for bringing *Amahl* back to the small screen; a kind gesture which I will ever remember. I've often thought of Britten's Red House and Menotti's Yesterhouse and the contrasting lifestyles of those two extraordinary men, Benjamin Britten's sparse and simple existence and Gian Carlo Menotti's rich-and-famous panache, both of which worked. Chacun à son goût.

The following year we had a bit more money for the studio opera which enabled me to stage and direct *Hansel and Gretel*. I chose Humperdinck's masterpiece because of its Wagnerian echoes. The extensive overture and scene-connecting orchestral interludes cried out for visual effects aka "TV magic". In the early seventies, the BBC's visual effects department wielded their sorcery through technological skills which were lavishly applied to *Hansel and Gretel*. During one interlude, the siblings fell asleep nestled in a giant leaf, which turned into a boat and sailed down a river. In another interlude, the witch rode her broomstick through the universe colliding with stars, planets, and other meteoric objects. Guess what? The boat never budged and the witch never flew. Each remained stationary. To cast the spell, I reached back to my television observations in Prague and employed the Chroma Colour Separation Overlay Technique. Chroma Keying is used to bring together two or more images or visual streams. By using a blue or green screen to trigger the effect, different backgrounds can be added as foreground, provided the colours blue or green are not in the foreground composition. Thanks to CSO we were able to create the illusion that the leaf boat was sailing and the witch was flying when in fact they were not. That's TV magic.

True confession. As gratified as I was working on *Traviata*, *Amahl*, and *Hansel and Gretel*, Wagner always was on my mind. Correspondingly, once Hansel and Gretel were safe at home, I put forth *The Flying Dutchman* as my next production. The 1969 Bayreuth experience with that magnificent work had deeply impressed me and I aspired to get my hands on it. John Culshaw enthusiastically green-lighted the project and the BBC granted my request, with one major hitch. A long-established BBC policy required that all operas originating from the studio had to be sung in English. *Amahl* was written in English, so no problem there. And *La Traviata* and *Hansel and Gretel* each had pretty good English translations. *The Dutchman* did not, which I discovered when I began looking at them. I didn't particularly like any of the versions and neither did Peter Butler, my colleague and associate. Adding to our concern, Gwyneth Jones and Norman Bailey, two of the world's finest Wagnerian singers, whom I'd been fortunate enough to engage for the production, preferred to sing in German. Rather than dither with any more translations, I asked the powers-that-be for what seemed a perfect solution. "Can we do *The Dutchman* in German with English subtitles on the screen?" Straightaway, the request was rejected sending Peter and me scurrying back to the English renditions. Nothing had changed, none of those attempts was good enough. At a dead end, we decided to grab the moment by creating our own English language translation. What a thoroughly satisfying task that turned out to be. Doing translations was simply another way of expressing my love of music. (This, by the way, wasn't my first experience with translations. At the request of his publishers,

I'd translated two of Martinů's operas, the previously mentioned *Juliette* and *The Greek Passion*.) Impressed with Peter's and my account of *The Flying Dutchman*, Gwyneth and Norman agreed to learn our English version. I then asked David Myerscough-Jones, another passionate Wagnerite, to create a concept and he did, a visual treatment that captured the haunted and haunting world of Senta and the Dutchman.

We began to visualize the production and could have set it off the coast of Scotland in a timeless period just as Wagner had indicated in his early sketches. Instead, we chose the 1840s, the period when Wagner was writing his score—the period of the beginning of the Industrial Revolution—the Age of Brunel. (Isambard Kingdom Brunel, the renowned marine engineer, became known as "the father of steam" after building the SS Great Western in 1838.) In homage to Brunel, David created a steamship with paddles for Daland's boat in contrast to the Dutchman's four master for Act I. Then, in Act II, instead of a room in Daland's home, David created a Jacoby-like workshop with the chorus grouped around looms, Jennies, belts, and bobbins. It was different, but it worked.

Several bastions needed to be stormed to get this *Dutchman* right. First, Richard Wagner wrote the opera without intervals but over time performances came to be divided into two separate acts. An outright sin since the interruption breaks Wagner's carefully crafted mood. Both David and I wanted to respect his original intention which meant getting a special time slot. The *Dutchman* playing time is around two and a half hours which didn't fall into the BBC's slots. A half hour, an hour, two hours, all worked separately but not lumped together. We went to the controller's office and, miracle of miracles, without much fuss, managed to get the oddball slot we needed. We had the time, now we had to have more space. The normal two-studio recording setup we'd used for *Traviata* and *Hansel and Gretel* wouldn't do, the *Dutchman* needed *lebensraum* and we spilled into three studios. Studio I, the largest production space in Europe, contained two huge ships. Studio II accommodated the conductor, the orchestra, and an unseen chorus. Studio III became the home/workshop for Senta and her spinning factory companions. This production obviously would cost a great deal of money and might not have happened had not David Griffiths, the producer of PBS's Great Performances in New York, agreed to coproduce *The Flying Dutchman* with BBC2. (I'd met David in Vienna in 1972 when I was directing the European premiere of Leonard Bernstein's *Mass*.) *The Flying Dutchman* made a big splash and received excellent reviews.

After the *Dutchman* aired, David Griffiths phoned and tantalizingly stated, "I've got something in mind that I'm sure would be mutually beneficial. Could you join me for lunch to talk things over?" We made a date. Lavishly praising the *Dutchman* telecast, David got to the point—he wanted to join with me in producing studio operas. "I'll bring in Sidney Palmer, a PBS colleague from Charleston, South Carolina, as my partner. The two of us will raise money and arrange for the programmes to be shown in the States." Good news, I thought to myself, a godsend out of nowhere. "There's one condition", added David. My heart sank. "What's that?" I asked, expecting to hear a deal breaker. "The operas", said David, "must be sung in the original language; no more English translations." I could have hugged the man when I heard those words. Of course, the final "yes" had to come from the BBC which, heretofore, had dismissed any appeal for original language operas. This time, however, the potential PBS alliance sweetened the pot. American dollars would strengthen the corporation's international position, a connection the BBC couldn't and didn't resist. With the English-only stricture lifted, I now could hire artists who were far more comfortable singing in the original language and couldn't or wouldn't be bothered with learning new words.

The following year (1977) we presented Verdi's *Macbeth* in Italian. The Bulgarian bass-baritone Nicolai Ghiaurov, the first singer I engaged, never would have sung Banquo in English. The *Macbeth* cast also featured Norman Bailey, Patricia Johnson, the London-born star of the Deutsche Oper, and the American tenor Neil Shicoff. I had to laugh, three out of the four leading roles in the BBC's first original language opera presentation were English-speaking. Ghiaurov included, these were singers of the highest order and gave our *Macbeth* production a totally international flavour. Ghiaurov felt very much at home in the BBC studio and quickly adapted to working to camera by reducing exaggerated stage gestures and concentrating on facial expressions. At the first recording session, he brought along his then partner, the Italian soprano Mirella Freni. I invited her to sit next to me in the control booth. Utterly captivated by her, I broke my ever-weakening resolution not to fraternize with performers. That chance meeting launched a forty-two-year friendship, one from which I greatly benefited in both my professional and personal life.

Macbeth, like its predecessors, had a good solid success. Later, when it aired in the States, the viewer numbers were staggering. Impressed by the response, David Griffiths and Sidney Palmer suggested we take our act on the road and transfer our efforts overseas. Both believed we were ready to reverse the procedure, i.e., do our work for PBS in the States and then share with the BBC. I had no objections. On the contrary, I looked forward to expanding

Norman Bailey and Patricia Johnson in the BBC2's
production of *Macbeth*, 1977

my connections and for a very good reason. After much
soul-searching and deliberating, I had decided to leave the
BBC and take my chances as an independent director. The
question remained, when?

Norman Bailey as the Flying Dutchman.
England's stalwart baritone brought opera
into homes across the UK through his
BBC television performances

Filming on the set of Wagner's
The Flying Dutchman in 1975

20

Yankee Doodling

In the summer of 1978, with the full support of David Griffiths, I made my America debut directing Ben Britten's comic opera, *Albert Herring*, at the Opera Theatre of St Louis. British soprano, Pauline Tinsley, and Scottish bass, David Ward, headed the Anglo-American cast. The co-production was aired on PBS in the States and on BBC2 in England and was well-enough received for PBS to send me to Minneapolis, Minnesota, to record the Peking Opera which, claimed the promoters, "contained the Treasures of China". The idea intrigued me. I even broke one of my fixed rules not to participate in productions using a language I didn't speak. Naturally, I requested an English-speaking interpreter. I met with him and learned a few pertinent facts. First, Peking Opera is not opera as we know it in the western world. Rather, it is a mélange of song, dance, and acrobatics. Second, the interpreter wasn't that comfortable in the English language. I explained that he had to cue me a few seconds before any action took place so that I knew where to point the camera. "For example," I said, "if there is a battle between one group on the right and another group on the left you must let me know when they'll be coming together." "Yes, yes, I can do this", the young man assured me. Guess what? He couldn't. The rehearsal began and the action was so fast that whatever he told me was about to happen, already had happened. Not since the days of the genuflecting priest racing around the church alter had I missed so many key shots. Obviously,

John Graham-Hall as Albert Herring and Pauline Tinsley as Lady Billows in Britten's *Albert Herring*, Glyndebourne Festival, 1990

I couldn't rely on him. My only alternative was to shoot the opera like a football match and follow the action as best I could. Needless to say, the video fell short of my usual standards, which is another way of saying it was a mess, a colourful one, but a mess, nonetheless. Still, the experience did introduce me to the world of Peking Opera and never again would I equate the Far Eastern with the European version.

Following the Peking Opera debacle, David suggested that we go to another regional house and after a bit of "shopping around", I wound up at the Houston Grand Opera where we presented *Willie Stark*, composer Carlisle Floyd's operatic setting of Robert Penn Warren's book, *All the Kings Men*. (I'll have more to say about this production later.) Happy with the results of our PBS/BBC rather than BBC/PBS collaborations, David got together with the CEO of the Opera Theatre of St Louis, an Englishman by the name of Richard Gaddes, to discuss future possibilities in other cities. Gaddes immediately proposed that we look to the Santa Fe Opera for our next venture. With the BBC's blessing and Richard's introduction, I flew to New Mexico and spent ten days in that breathtaking region attending rehearsals and performances while waiting to meet with Santa Fe Opera's founding director, John Crosby. The meeting finally took place in his office where I found myself face to face with one of the oddest men I've ever come across. He barely greeted me, sank into his desk chair, and hardly ever looked directly at me the entire time we were together. Brushing aside his seeming disinterest, I presented my reason for being there. "Mr Crosby, I'm here to speak with you about the possibility of BBC2 and PBS's Great Performances producing operas from Santa Fe." Although Crosby looked blank, I ploughed ahead and concluded with what I believed to be the coup de grace.

"I think this alliance would mutually benefit all three institutions and that it would make Santa Fe the Glyndebourne of New Mexico." Mr Crosby stood up, and angrily declared that neither he nor Santa Fe needed the BBC, PBS, or Great Performances. He especially seemed to be insulted by comparison to Glyndebourne. I politely tried to dissuade him but he remained unreceptive and summarily dismissed me. I left the office shaken and greatly puzzled that Crosby could not see what a boon such a collaboration would be to his company. Disappointed I reported back to David Griffiths. Calling Crosby's move "foolhardy", David urged me to "forget about it", and remained optimistic that other opera houses would happily join our scheme. One thing, though, he felt that since I'd be working with American technicians, cameramen, and stage managers in the future, it might be a good idea for me to join the Directors Guild of America. It made sense and under his auspices I became a member. With a union card in my pocket and productions in St Louis and Houston under my belt, I went in search of another American opera company.

During the 1980s, Beverly Sills, the much-beloved American soprano, held the post of General Director at the New York City Opera. With high hopes, I made an appointment to meet with her at the City Opera's Lincoln Center home. Presenting myself as eloquently as I could, I explained that I made opera relays for the BBC and wanted to enlarge the opportunity to work in the United States. "I've already done productions with two regional American companies and wondered if there was any way we could collaborate in documenting performances with your company?" Sills listened to what I had to say and when I finished, responded, "I assume that you are British and not American." I replied that I indeed was British and, in an attempt to inject a little humour, suggested that perhaps my accent might have given me away. Ms Sills wasn't in the mood for levity and before I got another word out, she took over. "Well, Mr Large, I'd like to point out that this is an American house. I run this house for Americans, American singers, American directors, American people. There's no place here for a British person such as yourself. I think you'd be better off taking your ideas back to England where you belong." Shocked at her response, I did manage to counter that, to my knowledge, at least two of the company's star performers, Plácido Domingo and José Carreras, were Spanish and wasn't that a good example of America's melting pot ethos? She brushed aside my comment and, as had happened in Santa Fe, I was precipitously dismissed. I left the general director's office both offended and depressed. Beverly Sills, America's Opera Sweetheart, had mowed me down. And I still can't figure out why? Maybe she just had an off-day and took it out on me.

A few years later, I was engaged to direct a gala for San Francisco Opera hosted by Leonie Rysanek and Beverly Sills. I knew and liked Leonie but wondered how Miss Sills would treat me. The day of rehearsal, I went into the dressing room to say hello to the hosts. Leonie greeted me warmly and turned to Sills, "Beverly, this is Brian Large." "Brian Large," trilled Sills, "how nice to meet you. I've so admired your work and it's such a pity we never had the opportunity to work together." That's exactly what the woman said to me, my word of honour. I went into a stiff upper lip British mode, answering, "It's a pleasure to meet you, Miss Sills." And that was that. I never saw her again.

My American directorial assignments ended and with my Director's Guild union card burning a hole in my pocket, I recrossed the pond and returned to England. Within a week, I received a letter from British stage director, John Dexter, which would not only bring me back to America but also, once again, change the course of my life.

21

A Dream Come True

By the late seventies, competition had grown fiercer among television companies. Finances ruled and "Auntie" no longer sat atop the airwaves. Major drama productions gradually left the studios and went to outside locations. Consequently, the iconic Shepherd's Bush Studios, so expensive to maintain, remained underused. In order to compete with commercial television, BBC2 no longer could afford to present programmes for a minority audience. That meant less rarefied programming and prestige productions such as my studio operas, *The Flying Dutchman* and *Macbeth*, no longer took precedence. All of which got me thinking about my own future. Back in 1969, my first away from home engagement with Georg Solti in Munich had started a trend. For the next half-dozen years, while the bulk of my efforts remained with the BBC in London, my range of activity expanded exponentially. Throughout this period of diversification, one destination remained my lodestar; I longed to return to Bayreuth and daydreamed of recording a *Tannhäuser* or a *Lohengrin* there. I even was ready to take on the *Ring*. I'd about given up hope of returning to the festival, let alone working there, when the opportunity presented itself.

In the latter half of the twentieth century, Bayreuth ruled the Wagnerian world. Everything about the festival was top-drawer, administrators, singers, production staffs, crews, and audiences. As far as the administration, beginning with its founder and right up to the present day, generations of Wagners have been running the show either by themselves or by hiring the best directors. In the beginning, Wagner created a musical ensemble by hiring principal players from Germany's leading opera houses (closed for the summer holiday season), a practice that has endured to the present day. As for festival audiences, they, too, are a special breed. Today, as in the past, the dedicated faithful don't simply go to Bayreuth, they "make the pilgrimage".

Since my initial visit to Bayreuth in 1969, I'd kept up correspondences with a few singers and staffers, among them Peter Windgassen, son of the outstanding Wagnerian tenor, Wolfgang Windgassen. In 1975, Peter wrote to remind me of the festival's upcoming centennial in July of 1976. An entirely new production of the *Ring*, conducted by Pierre Boulez and directed by Patrice Chéreau would open the celebratory season, an appropriate choice since the world premiere of the complete *Ring* had opened the festival's inaugural season. From the moment I received Peter's correspondence my mind raced. How might I return to Bayreuth and participate in this historic moment? Happily, my thoughts turned to the 1969 meeting with Wolfgang Wagner when he and John Culshaw had discussed the centennial. At that time John seemed confident that the BBC would be interested in creating a documentary for the event and Herr Wagner embraced the notion. With that exchange in mind, I decided to put John's brainchild in motion and craft a plan. I envisioned a two-and-a-half-hour history of the festival from its beginning to the present day. The film would be in two parts; the first from the building of the Festspielhaus up to its closing in 1944, the second from the reopening in 1951 to the present day. In sum, my dream project would be a panorama of the rise, fall, and rise of Richard Wagner's impossible dream.

I threw some notes together, outlined my strategy, and presented it to John, quite a switch from the usual drill of John presenting plans to me. "I'll do all the research and direct", I told him, "… and you'll write the script and narrate." (John's sonorous voice had enriched the narration of many programmes.) He was all for it. Together we presented the plan to Dietrich von Watzdorf, head of music at Bayerischer Rundfunk (BR) in Munich. Von Watzdorf, recognizing the national and historic importance of the occasion, gave us his blessing, subject to Bayreuth's approval. John then contacted Wolfgang Wagner. Herr Wagner agreed that the BBC could create the programme in co-production with BR, and with the proviso that he himself be named advisor and executive producer. Moreover, he wanted to include a major performance element shot from the Festspielhaus stage to conclude the documentary and suggested *Die Meistersinger's* dynamic final scene. John and I were thrilled with his suggestion. BBCTV and BR worked out the details with Herr Wagner and then officially named me as the director of the Bayreuth centenary documentary.

All things now go, Herr Wagner contacted me and soon proved himself a worthy confrere. Among other beneficences, he provided access to the Festival archives and introduced me to the Chief Archivist of the Bundesfilm Archives in Koblenz. In our preliminary conversations, Wolfgang Wagner spoke frankly about the purpose of the documentary. "I want you to tell the whole story of the festival, everything," he advised me, "… especially the Nazi years and that includes Hitler's relationship to the festival, to my family, and especially my mother. Everything! The world must know what happened here." Herr Wagner's candour impressed me as did his desire to reveal the underbelly of the unholy Bayreuth/Third Reich alliance. No whitewashing, just revelation. I eagerly accepted the challenge. With the BBC's blessings and Herr Wagner's carte blanche, I returned to Bayreuth, this time as an investigative researcher rather than a quasi-tourist.

Like Benjamin Britten's Aldeburgh, Richard Wagner's Bayreuth is a one-season town, both spring to life during their respective festivals. While The Red House and the Snape Maltings attract a smattering of visitors throughout the year, Aldeburgh is a ghost town except for the festival season. Give or take the guided tours of the Festspielhaus and Wahnfried, the Wagner home and museum, and a few good restaurants, the same can be said of Bayreuth. Music is the charm that compels crowds to either of these off-the-beaten-track towns. Upon my arrival in Bayreuth, I plunged into researching every aspect of the festival. Gudrun Mack, Herr Wagner's press secretary, later his second wife, assisted me and we worked together quite compatibly. After preliminary explorations in Bayreuth, I went to the archives in Koblenz and uncovered newsreels containing heretofore unseen footage of Adolf Hitler's many visits to Bayreuth. The reels included views of the citizenry lining the streets saluting and screaming in frenzied adoration. Less frantic footage revealed clips of the Führer, clad in white tie and tails, attending operas at the Festspielhaus and montages of intimate moments showing him, in civilian garb, relaxing at Wahnfried with Winifred and her four children, Weiland, Friedelind, Wolfgang, and Verena, all of whom called their Führer, Uncle Adolf. Rumour had it that Winifred might have been one of the Führer's girlfriends. Further gossip implied that she attempted to interest Friedelind in marrying him. Whether or not this tittle-tattle had any credence we'll probably never know for sure. Evidence, however, does suggest that Winifred specifically cultivated Hitler's friendship to keep her festival going and, at that, she certainly succeeded. She even convinced him to allow Jewish performers on the Festspielhaus stage after they were banned from all concert halls and theatres throughout the Third Reich. Whatever her ulterior motives, she defended Hitler and his cause to the end of her days. Even when removed from office following the Nuremberg Trials, she remained a constant reminder of Nazi iniquities and an unrepentant festival entity until her death in 1980.

Formidable as she was, I must confess that my dealings with Winifred Wagner were quite pleasant. I recall driving her up the hill to the Festspielhaus and chatting about festivals, past and present; she still spoke perfect English albeit with a slight Germanic inflection. As we motored along, she looked out the open window and surveyed the surroundings much like a sovereign regarding her fiefdom. Because of her relationship with Hitler, Frau Wagner no longer had the power, but she always retained a presence. To this day, watching newsreels of Der Führer in Bayreuth chills the spine. You cannot help paralleling the hero-worshipping propaganda with other film documentations of the time, the ones showing cities laid to waste and innocent men, women, and children being herded into ghettoes and concentration camps. There's no getting around it, Adolf Hitler created hell to the music of Richard Wagner.

After several weeks of intensive researching, I went back to England and turned over my notes to John Culshaw. When he finished writing the script, I returned to Bayreuth and began filming. My task was made easier by Wolfgang Wagner's support. By the way, for as long as I knew him, I always addressed Wolfgang Wagner as Herr Wagner. He never invited me to use a less formal salutation and I never presumed to address him in any other manner. I must admit, as much as I appreciated everything that Herr Wagner did for the centennial filming, I wanted more. The truth is, eager as I was to do the documentary, I ached to get television cameras into the Festspielhaus and video actual performances. A pipe dream, for sure.

During his years as director, Wieland Wagner had declined all offers to film performances in the Festspielhaus. He claimed that his low-key lighting was too sensitive and could never be preserved properly on film. At one point, for promotional purposes, he had allowed newsreel companies to film excerpts from *Meistersinger* and *Rheingold* rehearsals and, indeed, they did not reflect the subtlety of his lighting. Following his brother's lead, Wolfgang Wagner also believed that colour cameras could not capture Bayreuth's scenic effects. Reassuring him that everything would be close to, if not actually perfect, I somehow managed to convince him to change his mind. We taped the final scene of *Die Meistersinger* with colour cameras. Satisfied with the results, Herr Wagner unexpectedly granted me permission to shoot, in colour, a few selections from his final *Ring* production. As if that weren't enough, he stunned me by stating, "I think it is now time to talk about recording the new *Ring*." John told me that after Wagner saw the BBC/BR documentary, he said "This man has the stuff; I can trust him." My impossible dream had come true but, alas, had to be deferred for a few years.

Chéreau's *Ring* was so controversial it is not surprising its premiere was greeted with hostility and boos. It was reviled by conservative members of the public and denounced by leaders of the world's press. Despite this, Wolfgang Wagner believed wholeheartedly in Chéreau's vision. So much so he decided to delay taping the "new" *Ring* until Chéreau had time to refine his thoughts and the production had time to settle in. Traditionally, a *Ring* production runs for five years, then leaves the repertoire for a year or two during which a new version is fashioned. The new *Ring* then joins the schedule for the ensuing five years. My luck, I happened to hit a production with a multitude of kinks to work out before it could be filmed. Forced to cool my heels for three years, I concentrated on the documentary.

The centennial came and went and our two-part film, *The Impossible Vision* and *The Vision Renewed*, brought the Bayreuth story to television audiences in Germany, England, and the United States. At the same time, following the centennial hoopla and the subsequent censure of his effort, Patrice Chéreau began reworking and redesigning major portions of the *Ring*. By the time he finished, his and Boulez's interpretation had become a definitive version of Wagner's masterwork.

In June of 1979, the *Ring* was ready to roll and I took a leave of absence from the BBC to tape it. I asked Peter Windgassen to be my assistant. We arrived in Bayreuth to begin preparations and were off to a back to front start. Rather than *Rheingold*, for reasons known only to himself, Wolfgang Wagner insisted that we begin with *Die Götterdämmerung*, the last opera in the tetralogy. No one challenged Herr Wagner's choice because of the underlying Bayreuth rule established by his grandfather, to wit: "Whatever Wagner wants, Wagner gets." A lot was riding on the success of the *Götterdämmerung* test video. It had to be close to perfect or the entire project might be halted. Consequently, great pains were taken to ensure a successful outcome. We installed extra lights, put up towers where cameras could be mounted whenever needed and turned the Festspielhaus into a TV studio. There would be no audience, indeed no one would be admitted except for those directly involved with the production. Along with putting *Götterdämmerung* first on the recording list, Herr Wagner put one other condition on our project, each act had to be filmed from beginning to end with no stops. Once the red light came on, it stayed on. If a musical mistake happened, we'd confer with Boulez at the end of the act and, a retake, only of the error, would be re-shot. I heartily approved of this stipulation because it ensured the feeling of a "live" performance. We rehearsed for twelve days before shooting, then I, along with Chéreau and Boulez, Herr Wagner, his wife, and representatives from Bayerischer Rundfunk and Unitel watched the master tape together. *Gott sei Dank*, *Götterdämmerung* proved good enough to green-light the rest of the *Ring*. The hurdle had been cleared, the die had been cast; we were ready for *Rheingold*, *Walküre*, and *Siegfried*.

In June of 1980, everyone returned to the Festspielhaus "film studio". We rehearsed, relit, and, over a period of twenty-four days, recorded *Rheingold*, *Walküre*, and *Siegfried* as well as a retake of one flubbed scene in *Götterdämmerung*. The *Ring* was complete. Edmund Hillary had conquered Mt. Everest, Neil Armstrong had been the first man on the moon, and Brian Large had recorded the first ever complete Bayreuth *Ring* in colour. I truly believed that Richard Wagner, who himself said "every time you do something, do something new", would have approved.

The *Ring* aired and the floodgates opened. And, Bayreuth became a regular port of call for me. During the centennial madness, Herr Wagner had approached me with an irresistible proposal, "Brian," said he in his Franconian-tinged parlance, *"dies ist erst der Anfang. Ich möchte, dass Sie für jeden neuen Ringzyklus zurückkehren und sie alle aufzeichnen"* (... this is just the beginning. I want

you to return for each new *Ring* cycle and record them all).
Never had Herr Wagner's ear-bashing vernacular sounded
so sweet, *Musik in meinen Ohren*.

From 1979 to 1989, I became a Festspielhaus fixture as I
recorded and rerecorded the entire Bayreuth repertoire,
with one glaring exception. Although I was asked to do
Tristan and Isolde on two occasions, each time I had business elsewhere. As much as it hurt, I had to turn down
every offer. Fortunately, I did get to video *Tristan* on three
occasions in three disparate opera houses. Although I relished each opportunity, none of those productions could
replicate the distinction of filming the master's work in the
master's house.

Looking back, I'm still impressed by the Centennial *Ring*
recording. I learned so much working with Chéreau and
Boulez. No matter how many times I'd seen the score, no
matter how many times I'd taken it apart, I had to go back,
look for fundamentals, and share them. Chéreau trusted
me completely. My job was to build a series of pictures
which would grow dramatically as Chéreau finetuned the
details. Positioning myself beside him, I remained on the
floor with him as he reworked the production and put his
thoughts into actions. Being at his side enabled me to see
through his eyes. By taking his point of view, I was able to
appreciate what he was trying to get from the artists and
what he was trying to do with the intricacies of the production. Meanwhile, everything that was thought about,
shouted out, or discussed in rehearsal had to be put down
on paper. When that was done, we'd have meetings with
the cameramen so they'd know what we were trying to
capture. I tried to get the best angle and the best place to
position the cameras in order to achieve the most dramatic

effect. After much consultation and discussion came the camera dress rehearsal of *Rheingold, Walküre,* and *Siegfried* with Chéreau on the floor, fussing and fixing, while I, score in hand, followed along on the sideline. Everything I did was dictated by what Chéreau was doing and resulted in a vibrant confrontational communication. A piano accompanied the first rehearsals of each individual opera. At the next run-through, the orchestra took over and Chéreau and I left the floor to watch from the control room. Afterwards, we reviewed, made corrections, and tried to polish as much as we could to prepare for the next day's recording. As mentioned, there were no stops and starts, each act was recorded straight through. As a result, the viewing public saw what appears to be a "live" performance composed of Boulez's thoughtful and brilliant take on the music, coupled with Chéreau's painstaking staging, the artistic excellence of the singers, the arresting mise en scène, and the two shillings I put in for the taping. I've gone back to that *Ring* recording many times, and always find it fresh, vital, original, and down to earth. In actual performance the *Ring* can be daunting; seventeen hours of music stretched out over four days is a commitment and many avoid it because they fear it asks too much. But I believe that the Bayreuth Centennial production made the *Ring* accessible and acceptable to all music lovers not just Wagnerites. In honouring a treasured legacy, we were able to bring viewers as close as possible to one of music's greatest works. That's a laurel I'll happily rest upon.

Richard Wagner's
Das Rheingold and
Die Walküre, 1976
at the Bayreuth
Festival

253

**Behind the scenes
at the Centennial *Ring***

Patrice Chéreau and I

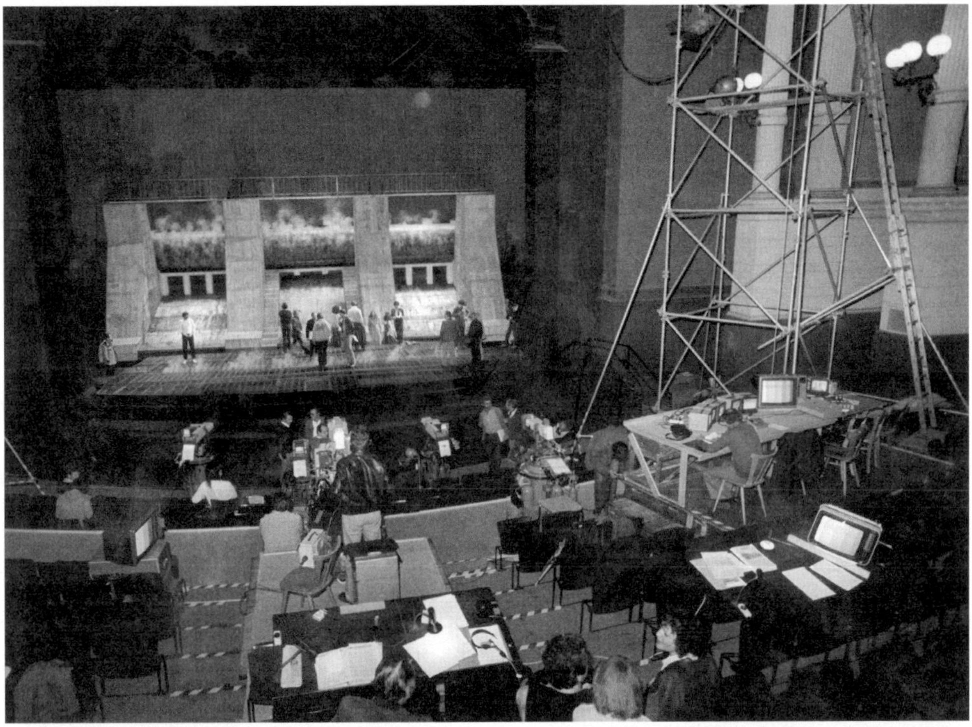

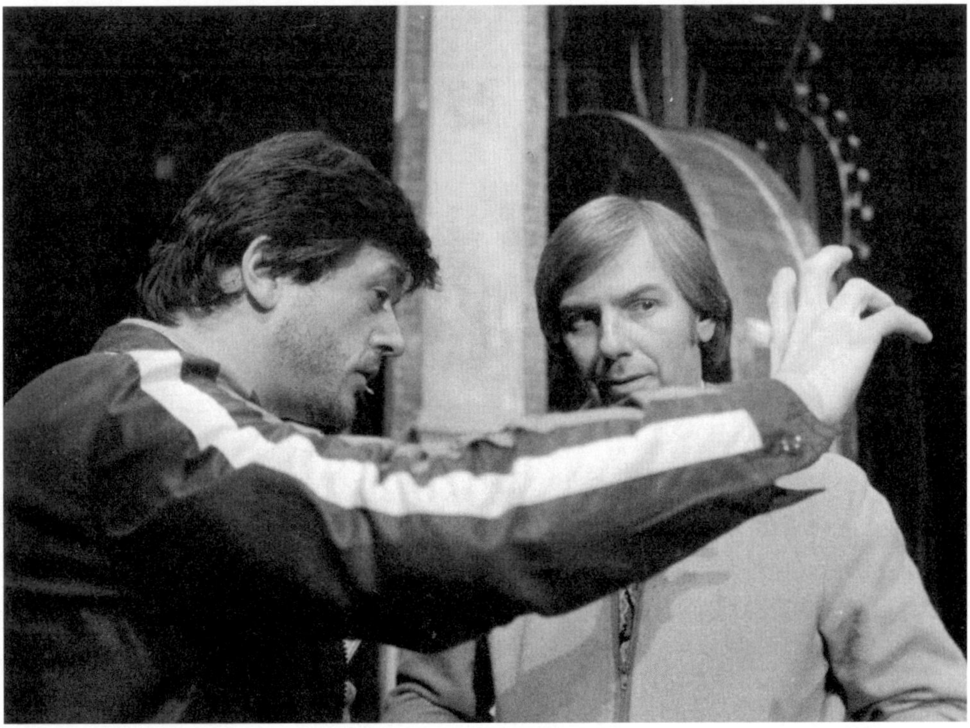

Zdenka Podhajská, Jack Mastroianni, Ruby Eileen and John James Robert Large

Anna Tomowa-Sintow, Cecilia Bartoli, Virginia Zeani

Judy Flannery and Hazel Wright, Mary Lou Falcone

ORF crew, Peter Windgassen, Yehudi Menuhin, Renato Zanella and the Vienna State Opera Ballet

Peter Pears, André Previn

John Culshaw, Colin Graham

VII

Elisabeth Soderstrom on the monitor, Richard Armstrong

Lorin Maazel, Benjamin Britten

Josef d'Bache-Kane, Steve Eveleigh, Van Cliburn

Virginia Zeani and Angela Gheorghiu, Seiji Ozawa, Maya Plisetskaya and Rodion Shchedrin,
Claudio Abbado, James Levine and Hildegard Behrens, Jonas Kaufmann, Catherine Malfitano,
Gabriela Beňačková, Ildebrando D'Arcangelo and Anna Netrebko

Birgit Nilsson, Oleg Prokofiev, Lady Valerie Solti, Martha Mödl,
Angela Gheorghiu and Roberto Alagna, Grace Bumbry, Riccardo Muti

22

A Confluence of Commitments

On the 5th of January 1980 BBC2 screened my last studio offering, Prokofiev's *The Love for Three Oranges* in the original French. I asked the composer's son, Oleg, if he would act as an advisor and introduce the programme on air. He agreed and proved to be not only helpful but a thoroughly delightful gentleman as well. *The Love for Three Oranges* like its predecessors, received excellent reviews and, after it aired, Oleg Prokofiev invited me to lunch. We chatted on various subjects when suddenly, he paused, then said, "You know Brian, I so enjoyed reading your books on Smetana and Martinů. You really captured each of them so brilliantly." Flattered by his praise I was taken more aback as he continued, "And it made me think ... I wonder, might you be interested in writing my father's biography?" What a surprise and what a tempting offer. My first impulse was to say yes, but further conversation with Oleg revealed a major obstacle. Sergei Prokofiev had left voluminous dairies, an invaluable source of material for any biographer but not for me since I could neither speak nor read Russian. Even when Oleg offered to work with me as a translator, I had to say no. The preparation alone would have taken two years and I never would have been at ease working outside my language comfort zone. More to the point, and what I could not say to Oleg, I didn't want to tie myself down with such a consuming project because I had more pressing demands with which to deal.

When the Met opened on 13 September 1966, the first applause went to the twelve chandeliers, a gift from the Republic of Austria as a token of gratitude to the USA for its role in post-World War II reconstruction

When the New York Metropolitan Opera opened on 13 September 1966, the first applause went to the twelve chandeliers designed by Hans Harald Rath, a gift from the Republic of Austria as a token of gratitude to the USA for its role in post-World War II reconstruction. The chandeliers are a tribute to the Space Age. It's always a hold-your-breath experience when they are raised to the ceiling at the beginning of every performance.

In 1975, John Dexter had been appointed Director of Productions at the Metropolitan Opera in New York. Previously he'd been Director of Drama at the Royal Court Theatre in London, and Associate Director of the National Theatre of Great Britain. Dexter staged plays and operas brilliantly. I greatly admired his work but lost track of him after he left London for the Hamburg State Opera. In 1977, Live from the Met, a series of TV opera transmissions, began with a production of *La Bohème* featuring Renata Scotto and Luciano Pavarotti. (In 1988, the series changed to a tape format and Live from the Met became The Metropolitan Opera Presents. In 2007, The Metropolitan Opera Presents lost its solo listing and was sandwiched into the Great Performances on PBS series. *Sic transit gloria mundi*.) A couple of years into John Dexter's Met tenure, I received a letter from him. In it, he wrote that the Met soon would be doing transmissions on a regular basis and, having seen and been impressed by my productions, he proposed that I fly to New York to discuss with him the possibility of joining the Met staff. As the old expression goes, you could have knocked me over with a feather. Although stunned and flattered by the offer, I really didn't want a full-time job at the Metropolitan Opera mainly because I wasn't that comfortable in New York City. I first went there in 1972/73 to work on

Bernstein's *Mass* and found Manhattan noisy, way too rat-a-tat for a "sedate" Englishman such as myself. During that initial stay, David Griffiths, the only person I knew in Manhattan, looked out for me. Among other things, he took me to a production of *Carmen* at the Met which I didn't particularly like. In sum, I simply couldn't warm to the Big Apple and had no desire to reside there. I wrote back to John Dexter politely citing my feelings about New York and in more formal words basically said thanks for thinking of me but no thanks. He immediately wrote back, "New York's a great place, you just have to get used to it. Honestly, I think you should come here and talk with me." There followed another exchange of letters. Finally, I broke down and agreed to fly over.

David picked me up at Kennedy Airport and seemed more excited about the Met's proposal than I. The next day I went to see John Dexter. I'd known him but only slightly and now here I sat in the office of the Metropolitan Opera's Director of Productions. John did a real sell job. "We're going to do at least four transmissions a year, Brian. We have an excellent television director by the name of Kirk Browning. But there are times when Kirk is not available and I'd like you to join us. In all honesty, there are certain pieces that would be more suitable for you. For instance, you speak German and Kirk doesn't." Apropos, John went on to explain that my first taping would be his production of Kurt Weill's *The Rise and Fall of the City of Mahagonny* making its Met debut in November of 1979. After that, in February of 1980, *Un Ballo in Maschera* with Pavarotti would follow. "Look Brian, before you decide, I want you to see how the Met works. I would want you to watch a rehearsal that I'm directing. I want you to meet James Levine and others on the music staff. Then make your decision." John Dexter had laid out a banquet, I had to take a bite. For a week, he wined and dined me and took me into every nook and cranny of his opera house. Incredibly impressed by everything I saw and heard, the building itself and the superb quality of the orchestra, the sound within the hall, I melted. Still, I hesitated at making a full commitment and told John that before doing so, I'd like to try a couple of shows and see how I would fit in. And so, I agreed to do *Mahagonny* and *Un Ballo in Maschera* as a test run.

As if my plate weren't full enough, at the same time I signed on with the Met, I received an offer from the Chicago Lyric Opera. The Lyric had engaged Mirella Freni, Nicolai Ghiaurov, Alfredo Kraus, and conductor Georges Prêtre for a new production of Gounod's *Faust* in September of 1979. I should mention that the production also boasted a full twenty-minute *Walpurgisnacht Ballet* choreographed by Georges Balanchine. The company was looking for a television director and Nicolai mentioned my name. Chicago called, I was contracted and flew to the Windy City to prepare for the taping. The video itself would be transmitted at a later date. During my time in Chicago, a plot began to develop and thicken at the Metropolitan Opera House. I'd been hired by John Dexter but neither Michael Bronson, the Met's television producer, nor his assistant, Clem D'Alessio, knew me. When Bronson heard about my Chicago gig, he decided the two of them should fly there to see me in action. The day before the scheduled taping D'Alessio contacted the Lyric Opera front office to set up the visit. I was immediately informed that Messrs Bronson and D'Alessio would be flying in the following day and joining me in the recording truck that evening.

The night of the taping, my colleagues and I were doing some preliminary work in the video truck when I received a phone call from the front office. "Brian, you know that we've been negotiating all along with Balanchine's agent about taping the *Walpurgisnacht Ballet*. Well, the negotiations just collapsed; it's not going to happen. Of course, you'll be taping the rest of the opera but to keep the peace we've sworn on a stack of bibles that all recording machines will be turned off during the ballet. I'm counting on you to act accordingly." I agreed to do as requested, hung up the phone, and apprised the crew of what had happened. Some grumbling ensued; we all were disappointed not to have the opportunity to record a Balanchine work. A few minutes later, the front office called again, this time informing me that the flight carrying the two gentlemen from the Metropolitan Opera had been delayed but they were on their way. Shortly before curtain time, Bronson and D'Alessio arrived and were quickly ushered into the truck. We said our hellos, shook hands, and the two of them sat down behind me to watch the taping. Everything proceeded without a hitch and then we reached the end of Act III. During the intermission, the Met duo stepped out for a break. I looked at the recording plan and of course, the *Walpurgisnacht* was front and centre at the beginning of Act IV. By nature, I'm not a prankster but I do enjoy a good laugh and like Faust, the Devil took hold of me. I called over the crew. "Look," I said, "those two guys from the Met don't know that the recording machines will be off when the ballet is on. Let's have a little fun and use every trick on the console to create a *Walpurgisnacht* to end all *Walpurgisnachts*. Just go along with anything I do at the controls and don't say a word." The crew was ready, willing, and able to assist.

Messrs Bronson and D'Alessio returned to the truck and took their places behind me. The act began and I proceeded to use the mixer to create on-screen pandemonium none of which would actually be recorded. First, I switched male and female body parts. A simple flip of a lever and ladies' upper bodies were placed on men's torsos and vice versa. These weird creatures whose bodies had morphed into each other could be made to stand on their heads, lie on the ground or leap through the air and stay there, technical tricks carried to the extreme. The men would come in from one side, the women from the other and we'd flip a switch so it appeared as though men in tutus and ladies in britches were jumping all over each other. The crew remained quiet but I heard strange sounds emanating from the dumbfounded Met duo behind me. I had a reputation for being business-like in my profession, a detail man who liked everything to go efficiently and smoothly would be an accurate description of my work ethic. No one ever would have suspected me of a Monty Python streak, least of all the two men representing my newest employer. The ballet concluded, the recorder was switched on and we were back in business.

When the performance ended, I turned to Michael and Clem. "How'd you like the ballet?" I asked, a huge smile on my face. Before they could answer, I told them the story and suggested we go for a drink. We settled in at a nearby bar where we reviewed the telecast over a few beers. Michael confessed that he sat through the balletic bedlam thinking, and this is the guy who's going to join the Live from the Met team? "Do you do this kind of thing often?" he asked. "No," I assured him, "I've never done it before and I'll never do it again." I never did, although I sometimes wondered how Mr Balanchine might have reacted had he seen my version of his *Walpurgisnacht Ballet*.

Faust finished, I returned to New York to prepare *Mahagonny*, my directorial debut at the Metropolitan Opera House. The experience proved to be thoroughly satisfying. John had

With Lotte Lenya

assembled a terrific cast including Astrid Varnay as Begbick. He'd also brought in Kurt Weill's widow, Lotte Lenya, as an advisor. What a privilege to meet and talk with the Widow Weill. Chain-smoking endless cigarettes, Lenya spun tales of her long and distinguished career and of her many collaborations with her composer husband. She, herself, had sung the role of *Mahagonny's* Jenny in 1927 and a year later created the role of another Jenny in Weill's *Threepenny Opera*. Her appearances on musical and operatic stages, in cabarets, and in motion pictures and television were studded with honours and awards including an Academy Award nomination for her role in the screen version of Tennessee William's novel, *The Roman Spring of Mrs Stone*. And she did an incredible turn as the villainous Rosa Klebb in the James Bond film *From Russia with Love*. Perhaps most notably, she received a Tony for her appearance in an off-Broadway revival of the *Threepenny Opera* in 1956; the only time that award ever has been given for a performance not on a Broadway stage. Conversing with Lenya, who exhibited the same style and wit in her narratives as she did in her singing and acting, I learned a lot about the international musical scene that she inhabited and dominated in the thirties. Lenya's lore and guidance provided invaluable insight into the opera itself. *Mahagonny* scored highly with the critics and my Met career was launched. I remember thinking on the flight back to England, maybe John Dexter was right, New York isn't so bad after all.

23

Bye-bye Auntie/
Hello, Uncle Sam

I returned to London and the BBC where I found myself growing increasingly frustrated at how my light was being spent. Established in the United States, in the midst of a twelve-year stretch at Bayreuth, the more I worked outside of my professional home, the more I thought about leaving it. The BBC had been my parent/teacher and like a good parent she'd given me roots and wings, but now my wings were being clipped. Auntie had changed. The old guard, Craxton, Culshaw, Attenborough, et al., who'd championed programmes of worth, had either retired or gone on to other venues. David Attenborough, for instance, never wanted to be an administrator; the role was thrust upon him. Retirement on the horizon, he upped and quit telling his friends, "I don't want to spend my remaining stretch administrating, I want to be out there creating."

At the time of Attenborough's departure, I was on leave of absence directing the Bayreuth *Ring*. When I returned, I reported to Robin Scott, the erstwhile comptroller of BBC Radio1 and Radio2, who had replaced David as comptroller of BBC2 and eventually became Deputy Managing Director of BBC television. I got along with Robin and we met on many convivial occasions. One touchy subject, however, often cropped up in our conversations. Somehow, no matter what we were talking about, Robin managed to slip in a remark about my "future". I never responded. Finally, he tackled the subject head on. "You've had a very successful career as a director, Brian, but directing is a young man's job and at forty-two you should be thinking of a more serious position in the corporation. You have other gifts that you can offer the BBC. I know you're tied up with Bayreuth, but once this *Ring* thing is over, I want you to think about coming into management. There's a place for you which has potential for a major position. If you're interested there's a future for you here."

Ring thing? Perhaps I was being overly sensitive but for Robin to dismiss what I was doing in such an offhand manner hit hard. I pulled myself together and promptly answered, "Music is my life, Robin. I love music, I believe in music and I believe in bringing music to as many people as possible. I thank you for thinking of me but I am not able in any way, shape, form, or manner to consider moving into management." A dyed-in-the-wool corporate gentleman, Robin didn't back off. "No rush, Brian, think about it, and let me know when you've made up your mind." I didn't want to tell him that I'd made up my mind the second he proposed the idea.

It's funny, I'd been agonizing over leaving the BBC and had just about given up the idea when Robin confronted me. I mean, how could I leave? I'd made a name for myself; I was in demand, and I made good money. I had security and at sixty-five I'd retire with a pension. Good heavens, how could I think of turning my back on all of that? How? The very word "management" made my skin crawl. I was a creator not a manager, period. Not wanting to offend Robin, I told him I'd give it some thought. And I did. I thought about nothing else. At one point I went to see my parents to talk things over. Being musicians, they knew how precarious making a living in the arts can be, that's why they'd been so elated by my BBC appointment fifteen years prior. Nothing had changed. "Are you crazy?" my father thundered. "How can you leave a job that's there for you till you're sixty-five, and with a pension, afterwards. You're going to throw that away?" For them, security meant everything. They'd lost all they had in World War II and could not accept the idea that their son might walk out on a life time sinecure. I didn't expect them to think the way I did but I wanted them to know what I intended to do.

Not long after my conversation with my parents, I arrived at work one morning and immediately called Robin Scott. "I'd like to talk to you", I told him. "Great", he answered. "Come on up at six and we'll have a drink and a chat." At the end of the day, I went to his office. I declined the drink he offered and, instead, got right to the point. "Robin, I have to tell you that much as I appreciate your offer, I'm unable to accept it. There's no way that I would give up directing for management." I took an envelope out of my pocket and handed it to him; it contained my resignation.

Soon, everyone knew about my impeding departure. Some BBC colleagues expressed their disappointment, not all, but enough to make my leave taking sting a bit. "We brought you in, we trained you, you've made a great success and now you're deserting us? Kicking us in the teeth, as it were. That's not what we expected." No use to try and explain that the company that had nourished me had changed, dramatically, and I didn't want to hang around while the wonderful world of BBCTV continued to change. I simply put down my head, suffered the slings and arrows in silence, and concentrated on whatever tasks remained. I had about three months to go before I could take my leave. Then it would be Goodbye Auntie, Hello World!

I should say "brave new" world because the entire industry in which I'd grown up was in a state of flux, not only in England but in Germany, France, and Italy as well as across the ocean in the United States. Videos were becoming increasingly important. Independent video companies sprang up and began recording performances and selling them to the highest bidder. As the networks faded into the background, a vibrant group of video entrepreneurs and their companies dominated the burgeoning industry. Unitel, headed by Leo Kirch, was among the first such corporations and a leading force from the beginning. The Bayreuth Festival was exclusive to Unitel, whatever Bayreuth presented was financed, serviced, and distributed by the Unitel company. Reiner Moritz, a brilliant producer and businessman, left Unitel and formed his own video corporation, RM Arts, based in Munich and London. Reiner linked up with institutions, such as the Bavarian State Opera, Paris's Théâtre du Châtelet, and the San Francisco Opera. By so doing, RM Arts created an exceptional line-up of first-rate videos. Another gentleman, Bernd Hellthaller, established EuroArts in Berlin and made strong connections with the Berlin Philharmonic Orchestra, the Deutsche Oper, and the Vienna Philharmonic. With the last named he established a yearly series of May Day Concerts. Polivideo, an outstanding company, originated in Ticino, a Swiss canton close to the Italian border. Polivideo built studios and editing facilities in cornfields surrounding Locarno and was linked to La Scala and the Verona Arena. In London, Julian Wills created the National Video Corporation and contracted with the Royal Opera House to record opera and ballet productions. As the video companies proliferated, the record industry took note. Philips Records, a Dutch firm, cornered the Russian repertoire by using their connection to the Kirov company in St Petersburg. In New York City, Columbia Artists Management created CAMI Video headed by Peter Gelb.

Oddly, the only country that seemed to be out of it was Austria. Although the Austrian TV networks were well aware of the treasures they had, the Vienna Philharmonic, the Salzburg Festival, the Mozart Festival, etc., they sat on the fence instead of incorporating and getting into the video business themselves.

I could not have picked a better time to become a free-lancer. I was invited everywhere from my old stomping grounds at Covent Garden to the Arena in Verona, the Châtelet in Paris, and overseas to New York, Houston, St Louis, San Francisco, and a few cities I'd barely heard of, including Minneapolis. From the early eighties on, I had my choice of projects all over the musical video world. I had made the right decision at the right time. I felt vindicated for going out on my own, especially when my parents called to apologize for giving me such a hard time about leaving the BBC. They were overjoyed that everything had turned out so well.

During my last few months with the BBC, as a courtesy, I agreed to direct one final opera, *Otello*, given by the Royal Opera Company on tour in Manchester (1981). At the same time, PBS had asked me to work on *Willie Stark*, a new opera by the American composer Carlisle Floyd. I knew nothing about *Willie Stark* but was eager to take on the assignment primarily because I well knew of and greatly admired its director. How could I turn down an opportunity to work with Hal Prince?

I believe that in the course of writing my story I've made it abundantly clear that music is my life and that opera is closest to my heart. But it's not only classical music that inspires me, I'm exceedingly fond of all musical theatre, especially the Broadway variety. And, for the last half of the twentieth century, producer/director Hal Prince personified that art form. Prince received a lifetime total of twenty-one Tony Awards for a multitude of musicals he either produced or directed (or both). All of them represented Broadway at its brightest and included *West Side Story, Cabaret, Candide, Company, Damn Yankees, Evita, Sweeny Todd, A Little Night Music, Follies, Fiddler on the Roof*, and on and on and on. Name a super hit and chances are Hal Prince had a hand in it. After seeing my work with the Met, Hal decided that rather having someone simply putting a camera in front of the stage, I might be able to bring a different perspective to the taping of *Willie Stark*. He contacted me and I accepted his offer. Bedazzled by the opportunity to work with Prince, I'm embarrassed to say I gave short shrift to *Willie Stark*'s composer, Carlisle Floyd. The penny dropped later when I discovered that Floyd, one of the foremost American composers of his day, was an especially gifted opera composer and a fine gentleman as well.

In many ways, Carlisle Floyd was a counterpart to Ben Britten. Ben wrote on certain themes, the tragedy and absurdity of war was one topic, reflections on his Suffolk roots was another. Carlisle Floyd, a Southerner, paralleled Ben by writing operas based on American topics, such as rural life and the Great Depression, and brought his Southern gentleman's outlook to bear on these indigenous topics. He wrote in an incredibly lyric manner which to me seemed *echt* American and his warm Southern charm permeated his music. Very different from Ben's music and perhaps more accessible. The fact that I actually learned something about music through working with Carlisle Floyd astounded me. I took on *Willie Stark* to participate in the project with one man, and came away with a profound respect for two men. A delightful bonus.

Even though I'd agreed to do *Willie Stark*, one hurdle remained. "Money makes the world go round" we're advised in Hal Prince's production of *Cabaret* and truer words were never spoken. Whatever the business—theatre, television, film, classical music, pop music, opera—everything in the entertainment industry is about money. Generally speaking, whatever you're trying to do always comes down to the bottom line. The *Willie Stark* video had to be paid for and Houston Opera was struggling to find funding. Negotiations with Exxon went on and on, they just wouldn't commit. Meanwhile, I had to go to Manchester to take care of the *Otello* and I flew off without knowing whether the *Willie Stark* deal would go through or not. Phone calls from Houston saying they hadn't reached an agreement came to my hotel room daily. The message was ever the same: "We're still waiting for Exxon to say yes or no." One evening after a day of rehearsals, I returned to my hotel and as I passed the front desk the receptionist, a dead ringer for Joyce Grenfell, the fabled English actor/comedian, stopped me. Her long face twisted in a look of sadness as she breathily told me, "I'm awfully sorry sir, but I have to be the bearer of bad news." "What do you mean?" I asked. "Well, sir, a telegram has just come in from America and I … I … I don't know how to say it but I'm so sorry, and may I extend my condolences." "What on earth are you talking about?" I demanded. "Here, sir, look at this", and she handed me a telegram. The wire came from the Houston Opera and read, "Sorry to tell you Willie died today", which meant of course that Exxon hadn't come up with the money. I burst out laughing and the receptionist looked at me as though I'd gone mad. I was in no mood for explanations so I just thanked her and went up to my room. I decided to put all thoughts of Houston out of my head and to concentrate on the *Otello*. Easier said than done. The next day, after rehearsals, I returned to the hotel and as I made my way past the front desk, the receptionist cried out exultantly, "Sir! Sir, I've got wonderful news. Look, look, you've another message. Willie's not dead!" Sure enough, this telegram read "Willie's alive and well." Obviously, either Exxon reconsidered or someone else had stepped in. I don't remember much about the *Otello* in Manchester but I'll never forget that while I was there, *Willie Stark* died and was resurrected within twenty-four hours.

As soon as the *Otello* taping finished, I flew to D.C. and joined Hal Prince at the Watergate Hotel where we began fashioning a TV treatment. Floyd's opera premiered in Houston, then had two performances scheduled at the Kennedy Center after which the production returned to Houston. In the same manner as the *Ring* had been videoed without an audience in the Bayreuth Festspielhaus, the *Willie Stark* recording would take place sans spectators in Jones Hall for the Performing Arts. Hal and I developed an easy working relationship right off the bat and working with him was a dream. At first, I simply watched what Hal did and took notes. In his hands, *Willie Stark*, an opera with major choral interludes and a politically motivated plot, received the same treatment as a highly bred Broadway musical, *Evita*, say, or *Sweeney Todd*. The approach was absolutely right and set off on-stage sparks. A monolithic block of steps dominated the set and Hal had created intimate moments, crowd scenes, and spectacular dramatic passages at the front of them. Immediately, I saw something and forthrightly spoke to Hal. "Look, these steps are striking but you're putting all the action at the front of them and it's flat. We need to take advantage of those steps. Why not use the back as well as the front of them? In other words, I can bring the cameras around and treat the stage like a film set. It'll give a three-dimensional feeling to the television screen." Hal loved the idea and that's the way we shot it. Another contribution the two of us made to Floyd's opera concerned its length. Hal felt *Willie Stark* needed cutting and managed to convince Carlisle Floyd to cut out a huge chunk of music. Asking a composer to blue-pencil his score is not something to be done lightly. I'm not so sure Ben Britten would have done it, but Carlisle Floyd respected our judgement and deleted nearly forty minutes of music which really improved the opera's flow. The abridged version did very well, reviews of the recording were good and Hal really enjoyed the process. He subsequently invited me to work with him in Vienna where he'd been assigned to direct *Turandot* at the State Opera. Alas, I had another engagement and had to decline the offer. It didn't work out but it pleased me that Hal Prince wanted to work with me again. Unfortunately, we never did have an encore; I only had that one opportunity for which I'm so appreciative.

Along with the rise of the video recording companies, the late seventies witnessed many changes and developments in the television and recording industries. In 1975, Sony introduced Betamax, the first home video cassette player and recorder. JVC produced a rival, VCR, in 1976/77. And, in 1978, Philips brought out VCR 2000. With prices slashed to meet public demand, VCR players became increasingly available and video stores with international franchises (think Tower Records) sprung up like weeds around the world. Home video was all the rage and the production of cassettes emerged as big business. Record companies supported the new craze. Philips made an exclusive deal with Valery Gergiev to record operas from the Mariinsky Theatre in St Petersburg. The Decca label signed up Luciano Pavarotti and later, Renée Fleming, as exclusive artists for both audio and video recordings. LPs were phased out to make way for the new software, the CD. Independent companies (Unitel, EuroArts, NVC, RM Arts, et al.) with the sole purpose of providing software, flourished. The video cassette ruled the video world. And who stood in the middle of this avalanche of technology? None other than Brian James Large. For a good, long time I was caught up in a mad, mad, mad, musical video world.

Post Script: When I left BBCTV in 1980 I never expected to return. Then, in September of 1994, I received an invitation to direct the 100th Birthday Prom honouring the Promenade Concerts' founder, Sir Henry Wood. And so, I once more found myself working within the cosy confines of the Royal Albert Hall. The concert featured music arranged by Wood himself and at the end, as the audience sang "Rule Britannia", a sublime feeling of pride and joy overwhelmed me. I was home.

ENGLAND 3-9 December 1977   Price 13p

Radio Times

Verdi's Macbeth

Norman Bailey and Patricia Johnson are
the murderous king and queen
in BBC2's production of the opera, also
in stereo on Radio 3, Saturday.
Back feature: the sounds and the fury

III

ACT

The Vienna Philharmonic: a New Year's Concert at the Musikverein

Jack and I seated with Grace Bumbry.
Standing, Max Strauss, Dominique Meyer,
Sissy Strauss, and Thomas Voigt, Vienna, 2017

24.

Be It Ever so Hectic ...

In November of 1979, I made my debut at the Metropolitan Opera with *The Rise and Fall of the City of Mahagonny*. My new "independent" state was anchored by my unprecedented twelve-year run at Bayreuth which kept me on my toes for a long time. I loved what I was doing and where I was doing it until, except for *Tristan*, I'd done all the repertoire at least once and sometimes twice over. At that point, the inevitable occurred. What had been so energizing no longer inspired me in the same way. I began to feel that I was repeating myself which for me always has been a sure sign to move on. Once again, the time was ripe.

Arriving at America's leading opera house I, like other newbies struggling to break in, came under the wing of the Met's legendary artistic liaison, Sissy Strauss. In the mid-sixties, the Met had hired Vienna-born Sissy to look after itinerant and permanent arrivals at the opera house. Making everyone feel at home was her job and she did it splendidly, ably assisted by her husband, Max Strauss, an exemplary host, himself. When Sissy heard about me, she sought me out and immediately embraced me, literally and figuratively. "You're the new boy, here, but don't vorry, I take care of you", she trumpeted in her never-to-be-lost-Viennese-flavoured English. And take care of me she did, along with all who luxuriated in the warmth of her purview. Sissy Strauss threw open the doors to both her houses, the Met and her residence a few blocks away. Whether guests gathered at the Strauss's huge round table for "intimate" dinners (never less than twelve, often more, and always prepared by the hostess herself, Hungarian Goulash being a favourite) or mingled with cocktail party crowds in the high-ceilinged living room of an apartment that in both layout and furnishings, seemed to have been plucked from Vienna's *Innere Stadt* and dropped onto Manhattan's Upper West Side. Dinner party or full-gala à la the annual Christmas celebration, assemblages at the Strausses rocked. There you met your peers, your betters, and any interesting hoi polloi whom Sissy happened to come upon. "At home entertaining" was her Viennese heritage and she carried on the tradition with zest and love. For four decades Sissy Strauss reigned as the Met's Den Mother. Sadly, in 2016, the times grew out of joint and faced with financial emergencies, the Met began stripping away "niceties" to cut costs. The position of artistic liaison was among the first to go. After forty-two years of making life richer for two generations of the Metropolitan Opera's extended family, Sissy Strauss's tenure ended as did her fabled get-togethers. The Strausses moved back to Vienna where the Met's loss became Vienna's gain. Another copacetic concurrence, their apartment is not far from mine; we are Vienna neighbours. It's been my experience that, whatever the venue, once you start eliminating the "niceties", you're usually saying goodbye to the heart and soul of your organization.

Sissy Strauss wasn't the sole source of comfort at my new home. Two other ladies also made life easier and I'd like to officially say thank you to Marilyn Shapiro and Sybil Harrington. Marilyn spent a quarter of a century creating and providing management leadership for the Met's modern development, planned giving, endowment, and marketing programmes. Put all those segments together and that's what fuels an opera house. Warm and welcoming, Marilyn became a friend and it was she who introduced me to Sybil, a philanthropist from Amarillo, Texas, and one of the loveliest, most generous persons one could hope to meet. In 1974, Sybil's husband and their only child, a daughter, died. The grieving widow and mother found solace in all manner of charitable works, including the Metropolitan Opera. Sybil donated at least $30,000,000 to the Met, underwriting sixteen productions and concerts and thirteen telecasts. She gave away as much if not more to hospitals, educational institutions and God knows how many other worthy causes. "Giving money away is hard work", she confided, "but I got a kick out of it. It makes me feel good." Passionate about opera, Sybil loved Wagner and had been to Bayreuth; little wonder we immediately bonded. A down to earth person, nothing about Sybil indicated her immense wealth. She smoked like a chimney, drank generously, and was great fun. We met in 1981, when she sponsored a telecast of *Traviata* staged by Colin Graham, designed by Tanya Moiseiwitsch, daughter of pianist Benno Moiseiwitsch, and directed for television by me. Sybil asked how the opera would be televised and immediately we invited her to rehearsals. She enjoyed herself so much, we extended another invitation for her to join us in the control truck during the live telecast. That day, Michael Bronson, the television producer, had everyone in the truck wear T-shirts with camellias on the front and "La Traviata. Thank you, Sybil", printed on the back. When she walked into the truck, we all stood up and turned around; Sybil screamed with delight. During the transmission she sat directly behind me, absolutely mesmerized by what was happening. In tears at the end, she announced, "So this is how my money is being used. It's wonderful. This has been one of the happiest days I've ever known. Having seen this,

Michael Bronson and I with the dowager empress of the Met, Sybil B. Harrington. Patron extraordinaire, her munificence was matched by her lively sense of fun

I'm sure that after death, there's got be some sort of life. But for now, let's all go to Studio 54 and dance up a storm!" I spent the rest of the evening and early morning swaying with Sybil Harrington in New York's wildest disco. Boy, could she dance.

That was Sybil Harrington in a nutshell. She took unthinkable personal sorrow and turned it into joy for others as well as herself. Our friendship continued strong over the years. We always remained in touch. During the Met season, she was a constant presence in New York, and I occasionally visited her in Amarillo. The Met eventually named its auditorium in her honour and put a plaque on the wall for all to see. If you're at the Met and happen to pass by that plaque, I hope you have a deeper understanding and appreciation for a great lady.

In September of 1980, I had begun work on John Dexter's production of Alban Berg's *Lulu* when the unthinkable occurred. The orchestra went on strike and the Metropolitan Opera closed its doors. Lines formed in front of the house not to buy tickets but to picket. Negotiations seemed to be going nowhere and word got out that the house would be shuttered indefinitely. Management called and advised me that because of the situation I was free to take on other work if I wanted to. Wanted to? I needed to. Immediately I used my slender contacts to find whatever I could. By a stroke of good luck, the legendary Philadelphia Orchestra needed someone to video a few concerts led by Riccardo Muti, the orchestra's outstanding music director. Elated, I told friends what had happened. Their responses were terrifying. "Muti? He's impossible to work with. He's so temperamental; he's so difficult", etc., etc. Well, Riccardo Muti and I got on like a house on fire. These concerts sowed the seeds of a friendship that flourished in Europe. He invited me to return to Milan to direct *Nabucco*, his inaugural opera performance as Music Director at La Scala. This was followed by the three Mozart/Da Ponte operas in Vienna as well as five appearances as conductor of the VPO New Year's Concerts. To cap it all, he invited me to direct the concert in Salzburg celebrating the 250th anniversary of Mozart's birth.

While in Philadelphia, I learned that the National Video Corporation in London planned to record a new production of *The Tales of Hoffmann* at the Royal Opera House in December. Immediately, I contacted Julian Wills, told him I was available, and was hired to tape the opening night. When the Philadelphia gig ended, I returned to London to begin preparations on the *Hoffmann*. A few days in, I received a phone call from the Met informing me that after eighteen weeks, the strike had ended and *Lulu* would take place. "Come back", I was told. "I think we may have a problem", I replied, and went on to explain that I'd accepted a contract to work at Covent Garden on a new *Hoffmann* and was in the thick of it. "But you have a contract with us", the Met answered. "Yes, but you cancelled the contract because of the strike, so I signed an agreement with NVC." "You've got to do the *Lulu*", insisted the Met. I felt bad, especially since John Dexter was counting on me. I couldn't walk away. "Okay, let me talk to the Royal Opera and I'll get back to you." I called the administrative office at Covent Garden and explained what had happened. They were sorry but refused to let me out of my contract. What a pickle. Each opera house had an agreement with me and neither of them would yield. They say one pair of feet can't dance at two weddings, especially, as in my case, if those "weddings" are on two different continents. Undaunted, I did it, by figuring out how to handle both assignments at the same time.

Remember Frank Whittle, the inventor who was testing the world's first jet engines the year I was born? Well, by the time *Lulu* and *Hoffmann* were vying for my attention, the Concorde was flying the Atlantic in two hours and fifty-three minutes, cutting the flight time of ordinary jets in half. Three hours was a doable commute. I contacted the Met and Covent Garden and agreed to work in both their houses at the same time.

Starting in London, my schedule went something like this: I'd catch the morning Concorde out of Heathrow and arrive at Kennedy early in the a.m. Eastern Daylight Saving Time. I'd grab a taxi, go straight to the Met and do a morning and an afternoon rehearsal which would end between 4 and 6 p.m. Next, I'd take a taxi to Kennedy and board a British Airways night flight during which I'd grab a catnap and go over my notes. I'd arrive in London at 8 a.m., take a taxi to Covent Garden, and do rehearsals for *Hoffmann*. That evening I'd go home and sleep in my own bed. The next morning I'd go to Heathrow, catch the morning Concorde and repeat the previous day's routine. I had no luggage, just a briefcase containing toiletries and two scores, the three-act version of *Lulu* which I was learning, and the *Hoffmann* which I was reviewing. Best of all, the Met and Covent Garden agreed to split the cost of my flights. The whole process took about eight days, at the end of which I stayed on in New York. *Hoffmann* was going to be transmitted live on New Year's Eve so I was able to see *Lulu* through to the finish.

Around 3 p.m. on *Lulu's* opening day, Teresa Stratas cancelled. Her understudy Julia Migenes took over and after some intense, last-minute, run-throughs went "onstage an understudy and came off, a star". The reviews were very, very good. *Lulu* in the can, I returned to London, celebrated Christmas, and a week later directed the New Year's Eve *Hoffmann*. Sybil Harrington came to London for the occasion and after the performance, hosted a fantastic New Year's Eve party complete with a gaggle of bag pipers blasting in 1982.

25.

... There's no Place Like the Met

Early in 1980, rehearsals began for *Un Ballo in Maschera*, the second opera in my two opera "deal" with the Metropolitan. I arrived at the opera house and was told to report to John Dexter's office. John greeted me warmly and invited me to sit down. "We've had wonderful news, Brian," said he with a big grin on his face, "Birgit Nilsson will be singing *Elektra* here in January." "Wow," I responded, "that is wonderful news." Nilsson had been an illustrious fixture at the Met from the early sixties to the mid-seventies. Then, the Internal Revenue Service discovered that, somehow or other, she never had paid any income tax.

Uncle Sam told Nilsson to pay up or shut up. She didn't pay and forthwith was banned from singing in the United States. In November of 1979, after a nearly five-year absence, the diva's debt had been cleared and she returned to New York for a sold-out concert at the Met. Now, she'd be returning to sing one of her signature roles which required a bit of schedule juggling for the Met.

Like most opera houses, the Met's calendar is planned three years in advance but taking into consideration Nilsson's age and the extreme demands of the Strauss one-acter, there could be no guarantees that she'd be up to singing it three years hence. With that in mind, the Met boldly removed four performances of *Lohengrin* from the upcoming season and replaced them with four performances of *Elektra*. Rescheduling within a couple of months of the performance was an incredible gesture.

But, as John Dexter explained, they wanted to do this as a kind of farewell gift for all that Nilsson had done for the Met. Of course, her return also would generate highly-visible publicity and a bonanza in box office receipts. Having set the scene for me, John continued. "I want you to do the *Elektra* video, Brian. Would you like to?" Again, I'd been presented with that iconic, ironic query, "would I like to?" I didn't waste time and simply said yes. "Excellent," replied John, adding, "the performance is on the 16th of February." That date resonated with me. "The 16th? But that's when I'm doing the Pavarotti telecast. Have you rescheduled the *Ballo*?" "No," replied John, casually, "actually, the 16th is a Saturday. Basically, I'm asking you to do a taping of the *Elektra* matinee and to follow it up with the live *Ballo* in the evening. It's a lot to ask. Are you still willing?" My answer came swiftly. "Nilsson in *Elektra*? Pavarotti in *Ballo*? Are you kidding me? And by the way, the 16th of February happens to be my birthday. This is about the best present I can imagine."

And so it happened that on my forty-third birthday I taped a live *Elektra* performance with Birgit Nilsson and, two and a half hours after she finished singing, I returned to the truck to direct a live PBS transmission with Luciano Pavarotti. Occasions such as that incredible 1980 double bill have made me believe that some sort of force always has been with me. Call it what you will, destiny, fate, whatever, it's been my subliminal guide. Why did John Dexter write me a letter when I was questioning whether or not to leave the BBC? And why, when I declined to join the Met, did he insist that I give it a try? Which I did. Working at the Met was so energizing, so inspiring, what else could I do but stick with it?

My pilgrim's progress from the UK to the USA officially took place in the late fall of 1981 after which the Metropolitan Opera House became my second home for the next thirty years. During my apprenticeship, the BBC had provided me with the ideal training ground in which to create a visual style recognizably mine. From the beginning I balked at plonking down cameras and just letting them run. I wanted to enhance rather than reproduce, to treat the scene like a canvas, to paint on it like an artist with his brush. And, through lighting techniques, and by composing shots in a variety of intensities—close-ups, medium shots, and wide angles, to underline the drama in the words and/or the music. Indeed, one of the main reasons John Dexter brought me to the Met had to do with the way I translated opera in visual terms. In order to recreate my personal style in my new artistic home, I had to have the support of an understanding and responsive camera crew. Which meant that before I could do anything, I had to get to know the Met's camera operators, not just as technicians, but as individual personalities and fellow artists. Which I did, and in the process, I grew to greatly admire them. Those men made it possible for me not only to recreate my style, but to refine and enlarge it. Having trained in London, I came to New York with a rather rigid, traditional way of shooting and directing. Once in the New World, I was blessed to be able to exploit and benefit from the varied palette of the Met's outstanding virtuoso camera crew. And when I say "varied", I mean varied. A few of them worked in soap operas as well as classical opera and, without my realizing it, a bit of "soap opera technique" brushed off onto me, a freer, looser approach along with the speed that's essential in creating revolving dramatic characters and situations. Never did one lucky man have so many incredible right hands, and I want to introduce them:

Manny Gutierrez, a specialist in crane and jib operation and a sensitive and passionate lover of music and opera; Juan Barrera, a brilliant handheld camera operator with an eye for creating dramatic tension filled with close-ups of telling beauty; David Smith, who had a natural gift for capturing movement whether classical ballet or modern dance; Jacob Ostroff with his sensitive eye for framing close-ups and who, along with John Feher, Charles Huntley, Larry Lieberman, and Ronnie Washburn who had years of experience working in daily commercial "soaps". Last, but by no means least, Jay Millard became my personal assistant and was with me from 1981 to 2010. Our team grew and worked together like a family, not only at the Met, but overseas as well, especially in Eastern Europe. Our international activity began when invitations came to me from Moscow and St Petersburg. I accepted but insisted upon bringing my team of cameramen with whom I could communicate rather than struggling with a Russian-speaking group. In those days production companies usually had sufficient funds to cover the cost of necessary luxuries, so I had no qualms about making such a request. All told, we were responsible for a number of superior productions in Russia and later in Spain and Italy. Some of my cohorts had never been to Europe and I took particular delight in introducing them to the "Old World". To sum it up, no one could have asked for a better group of associates; I never could have accomplished what I did without them.

At first my chores were prescribed. Kirk Browning and I split the PBS opera broadcasts each year and, when Kirk retired, I took over his as well. Moreover, when I wasn't working at the Met, I plied my trade in other cities, San Francisco, Chicago, Los Angeles, etc. And, when I wasn't in the States, I worked in Germany, Italy, Austria, France,

England, any place in Europe that wanted me. My Met career began with John Dexter's provocative production of *Mahagonny*. After which I was presented with the opportunity to work with two of opera's most illustrious stars, Birgit Nilsson, outstanding in the German repertoire, and Luciano Pavarotti, acknowledged as one of, if not the "greatest male opera singers of the twentieth century".

"Flashing" the Rheingold Ring from the Met Opera production

Met camera crew wearing eye patches at the last *Ring* rehearsal. Everyone wanted to be Wotan

26.

Hoi Jo to Ho!

John Culshaw had introduced me to Birgit Nilsson at Covent Garden and while I'd heard her sing and occasionally saw her socially at Bayreuth, we'd never worked together until the *Elektra* fell into my lap. The minute I got the good news, I rang up Birgit's manager, Edgar Vincent, and asked if he could arrange a meeting with her. I told him I wanted to address any questions or concerns she might have about my work method. "Good idea", he replied. "I'll set up something." Birgit happened to be staying in Plácido Domingo's apartment in the Essex House on Central Park South. (Throughout his career, Domingo bought multiple residences in cities where he often sang. When he wasn't there, he rented them out to fellow artists.) Birgit invited me over and we quickly renewed contact. Warm, friendly, funny, but nervous, too, she wanted to work out the snarls of doing a live TV recording. She admitted to being terrified. "You see, Brian, I have no experience in this video thing. I grew up in Europe long before opera became a common occurrence on television. I did a couple of recitals for Swedish TV and I've sung arias on The Bell Telephone Hour here in America, but I've never done a full live performance. What if I do something wrong and there are no retakes? And what if I can't sustain my energy? And I'm really worried about this production. I did it seven or eight years ago, I know the ups and downs of this multi-level set and there are problems. I'm sixty-one years old and I'm not sure I have the staying power. This is too scary. Please

Birgit Nilsson as Elektra and Mignon Dunn as Clytemnestra
during a high voltage daughter/mother confrontation,
Metropolitan Opera, 1980   293

help me." Whew! I hadn't expected this particular *prima donna assoluta* to be so utterly vulnerable. Realizing that her fears might get the better of her, I thought it best to tell her exactly what I planned to do. First, I reassured her. "You've every reason to be concerned but there's no need to worry. My job as television director is to take a stage director's work and make it fit a different medium. I'm not going to treat *Elektra* like a stage opera, this is a TV music drama, everything has to be scaled down. You can't think in terms of reaching the back row of the gallery, you're playing to an unknown audience watching a television screen at home. In other words, you have to adjust your facial expressions and the way you use your body. You can throw your arms out wide on stage but you can't let them fly out at a 180-degree angle on television, they've got to go forward, 90 degrees to fit the screen format. Everything has to be contained. I can help you control your expressions and your gestures." "That's good, that's good," Birgit responded, "what you say makes sense. But what about the visualization, how will you treat that?" "Good question", I replied. "As I mentioned, I want to treat this like a drama with music. I'll create a visual treatment, much like a movie script, showing a series of shots depicting the *Elektra* story." I went into technical details and explained that one of the cameras would be used to show the other performers responding to Elektra's actions. Birgit smiled, "I understand. And I like this but what about specific scenes?" "As far as specific scenes, there are two primary occurrences for you, the confrontation with your mother, when Clytemnestra can't sleep and is describing a nightmare, and the recognition scene with your brother, Oreste." Once more, I pointed out that the television camera provided the intimacy that the stage normally couldn't and that's why reactions are so important. "Everything has to be contained within the framework of the television screen and, generally speaking, big is bad."

Birgit really got it and loved the moments when I explained precisely what the camera would be showing and where close-ups would be used. She seemed fascinated by the procedure and impressed me with her intelligent questions and her willingness to go with my suggestions. When I finished, I asked her what her biggest fears were apart from the energy concerns. "Well, there are three of them", she explained. "The first is to keep my voice lubricated. When I sang Elektra in Vienna and London and when I sang Wagner roles like Isolde in Bayreuth, there were always places where I could keep a bottle of beer handy. Like the Bayreuth *Tristan* where I had one hidden behind a boulder." She then proceeded to describe the scene I had witnessed from the lighting tower when she downed a beer and belched. (I decided to keep quiet about that; I didn't want to come off like a Peeping Tom.) Birgit, a savvy person, realized that television couldn't provide the "hiding places" she was used to. We had to find a discreet way for her to keep her throat moist. Amazingly, she herself came up with the solution, "Brian, do you know those chocolate capsules candies with liqueurs in them? I can't remember the name but you break them open, drink the inside, and chew up the outside." "I think they're called Cordials or something like that. Well, maybe we could have the costume department design little capsules to look like beads or ornaments, fill them with water, and attach them to my costume. *Elektra's* behaviour is erratic, often neurotic, and when I start to get excited, I could tear the capsules off my dress, break them open, swallow the water, and drop the outer shell." "Brilliant", I said. And, that's exactly what was done. The costume department crafted a multitude of water-filled beads which looked like buttons, and sewed them onto her costume. In performance, she'd rip them off and down the contents whenever she needed to wet her whistle. Each bead contained a few sips of water, just enough to assuage the dryness. That problem solved, we tackled the next.

At the very end of the opera, after ninety minutes of singing, and after her brother has murdered their mother and stepfather, Elektra goes into an ecstatic dance of triumph. Birgit balked at that. "I'm too old to do a choreographed dance. I'd rather create a body movement based on the rhythmic stamping in the score." She then showed me the musical accentuations Strauss had written in the score. Birgit wanted to match her pounding feet to the stabbing chords in the orchestra. Again, a perfect solution. We now addressed her final concern, Elektra's collapse and death. "Believe me, Brian, after ninety minutes of singing, I feel like I'm dying but mostly I'm lying there huffing and puffing. I can't be shown like that, it would destroy the scene." "You're right, Birgit, seeing the dead Elektra gasping for air would be disastrous. But the whole point of the scene is her death. You've got to be shown stone-cold dead. One way to do it is for us to set up an extra camera on a lighting tower and use it to shoot the death scene in close-up. Then, in post-production I can freeze that frame on screen. Believe me, you'll look dead." "But this is perfect", Birgit cried, clapping her hands. Within an hour or so we'd established an enduring, productive working relationship.

Of the four *Elektra* performances, we taped the second and the third as rehearsals and a final recording of the fourth. Once we had the first two tapes on VHS cassettes, I went back to Birgit's apartment to watch them with her. We spent several hours going over the second performance and then repeated the process for the third. She would stop and start the viewing machine to critique her own performances and mark her score. And by the way, she'd politely critique my efforts as well. "I like that", she'd say pointing to a scene on the screen. Or, pointing to another scene she'd say, "I don't like that", and tell me why. Most important, in the end, she trusted me. She knew what I was going to do and I gave my word that I'd only do what we'd agreed upon. By the time we got to the final matinee, Birgit had complete control of *Elektra*. When the curtain came down on the last performance, the audience went wild; applause went on like a ticker-tape for twenty-nine minutes. Confetti rained down from the galleries as Nilsson took her final bows in the house that had become her musical home.

Years later, after Birgit had retired, we had a delightful reunion at a reception given by her record company in London. Moving off from the crowd for a while, we spoke privately. Unsurprisingly, *Elektra* entered the conversation. Birgit recalled our collaboration, remembered it vividly, and expressed her gratitude. "I told you then and I tell you now, this *Elektra* was very important in my career, Brian. Because of you, it wasn't too late for me to become part of video history." I thanked her and commended her for recognizing the power of television and for her willingness to participate. Although I directed *Elektra* several more times, none came near the unique experience of guiding Birgit Nilsson through that tangled tale.

Performers such as Birgit Nilsson don't simply go out and sing, they prepare. Don't get me wrong, all singers prepare, it's just that some don't choose to dig as deep as they might. While I always offered to assist artists to paint a fuller portrait, not a few brushed me off. Not Nilsson. The preparation we did together provides a good example of my directorial approach. Now on to the next opera immortal. Without question, of the multitude of artists with whom I worked, the most illustrious would have to be Luciano Pavarotti.

27.

Non Cacio Così

*Everybody adored him, as did I, but they didn't have to deal
with him and, eventually, that made a difference.*

In March of 1977, the inaugural broadcast of "Live from
the Met", a telecast of *La Bohème* with Renata Scotto as
Mimi and Luciano Pavarotti as Rodolfo, appeared on
America's Public Broadcasting Service. Although not
the first Met telecast (*Don Carlos* had been transmitted
from the old Met in November of 1950), *Bohème* did mark
the beginning of regular opera transmissions from the
Metropolitan Opera House. My working relationship with
Pavarotti began with the *Ballo in Maschera* in 1980. From
then on, we collaborated regularly at the Met and other
opera companies. Wherever we were, the routine remained
the same. During rehearsal period, Luciano would call and
ask me to drop by his apartment or hotel suite to explore
the video aspects of the pending production.

In November of 1990, I went to his Hampshire House
apartment in Manhattan to discuss the upcoming telecast
of his Thirtieth Anniversary Gala at the Metropolitan Opera House. As did all our tête-à-têtes, the meeting began
in the kitchen. An oversized pot of boiling water bubbled
on the stove and Luciano, enveloped in a capacious bath-
robe, stood over it. He greeted me effusively with the pet
names by which he always addressed me. "Eh, *Briano,
Brianino, come stai*? How are you doing? *Cosa c'é di nuovo
su Rialto?* What's the gossip on the Rialto? *Dimmi tutto.*

Ridi, Pagliacco in veritas.
Luciano Pavarotti, Naples, Italy, 1996

299

Tell me everything." After I shared a few current stories, Luciano began to pick my brain about the gala even as he prepared and served perfectly cooked spaghetti topped with tasty Bolognese sauce. After dinner, we proceeded to the bedroom where he flopped down on his bed, flipped on the huge TV at the foot of it and with me seated in a comfortable armchair, the two of us watched an archival recording of Donizetti's *L'Elisir d'Amore*. Luciano lay there, propped up on the pillows and surrounded by munchies—potato chips, nuts, candies—which he nibbled on for the rest of the evening. His appetite was as prodigious as his talent.

Luciano always got a kick out of viewing himself on the screen and particularly enjoyed his portrayal of Nemorino, the bucolic bumpkin with a heart of gold. At one point, he turned to me saying, "*Brianino*, you see this Nemorino? *Ecco*, that's me, that's who I am." Indeed, in the beginning, that's who he was, an affable, fun-loving, quick-witted peasant who delighted in being seen as the country boy. Yet underneath his erstwhile rustic persona lurked a darker character whose presence steadily asserted itself as Luciano became more wealthy, more famous, more powerful, and more physically challenged.

When the video ended, Luciano leaned over and said with utmost sincerity, "*Brianino*, it is my opinion that you cannot underestimate the power and importance of television." "I never do", I answered. "I am not kidding, *Briano*. Look at me, I am the best example of this. I need television but I didn't fully realize it until the Met broadcast of *Bohème* twenty years ago. The day before the telecast nobody knew me; the day after, everybody knew me. People stopped me on the street to say hello and tell me how wonderful I'd been. This was my eye-opener."

Leave it to Luciano; he'd sized up the situation early on and continued to use TV's intense potential to his advantage for the rest of his performing life. Ben Britten had to be led to television, Luciano Pavarotti dove into it. Aware that his body wasn't exactly telegenic, and that aside from his voice, his greatest gifts were his genial grin and his sparkling eyes, he made sure the camera captured his assets by insisting on close-ups. He knew instinctively how to turn anything to his advantage, from camera angles to props. For example, during a recital someone handed him a large white handkerchief to mop the sweat from his brow. Luciano immediately turned the handkerchief into an ever-present visual signature. In formal dress, he stood by the piano, the white handkerchief clutched in his hand, dabbing his forehead even as he sang. No doubt about it, television completely enhanced Luciano Pavarotti's persona, a magic carpet that carried his career from its robust beginnings to its crippled end. He needed the media to stay in touch with his vast public, especially when his deteriorating physical condition prevented him from travelling or performing as much. And no one filled a screen better than he. Everybody loved the bigger than life singer whose God-given gift had no equal. Mind you, there were plenty of good tenors around, but when you came right down to it there was only one who just had to open his mouth.

At the peak of his popularity, Luciano Pavarotti could get away with just about anything. Howsoever he acted or reacted, his basic honesty kept him on the straight and narrow … somewhat. He'd always manage to find a gimmick that benefitted him. For example, his payments became astronomical but taxes pulled him back down to earth. Luciano met the challenge by devising different ways of receiving payment, especially for his many charitable appearances. I believe his legal waffling began when he gave a benefit concert for an opera house in Texas. Rather than accepting a fee, Luciano asked for "payment in kind", specifically a very expensive white Arabian stallion which he much admired. Houston Opera bought the horse which was delivered to Luciano's home in Italy. In the end, no taxes to worry about for Luciano or for the horse, either. Luciano arranged other payments in kind, among them two race horses in Oklahoma. In Berlin, when he sang for the Deutsche Oper's Twenty-Fifth Anniversary Gala, he took his fee in animal stock. Clever man.

In September of 1981, I directed a live telecast of *Aida* for the San Francisco Opera, simultaneously transmitted to Germany thus establishing SFO's first overseas telecast. The reason for this worldwide hook-up can be stated in two words, Luciano Pavarotti. Luciano would be singing his first Radames, reason enough for an international viewing. Lucianno's wants had become a command. And, lucky me, I had become someone Luciano wanted. Impressed with my work on the Met's *Ballo* and *Idomeneo,* he believed that I was the one who best captured his brilliance on video. Even after my reputation had been solidly established, I had Luciano to thank for my participation in many endeavours. In this instance, he actually demanded my presence and told San Francisco that I had to be involved or he wouldn't do it. I admit to being very flattered and very grateful.

Kurt Adler, managing director of the SFO, went all out for *Aida.* He put actor/director Sam Wanamaker in charge of a massive production, two hundred fifty-nine extras and choristers, elaborate costumes, sets dripping with Hollywood-like effects, and culminating in a Cecil B. DeMille version of Verdi's grandest of grand operas. Because of the MGMish aspects of the production, I expected that problems would abound but except for a few technical knots, the

major stumbling block turned out to be a continuing con-
tretemps between Radames and his Aida, Margaret Price.
Pavarotti and Price did not hit it off; quite the opposite.
The situation grew worse as Luciano endlessly contrived
to put himself in the limelight. Price, a down-to-earth
Welshwoman, had little tolerance for Luciano's antics.
Among many clashes, during a rehearsal of the tomb scene,
Pavarotti put his hand over the soprano's mouth to muffle
her singing. Unfazed, she bit him. Despite the tension between the warring leads, we managed to get through the
rehearsal period and the challenging difficulties of trans-
mitting the opening performance to Germany. The broadcast went smoothly, the production was highly praised, and
the San Francisco Opera became a participant in intercon-
tinental broadcasting.

Following the transmission to Germany, I had to record
and edit the *Aida* for PBS to broadcast. A performance
had been selected but Margaret Price suddenly became ill
and the video had to be postponed. Meanwhile, another
soprano had to be found. They found one, and what a
one! Leontyne Price agreed to replace the ailing Margaret
Price. ("Two for the Price of One", read the headlines.)
Leontyne sang just one performance which we could not
record because the contract belonged to the Welsh Price.
She recovered and returned as did the stressful relationship between her and Pavarotti. The show, however, had
to, and did, go on. No love lost between the leads still, the
recording became a PBS broadcast and then a successful
DVD.

Another Luciano occasion worth noting involved a production of *La Bohème*. I had the great good fortune to
video Puccini's beloved opera four times, at the Royal
Opera House, Covent Garden (1982), the San Francisco

War Memorial (1988), the Seebühne Bregenz Festival on a floating stage on Lake Constance (2002), and the Salzburg Festival in 2012. Each was special but the San Francisco production distinctively so. Mirella Freni and Luciano Pavarotti led the cast and that says it all. Freni and Pavarotti, both born and bred in Modena, Italy, had known each other from childhood, allegedly they'd shared the same wet nurse. They often appeared together and became famous singing *Bohèmes* all over Europe. Now they'd arrived in San Francisco to reunite as Mimi and Rodolfo for the first time in twenty years and the much-hyped reunion became the hottest ticket in town. Reiner Moritz's company had been contracted to do the videoing and, per usual, Luciano demanded my services. Reiner, an old friend, quickly agreed to my participation. Reiner and I had worked together many times including the San Francisco *Aida* and the two of us got along well, extremely well. We needed to because Luciano became more and more demanding. His weight was way up and his knees were riddled with arthritis. Much as he wanted to have his *Bohème* documented, he didn't want to move around on stage. On the contrary, he just wanted to sit in a chair thus wreaking havoc with the staging. It might be reasonable for Mimi, a tubercular, to take it easy, but Rodolfo is a robust young man, hardly someone who'd be involved in passionate love scenes while seated. Luciano didn't care about character veracity and threw tantrums when he had to stand up and participate. Lotfi Mansouri, general director of the San Francisco Opera and stage director of *Bohème*, couldn't take the stress and strain of working with the ever-demanding tenor. Pleading that he was too busy with company matters, Mansouri handed the production over to a young female assistant. She followed Mansouri's book and tried to make the artists do as he'd written. The day the assistant showed up, Pavarotti realized she was directing for the first time and bristled at being guided by a fledgling. When asked to do something he invariably responded, "*Non cacio così*" (a colloquialism meaning, "I won't do it", "I don't play like that", or, in this instance, "the hell with it"). He repeated the phrase so often the stagehands picked it up and whenever they were asked to do something they'd good-humouredly reply "*non cacio così*". The phrase became a resounding in-joke.

Luciano could be the biggest pain in the ass but the crew always gave him leeway. They loved him. A sweet note: About as superstitious as anyone could be, Luciano would not go onstage at the Met (or anywhere else) if he did not find a bent nail before the performance. For Luciano, a bent nail brought good luck. Knowing this, the stage crew would plant three or four of them on the stage floor. Luciano always managed to find at least one of them. Sometimes he'd nab them all. Did he know the drill? I rather think he did.

As for dealing with him, only one person in the entire company knew how to do that, Mirella Freni. The two of them spoke to each other in Modenese dialect and during their exchanges, she'd let him huff and puff but would stand her ground when he became too obstinate. Mirella knew Luciano would attempt to take advantage of any situation and when he did, she cut him down to size. How many times did I see him try to finagle her into helping him get his way? She'd say "no" and that was that. Luciano could con everybody else but he never got the better of his *amica d'infanzia*.

Despite the ups and downs and ins and outs of Luciano's manipulating, we came to the final recording of *Bohème*. After the taping, I went to congratulate him. Brow furrowed, he began to complain. "*Briano*, I am not content. My voice was not in best form. We have to do another take. Get everyone back and we'll record one more performance." Coolly, I explained that the technical crews were de-rigging and disconnecting cables from the cameras. "I can't call people back. It's finished, Luciano." "*Briano*, I am not a convenience performer", he answered. "If you want my Rodolfo you need to do something about it. I demand a retake. Basta!" He would talk no more and waved me out of the room.

I stood outside the door and thought, "What the hell am I going to do now?" The budget allowed for two rehearsals and one performance; we didn't have the money to do any more. The crew was on the way out. Suddenly, the answer hit me. I went back into the dressing room and addressed Luciano. "Okay, I persuaded everyone to come back and do one more take." Instantly he cheered up. "This is good news, *Brianino*." "Yes, it is, but there's a problem." "What problem?" "I don't have one hundred and fifty thousand dollars which it's going to cost. If you want another go, you'll have to pay for it yourself." Punching him in the money belt was a low blow but absolutely necessary. I knew he'd never part with a cent to do a retake. Luciano looked at me, paused, smiled, pointed his finger at me, then pointed his finger at himself, and then up to heaven. He laughed and exclaimed, "*Non cacio così!*" He knew he'd lost and accepted it. For a moment, Nemorino had returned.

As time went on, pain and decreased mobility exponentially increased Luciano's demands. For example, when he renewed his Decca exclusive contract, he inserted a clause stating that whenever he was in America, no matter for how long and wherever he was, the recording company had to give him exclusive transportation day or night to any location he wanted. He simply couldn't get enough perks; he wanted everything. At the same time, he worried incessantly about his health. In and out of hospitals, once he was released, he'd continue to wear his patient identification wristband till it fell off. On one shoot, I grabbed his hand and said, "Luciano, you've got to get rid of this. You can't appear on camera with a hospital ID." He pulled his arm away and sneered at me. The last time I saw him, a ragged white strip stating his identity still circled his wrist.

Concurrent with his health scares, his appetite expanded and his weight, always a problem, soared. Further, he became obsessed with staying young and, in a desperate attempt to stave off the inevitable aging process, began to blacken his thinning hair and beard. He surrounded himself with young people hoping somehow their vigour would rub off on him. Whenever members of his staff left, whether secretaries, cooks, or trainers, younger and younger persons replaced them. I remember visiting him while he worked out with his latest trainer. "*Brianino*," Luciano called out, "get down on the floor and do some push-ups with me." I did as he asked and it was fun but there was something forlorn about the whole picture. Having to watch this singing miracle go to any extreme to recapture his youth made being around him hard to bear. I worshipped the artist but I began to look askance at the man.

His success firmly established, Luciano became more commercial, which is not a criticism, it's a fact of life. No longer the country bumpkin, he emerged as the great matinee idol and could be seen everywhere—astride a horse leading a parade or singing Italian duets onstage with Elvis Presley. He had to keep up the image, the charisma, the good humour. And most imperative, he had to maintain his vocal prowess even as it became progressively difficult to per-form effortlessly. Certain vocal passages that he'd coasted through all his life became challenges to which he had to adjust. He had to work harder and as he did, he became frightened. He'd pull me aside and say with heartbreaking honesty, "*Brianino*, not too close, not too close with the camera. No more close-ups. I don't want them to see me struggling."

The illusion of a vigorous Luciano had to be maintained and re-staging became mandatory. During a recording of *André Chénier* at the Met in 1995/96, we had to figure out how to keep the action going without him having to move across the stage. Dramatic authenticity ceased to exist. No matter what occurred in a scene, Luciano remained seated. Sometimes we put him at a round table where he sat as the other characters circled him. He still could be charm-ing and lovable, but hell on earth if he didn't get what he wanted. I began to dread his phone calls telling me he was going to record an *Elixir* or a whatever and that he wanted me to do it. "Oh wonderful. Thank you, Luciano", I'd answer, but I groaned inside because I knew what it meant. Luciano would use his pain and his charm to get what he wanted, to remain on his "throne" and have the entire production revolve around him. Visually and dramatically it's really nerve-wracking when you can't show someone in relation to the other characters. I had to use every trick at my command to make him part of the action. And when I'd reach the end of my rope, he'd call me over and whisper, "*Brianino*, save me. I'm in pain. Don't show me like this. Help me." And I did the best I could. My heart went out to him because he felt compelled to be the young Pavarotti. The mind was willing but the flesh was weak; the smile, the good humour was surface level. He played the clown but beneath the façade, fear resided.

In 1999, Luciano appeared in a giant gala concert in Madison Square Garden. And thanks to him, I made my directorial debut in New York's fabled showcase for sports—boxing and wrestling matches, basketball and hockey games—theatrical events, and classical and pop music concerts. Nineteen thousand seats were filled for Luciano's sold-out appearance. Still, Madison Square Garden wasn't an ideal place for shooting a video. Recording the concert, a potpourri of arias and duets which he sang with his girlfriend, Madeline Renée, wasn't a very satisfying experience for me. Luciano had his problems, too. The weight, the buckling knees, the simple act of moving around, all had become arduous, sometimes impossible. And, of course, as his physical woes intensified so did his demands. At the time of the Garden appearance, barely able to walk, he needed to control everything. He insisted on being transported from his dressing room to the stage in a gleaming white stretch limousine. The distance was short and could have been done surreptitiously in a golf cart. But no, he needed to be pampered, it had to be an ostentatious chariot with lights and cameras following his every move.

On 13 March 2004, Luciano Pavarotti made his last appearance in an opera singing Cavaradossi in *Tosca* at the Metropolitan Opera House. On 1 December of the same year, he announced his farewell tour. The farewell became a series of tours including an "Australasian" final run at the end of which, in December of 2005, he gave his final full-blown concert in Taiwan. In February of 2006, he sang "Nessun dorma" at the opening ceremony of the Winter Olympics in Turin. The truth is, he really didn't sing. Initially, Luciano had turned down the invitation but finally was persuaded to take part when they allowed him to prerecord his signature aria. The orchestra pretended to play and Luciano pretended to warble; the actual performance had been recorded some weeks prior.

In July of 2006, Luciano was diagnosed with pancreatic cancer. He wouldn't yield to old age or to cancer. He chose to fight, underwent major abdominal surgery, and battled for his life. By a weird coincidence, not long after his diagnosis his long-time colleague and friend, Marilyn Horne, also fell victim to pancreatic cancer. She, too, underwent surgery and during recovery often chatted with Luciano over the phone. He told her about a new treatment in development at The Johns Hopkins Hospital adding that he hoped to join the programme. "Why don't you try it, Jackie?" he suggested. Horne, known to family and friends as Jackie, took his advice and contacted Johns Hopkins. She got into the programme, ironically, Luciano did not. He couldn't meet the necessary qualifications, which is another way of saying he was too far gone for the treatment. Horne survived the ordeal and was cured; Luciano succumbed and died at his home in Modena on 6 September 2007. The funeral took place at the Modena Cathedral. After the hubbub of the day's activity an air of sadness hung over the city. Later, Mirella and I visited the Pavarotti family tomb to pay our last respects. Tears clouding our eyes, we stood together, arm in arm, and said our goodbyes.

In 2019, Ron Howard made a documentary about Luciano which I very much enjoyed. The film was kind and honest, portraying Luciano with many if not all his warts. I admired the fact that they interviewed his first wife, Adua, and their three daughters. Adua had given up everything for her husband; she ran his home, raised his children and, at the same time, became the force behind his professional life. While she served, he philandered. Eventually he left her and after a series of affairs married one of his young assistants, thirty-four years his junior. Adua bore it all with dignity and reserve, yes, and even compassion. She visited him as he lay dying, and at the request of the second Signora Pavarotti, prepared and brought him a dish of his favourite pasta, Spaghetti Bolognese. After all she had endured, she came to him.

According to his former manager, Herbert Breslin, Luciano Pavarotti "loved music, women, food, and football—in that order". I like to think I'm not a judgmental person but when I heard that, I shuddered. I wasn't crazy about his behaviour and yet I continued to answer his beck and call. Why did I stand by a person whose behaviour appalled me? The answer is clear: music came first for Luciano as it does for me and that made it possible to assist the peerless artist and overlook the self-indulgent man.

Recently, I came across the video of *Un Ballo in Maschera* I recorded with Luciano in Vienna (1986). Not planning to watch the whole show, I took the album off the shelf and slipped the disc into a player for a brief pick-me-up. That was my intention. Once I began watching and listening, however, I could not turn it off. Luciano is at his best. His whole being shines as he approaches each phrase with ecstatic abandon and his sheer joy in singing is palpable. Has there ever been another who sang with such rapture? The man's life ended. Apollo's song, Luciano Pavarotti's "profuse strains of unpremeditated art", remains.

28

The Nightingale and the Lark

During that San Francisco *Aida*, when Leontyne Price stepped in for Margaret Price, I had hoped to at least meet the fabled American soprano. I didn't, a big disappointment as I yearned to video this incredible artist. Seven months later, the gods smiled. In March of 1982, Sybil Harrington sponsored a gala concert at the Metropolitan Opera House featuring Leontyne Price and Marilyn Horne, accompanied by James Levine and the Met orchestra. An unabashed admirer of both singers, I barely could contain my delight at the opportunity to meet them and, more important, to record them. Price and Horne were such superstars I felt uncharacteristically nervous. Perhaps if I had been working with one or the other separately, I might have remained calmer; the two together put me a bit on edge. When we were introduced, Price was gracious, "How do you do, Mr Large", she said warmly as she shook my hand. Still, she continued to address me formally as Mr Large. I, in turn, called her Miss Price. Horne, on the other hand, was completely informal. She didn't like using "Mr" and from the beginning called me "Brian … Large", pausing between my first and last name. Horne, possessed of a wicked sense of humour, couldn't resist fooling around with the implicit pun in my name. If by some miracle you haven't yet noticed, say my name quickly and Brian Large becomes "by and large". You can imagine what fun that was for me as a schoolboy. I forgave her the minute I heard her sing "Non temer un basso

Marilyn Horne and Leontyne Price in concert at
the Metropolitan Opera, 1982. Absolute proof that
"music is the speech of angels"

affeto", an aria from Rossini's *Siege of Corinth*. I didn't know the aria, I didn't know the opera and when I looked at the score, I wondered how anyone could sing all the notes in the impossibly florid music. Horne could, and I was blown away by a brilliant and breathtaking musical experience. Another moment in the rehearsal also got to me. The programme included the "Mira o Norma" duet from the Bellini opera. Horne had made her sensational Metropolitan Opera debut in the role of Adalgisa opposite Joan Sutherland's Norma. Although urged to do it, Price never essayed Norma, one of the greatest soprano roles in the operatic repertoire. (Wagnerian soprano, Lilli Lehmann, claimed it was easier to sing all three Brünnhildes than one Norma.) At rehearsal, the two divas stood in front of the orchestra and sang the duet. When it ended, Leontyne broke into tears and fell into her colleague's arms. "I should have sung that role", she whispered to Horne. The concert itself was a little miracle, or a big one if great singing affects you as it does me. As an added bonus from this brilliant concert, I established a good relationship with each of the singers.

I next worked with Leontyne Price on an *Aida* at the Met in January of 1985. We were recording the final performance, a matinee. That afternoon I went to her dressing room before the curtain went up. Adhering to the formality of our relationship, I said, "I've come to wish you good luck, Miss Price and I'll be back to see you after the performance." "Thank you, Mr Large", she replied. I left the dressing room and took my place in the television truck. The curtain went up on one of the greatest performances ever seen at the Met, and everyone in the audience knew it. True, Leontyne Price had passed her prime, but her "passed the prime" surpassed a lot of singers' "primes". At the end of the third act aria, "O patria mia", the house went wild and, though it only lasted minutes, the clapping and shouting seemed to go on endlessly. Price stood there as wave after wave of applause washed over the proscenium. I had the camera brought in on her face in a full screen close-up. Instantly, I decided to hold the shot, which I did even as my colleagues sitting behind me cried out, "Cut away, cut away, it's too close to her, too close." I paid them no heed. I'd made up my mind to keep that incredible woman in full close-up until the applause ended. Attention had to be paid. The others unrelentingly urged me to move on. "Come on, Brian. This is boring, cut away. Let it go." I held fast and I'm very glad I did. Her head held high, her eyes filled with tears, her lips occasionally trembling, Leontyne Price stayed within her character, the enslaved Ethiopian princess torn between allegiance to her lover and to her country. The majestic manner in which she received her homage was soul-stirring. Yet, as composed as she remained, Price could not help being moved by the tumultuous reception afforded her. With utmost grace and dignity, she blended her personal thanks with Aida's angst. I never witnessed anything like it. That headshot of Leontyne Price turned out to be a first of its kind. To state plainly, and sad to say, never had an artist of Black heritage and of this calibre been held in that kind of close-up for that long. The opera ended and, as promised, I returned to the star's dressing room, knocked on the door and announced myself. "Come in", Price called out. "Well, how was it?" she asked as I entered the room. "Wonderful, Miss Price, simply wonderful." "Are you sure it was wonderful, Mr Large?" "Absolutely", I asserted. Price smiled. "Well, I'm glad it was wonderful, Mr Large, because—and you're the first to know, that was the last time I'll ever sail down the Nile." Wow. I had just recorded Leontyne Price's final

Aida. I stammered a mixture of compliment and regret. When I finished, she threw her arms around me in a quick, spontaneous hug. We exchanged a few more words and I took my leave. As I reached the door, she called out. "By the way, Mr Large, I don't know when we'll meet again but when we do, call me Leontyne." I walked out of the dressing room and into a battalion of Leontynites clamouring to see their idol, "our" idol. True to her word, she never sang Aida again and the close-up of that magnificent artist in her final portrayal of the Ethiopian princess became part of television history.

Thanks to Reiner Moritz and his passion for recording off-the-beaten track operas, I crossed paths with Marilyn Horne when Reiner decided that Vivaldi's *Orlando Furioso* had to be recorded. The San Francisco Opera mounted the production and I was contracted to do it. I'd never heard a Vivaldi opera in my life and became completely fascinated by this incredible piece. Adding to the pleasure of trying my hand at Baroque opera, Marilyn would be singing the lead role with Sir John Pritchard conducting. I knew John from my BBC days; Marilyn made her Covent Garden debut singing Marie in Berg's *Wozzeck* under his baton. What looked to be a joyful reunion of colleagues and friends turned out quite differently.

For some time, rumours had been circulating that Pritchard was ailing. During rehearsals, it became obvious he wasn't "ailing", he was seriously ill. Nevertheless, he insisted upon conducting every piano rehearsal. He'd sit in the pit barely able to hold the baton let alone beat two of three. Clearly in distress, he refused to yield. One afternoon, Marilyn and I were seated together in the back of the auditorium watching a scene on the stage while Sir John struggled to carry on. The procedure became unendurable.

Without saying a word, Marilyn got up and went down the aisle to the pit rail. She leaned over the rail, and as I later learned, reassured Pritchard that *Orlando* was going to be a splendid production, then suggested that since the rehearsals were going so well, he really didn't need to be there. Better to save his energy. Somehow, she got through to him. Gently assisting him out of the pit, they stood arm in arm in the aisle for a few moments. Then, still linking her arm in his, she slowly propelled him up the aisle to the exit door and through to the street where she helped him into a taxi. Two days later, Sir John Pritchard died of AIDS. Deeply affected by her friend's passing, Horne's strength of character allowed her to complete the task of documenting *Orlando Furioso*. Well-liked by her colleagues, everyone knew Marilyn Horne could be a tough cookie. On this occasion, I bore witness to another side of that great diva, her kind and generous soul.

Our next reunion took place in 1986 when she returned to the Met in a delightful Ponnelle production of Rossini's *L'Italiana in Algeri*. In terrific form, vocally and physically, Marilyn had slimmed down amazingly for one of her semi-glamorous, non-trouser roles. Knowing the production would be televised and documented, Horne wanted to present herself in an elegant and stylish manner and asked me to help her do so. I immediately agreed. We recorded bits from various rehearsals and then met in my office to look at them. I played the tape and she liked it. I didn't. From an acting and television point of view, I found Horne's interpretation devoid of subtlety but what was I going to do with that? Though we didn't know each other well, we had a good working relationship which I wanted to continue. Still, I felt that I had to comment, truthfully. Drawing upon all my courage, I took a deep breath and spoke. "Marilyn, please excuse me for saying this but I think you're playing a sprightly Italian girl more like Ethel Merman on Broadway." Her eyes narrowed and I panicked. I wasn't meaning to put her down by comparing her with Ethel Merman, far from it. Merman was a magnificent performer but her brand of brashness didn't suit Isabella. A long pause ensued during which Marilyn said nothing. Had I not chosen the right words? Had I been indiscreet rather than helpful? Had I been rude? I hadn't meant to be any of that but, oh boy, the woman just glared at me. Finally, she spoke. "So that's what you think?" "Yes, it is." "Okay, play the tape again." I did as she asked. "Again", she said when it ended. At this point, I half expected her to pull the tape from the machine and wrap it around my neck. Again, she watched intently. After a moment or two of silence, she spoke. "I think I know what you mean, Brian. I think you're right. I know I can do it differently. I'm sure I can. Thank you for being honest with me." She left the office. The door closed and I heaved a sigh of relief. We taped the next rehearsal and watched it together. What a difference. She'd lightened up, turning her portrayal into something subtle, refined, and delightful. She smiled more and longer and thus became better able to match her demeanour with her dazzling coloratura. Expressive as well as funny, she'd brought a whole new perspective to her character. Horne had taken my criticism the way I intended it, constructively, and with no hard feelings. Not only that, after the recording, she treated me to one of the best imitations I'd ever heard of Ethel Merman singing "You're Not Sick, You're Just in Love".

Rossini again brought Marilyn back into my life in October of 1990. *Semiramide,* an elaborate opera seria, provided Horne with a memorable military trouser role. Indeed, she portrayed so many heroic warriors they called her

"General Horne". *Semiramide* dazzled. June Anderson in the title role, and Marilyn and Samuel Ramey as her suitors, gloriously commanded the vocal pyrotechnics. I got to know and like Sam, a man of few but often choice words and an incredible singing artist. Whether playing a real devil like Mefistofele, or a human version, like Don Giovanni, he commanded the stage. And, his vocal dexterity in the Rossini repertoire remains breathtaking.

My last professional encounter with Marilyn Horne came in October of 1992 in the Zeffirelli Met Opera production of *Falstaff*, and what a delicious portrayal of Dame Quickly she gave, really amazing. From the beginning of our association, I pegged Horne as a straight shooter, someone who could take criticism and use it to her advantage. I was right.

Of all the productions in which Marilyn and I were together, one stands out although not for professional reasons. *Semiramide*, a joint effort of the Met and Japan's NHK Television Service, had to be edited in Tokyo. I'd never been to Japan and looked forward to going there. Since no direct flights over Russian territory existed in the early nineties, I had to fly from London to Anchorage and from there to Tokyo, an arduous journey. The flight, however, didn't concern me as much as my mother's health. Her condition continued to deteriorate and the trip would take ten days. On the one hand, I didn't want to break my word to NHK, on the other hand, I didn't want to leave my mother. The doctor assured me she'd be around for at least another three months and my mother, herself, wouldn't hear of my not going. "You have a professional obligation", she admonished. "You can't let them down." My father, too, pressed me to get my work done. And so, I took off. "I'll call you from Anchorage", I'd advised my mother when I left, and immediately rang her up when I arrived there. My father answered the phone calmly informing me that my mother had collapsed after I left and was in hospital. I quickly said I'd grab a return flight. "There's nothing you can do here. Continue on to Tokyo", rejoined my father. I said I preferred to come home but he wouldn't hear of it. I gave in, adding that I'd come right back if anything went wrong. When I phoned him again from Tokyo, in tears, he told me my mother had died two hours before. Crushed, I cried out, "I never should have left. I deserted her." My father would have none of that. "Your mother wanted you to go, she told you to go. Don't blame yourself. She made the decision."

I had a lot of thinking to do. I remembered way back when my mother cautioned me about becoming a musician. "If you're going to be in the profession, you have to be hundred per cent honest with yourself and others. You have to be hundred per cent professional, every single time." She and my father had instilled that ethic in me and made sure I lived up to it. Ruby Willis Large practiced what she preached. She pressed me forward, always. I owe so much to her and my father. Whatever I've accomplished, my parents' honest, loving auspices paved the way.

29

The Emperor of Salzburg

During the Metropolitan Opera's 1981/82 season, I experienced another intense musical moment, well, at nearly four hours, a lot more than a moment. Back in 1957, Sybil Harrington funded a new production of Verdi's *Don Carlos*. The opera, resurrected by Met general manager Rudolf Bing, has remained in the repertoire ever since. In 1983, *Don Carlos* was revived with a cast including Plácido Domingo, the recently married Mirella Freni and Nicolai Ghiaurov, Grace Bumbry, Louis Quilico and James Levine conducting the great Met orchestra. Best of all, John Dexter masterminded the staging. For me, this production represented the pluperfect presentation of Verdi's towering masterpiece. Getting that brilliant show on tape is one of my proudest Met achievements. All told, 1983 proved to be a bonanza year.

The *Don Carlos* a done deed, I next received an invitation from the Salzburg Festival to video Jean-Pierre Ponnelle's production of *The Magic Flute*. First seen in 1975, the Ponnelle version had been performed in Salzburg almost every summer since its premiere. Ponnelle, with whom I had worked, wanted me to tape it. What a smashing opportunity.

Ponnelle adored Salzburg, the city Austrian poet Hugo von Hofmannsthal called "the heart of the heart of Europe", and relished working in the 1500 seat *Felsenreitschule* (Winter Riding School) theatre. The *Felsenreitschule* had been carved out of the Mönchsberg

Herbert von Karajan conducts the Berlin Philharmonic Orchestra, 1968. I botched my opportunity to work with him at Salzburg and never regretted it mountain in 1926 when Max Reinhardt ran the festival. Its forty-metre stage is the largest in Europe and Ponnelle's ingenious "Cinemascope" production of *The Magic Flute* covered not only the stage's length and breadth but also integrated the alcoves and arches which had been carved into the mountain backdrop. The cast, Peter Schreier, Ileana Cotrubaş, Edita Gruberová, Martti Talvela, and Christian Boesch, had been performing together since 1978. They all were excellent but in the role of Papageno, Boesch stole the show every night, not because he was an Austrian but because of his brilliant acting and singing. Amazingly, James Levine conducted the production. I say amazingly because Herbert von Karajan, head of the festival and chief conductor, rarely welcomed competitors. The fabled maestro happened to be a power freak who micromanaged everything. Born in Salzburg, von Karajan viewed his hometown and its festival as his kingdom and his glory. I couldn't help wondering how Ponnelle managed to squeeze Levine (and me) into the picture. I'm sure that Ronald Wilford, head of CAMI, had a hand in it. Wilford, *the* power broker in those days, guided a powerful roster of megastars including von Karajan, James Levine, Seiji Ozawa, Claudio Abbado, Kurt Masur, Colin Davis, Mstislav Rostropovich, Vladimir Horowitz, Maurizio Pollini, Marilyn Horne, Kathy Battle, etc. etc. My guess is Wilford persuaded von Karajan to allow Levine to conduct and me to do the taping. Whatever the reason, we were in Salzburg where we made a very successful live transmission of *The Magic Flute*. Pleased with the results, Ponnelle and Levine went on to their next projects. I remained to attend some concerts. I tend to hang around festivals (cf. Bayreuth) often with unexpected consequences.

Shortly after my confreres departed, Herbert von Karajan's secretary telephoned to advise me that the maestro wanted to meet with me. Stunned, I quickly made an appointment. On HvK Day, I went to the administrative headquarters and was shown into the director's chamber, a well-appointed room adjacent to his office. I sat on a sofa until von Karajan entered. His appearance shocked me. I'd only ever seen him in action on the podium where he loomed like a Goliath; up close he was short and slight. "Mr Large", he said. I stood up and sputtered, "Yes. Maestro." To which he replied, "I guess we will speak in English as you don't speak German." I quickly answered, *"Es ist nicht notwendig. Ich spreche deutsch."* (Touché) I could see my rejoinder took him aback. He did not answer but sat down in a chair opposite me as I dropped back onto the sofa. "Herr Large," he began, switching into German which we spoke for the rest of the interview, "I saw *The Magic Flute* on the television. It was not good. I tell you it was not good, but it was not bad." "Maestro, I'm flattered that you found the time to actually watch it and I appreciate your doing so." "Yes, yes, as I said it wasn't good but it wasn't bad. Tell me about yourself. Do you read music?" "I do." "You do read music?" "Yes. I trained in music at the Royal Academy. I have a doctorate in music. I'm a pianist and conductor, and was a performer as well as a teacher. I do read music." "Good, good. I have an idea I wish to share with you. You know Salzburg is my city. I was born here! I run the festival. I'm the producer and the organizer. I do everything. I choose the operas and cast them. I design the scenery, the costumes, and the lighting." "I know, Maestro. It's simply mind boggling. I don't know how you can do it", I said. "Yes, it is amazing. And, also, I do my own films and I do my own television." "That's even more incredible", I responded. He stopped, looked at me fixedly and again asked, "Do you read music?" "Yes, sir, I do." What was he up to? How many times did I have to tell him I read music? To play it safe, I decided not to question his questions but simply answer them. "Herr Large, are you sometimes available in the summers?" "Yes, Maestro. I don't have an agent and I myself accept engagements of significance and musical value." "Good! Good. I have an idea ..." "You do read music, don't you?" "Yes, I do." "You speak German?" "Yes. We're speaking German right now, Maestro." "Yes, yes. When I make an opera, I want it to be filmed to show on television. I write the script. And the cameras come in and I tell the cameramen what they should look at and I write everything down in the score. You can read a score, can't you?" The man kept repeating himself and I just sat there looking at him, nodding my head like one of those toy dunking birds perched over the edge of a drinking glass. The braggadocio and the repetition never ceased. If I hadn't been in the presence of the all-mighty Herbert von Karajan, I'd have been out the door the third time he asked if I could read music. But I sensed that a job might be in the offing and hung in. At last, it came. "I think from what I saw in *The Magic Flute,* maybe we could work together." *Finalmente,* there it was, a possible position at the Salzburg Festival from von Karajan himself. "It would be beyond my wildest dreams to come to Salzburg and work with you." I exclaimed, and plucking up my courage continued. "I'm curious, Maestro. Could you tell me exactly what you have in mind?" Unwittingly, I once again opened the floodgates. "Yes, yes. I would write the scripts, choose camera positions and tell the cameramen and the lighting people what I want. My designs would be laid out perfectly, the costumes and the make-up also would be my design. I would give you the script and the score. You would work with my assistants and you would be the one to press the buttons that I have marked in the score. Herr Large, I think you are the person to join my team." He stopped talking and stared at me. I took a deep breath. "Maestro, I guess I should be flattered by your invitation but first, may I tell you a little bit about myself?" I didn't wait for him to say yes or no but plunged ahead. "In 1980, I directed the first televised *Ring* from the Bayreuth Festival; I've worked at the Royal Opera House, Covent Garden, La Scala, Vienna, Verona, Paris, San Francisco and I am currently at the Metropolitan Opera House in New York. Maestro, quite honestly, and please don't be offended, while I appreciate your considering me for the job, I am not a button pusher." Silence. Von Karajan stood up and stared down icy eyed. If looks could kill I'd have dissolved right then and there. "That will be all, Mr Large", he hissed in English, enunciating each word like a gunshot. Turning on his heels, he resolutely marched out of the room.

I left the Festspielhaus and walked along the banks of the Salzach River musing over the past half-hour. What had I done? Perhaps I should have accepted his invitation and given it a shot. NO! Why try to convince myself? That little squirt wanted to enlist me in his army of yes-men. I did the right thing. A button pusher? Me? I wouldn't have it. All well and good but Lord knows this would be the end of my career in Salzburg. Worse, it could be the end of my career, period. Herbert von Karajan was a very powerful man. I was half-right in my prediction. While I continued to work elsewhere in Austria, I became persona non grata at the country's foremost music festival. Banished from Czechoslovakia and now, expulsed from Salzburg, a bitter pill, indeed.

Over the years various directors wanted to work with me in Salzburg but von Karajan turned them all down. While he could bar me from his festivals, he couldn't prevent me from attending them. (Whatever I felt about von Karajan as a human being never affected my respect and admiration for his artistry. A P.T. Barnum of classical music, he put on shows that never have been equalled.) I especially wanted to tape Jean-Pierre Ponnelle's much lauded production of Schoenberg's complicated masterpiece, *Moses and Aaron*, which premiered in 1987 and was repeated in 1988. It did not happen. Tragically, while in Israel preparing a production of *Carmen*, Ponnelle stepped backwards, fell off the stage and hit his head on the orchestra pit floor. A few days later, he died in Munich on 11 August 1988, at the age of 56. I was greatly saddened. We had become good friends since he introduced himself to me after the 1980 Bayreuth *Ring*. He'd asked me to work with him on Aribert Reimann's opera *Lear* in Munich, which I did. And we later collaborated on *Figaro* and *L'Italiana in Algeri* at the Met, and Hindemith's *Cardillac* in Munich. Salzburg's 1988 production of *Moses and Aaron* became a fitting tribute to a great artist and a great director.

I might have continued in my role as spectator at Salzburg had not the impossible occurred. During the summer festival of 1989, Herbert von Karajan, despite all the rumours of immortality, died of a heart attack. The Salzburg officials asked Georg Solti to return as chief conductor and to assume von Karajan's directorial position. Solti accepted. Soon after, he phoned me. "I need you, Brian. You've got to come back here." And back I went.

In August of 1990, I returned to Salzburg for a production of *Ballo* directed by John Schlesinger. Schlesinger, originally a documentary film maker for BBC television, had become a distinguished film director with many successes, including *Midnight Cowboy*, *Marathon Man*, and *Sunday Bloody Sunday*. I'd worked with him at Covent Garden on two major operas, *Hoffmann* and *Rosenkavalier*.

A true story teller, John directed operas as though they were films. He'd refer to the "takes" and use other cinematic terms that really didn't apply. He only stopped short of sitting in a folding director's chair and shouting directions through an old-fashioned megaphone. Whatever he did, though, it worked. The cinematic details in that Salzburg *Ballo* were exceptional. Not only did he fashion stories for the leading roles, he devised narratives for the *comprimarios*. I very much enjoyed my time with Schlesinger, not only for his artistic excellence but also because we shared the same birthday. From then on, whenever we were on a joint project, we'd always crack open a bottle of champagne to celebrate our mutual natal day.

After the *Ballo*, Solti asked me back to Salzburg for the next year to tape a new production of *The Magic Flute*. We had Ponnelle's version on record which had made it easier to say goodbye to his splendid interpretation. I came back again in 1992 to record Strauss's *Die Frau ohne Schatten* directed by Götz Friedrich and featuring Éva Marton. Year after year, I returned until, in a situation reminiscent of my move from the BBC to the Metropolitan Opera, I swapped Bayreuth for Salzburg. I never regretted the exchange. Bayreuth will remain close to my heart forever but I'd given my all to the Festspielhaus and rather than redoing endless repeats, I embraced the diversity of Salzburg's agenda. I even did double-duty by adding the Salzburg Easter Festival to my schedule.

Of the many operas I recorded in Salzburg the first two stand apart for reasons already expressed, Ponnelle's *Magic Flute*, and the 1992 production of *Die Frau ohne Schatten*. I had anticipated an interesting artistic blend between Éva Marton and Georg Solti expecting that as fellow Hungarians they'd unite not only in spoken language but in musical language. An ideal Magyar marriage, as it were. How wrong could I be? The two of them addressed each other in their mother tongue all right, but far from politely. The results were more tongue lashings and shouting matches than conversations and no one knew what they were screaming about. A good guess? Solti had his ideas about how the opera should be sung and conducted and Marton had hers. As for the production itself, although getting through the preparation had been hard going, the result proved worth it. A challenge, for sure but throughout my career I sought challenge. All told, I would spend eleven noble summers atop the Green Hill in Bayreuth and twenty-seven delightful ones at the foothills of the Bavarian Alps.

30.

The Return of the Native

During the early 1980s, I kept very busy. A highlight had to be my La Scala debut, Puccini's *Il Trittico*, in 1983. Now I could say "been there, done that" when it came to opera's most hallowed house. Also significant, in 1984, I captured *The Trojans* at the Met; I was flying along the opera fast track. Then, late in 1985, I was plucked out of the opera world and thrust into a totally unexpected and electrifying endeavour. The saga began with a phone call from Peter Gelb, at that time a personal manager at Columbia Artists Management and president of CAMI Video. He wanted to meet with me regarding a project he had in mind for his client, Vladimir Horowitz. I knew Gelb by reputation, at thirty-three he'd been dubbed "the whiz kid of CAMI Video", but this would be our first in person encounter. Within the week, I arrived at his office. After a few polite introductory exchanges, Peter stated that he'd had an inspiration and wanted to explore his idea with me. He then outlined a project centred on his illustrious client Vladimir Horowitz. Horowitz, a Russian expatriate, had left his homeland some sixty years earlier vowing never to return. "I don't like the Russian approach to music, to art, to anything. I never want to go back and I never will" were his very words. And he'd abided by them for well over half a century. Peter, however, imagined a different scenario. Times had changed, the Soviet hard line had softened, somewhat, and contrary to what the pianist himself believed, Peter felt that his client not only could go home

Vladimir Horowitz photographed in his Manhattan
home, 1988. Martha Argerich called him "the best lover
the piano ever had"

again, but that his return, including a recital in the Moscow Conservatory, could be fashioned into a worldwide event. Peter envisioned a film crew following the 83-year-old pianist's every move, from his departure in New York to his arrival in Moscow and culminating in his appearance at the very concert hall where his career had begun. At the end of his explanation, Peter asked me to direct that concert. Euphoric at the prospect of being part of a stupendous project, I did have a slight trepidation. Though I never had heard Horowitz in person, I well knew his recordings, especially the Rachmaninov piano concerti, which were brilliant. Then, in May of 1982, I'd watched a television relay of a Horowitz recital in the Royal Festival Hall. Horowitz hadn't played in London for more than thirty years and his much-heralded return took place in the presence of Prince Charles. Alas, the pianist was not in top form. Throughout his career Horowitz suffered incapacitating periods of depression which affected his playing. (The worst siege took him out of the public eye for twelve years.) Not long after that London appearance, Horowitz stopped performing and recording for two long years. He recovered, returned to the stage in 1985, and continued playing to critical acclaim. Peter Gelb, understandably, wanted to make the most of the situation. Ergo, the "Return to Moscow". My fleeting thought was, all well and good, but what if Horowitz wasn't at his best vis-à-vis the Festival Hall concert? Not wanting to upset the exceptionally ripe apple cart, I brushed aside my reservation, kept my mouth shut, and eagerly grabbed the opportunity to document one of the greatest pianists of all time.

Scheduled for April 1986, Horowitz's appearance was an early cultural attempt to thaw relations between the Soviet Union and the western world. The Horowitz concert had been proposed during the Geneva Summit, allegedly at the request of President Ronald Reagan. In November of 1985, Gelb and I flew to Moscow and met with senior members of Gosconcert, a government agency that controlled the entire musical life of the Soviet Union. You could have cut the air with a knife. Openly suspicious, the Russians clearly believed that the concert was a pretence, camouflage for something else. Convinced that we planned to foster insurrections rather than to connect on an artistic level, they were loud and rude. I was nervous as a cat in a roomful of rocking chairs, yet I couldn't help but admire the way Peter handled the situation. Faced with such obvious enmity, Peter met them on their own ground. He shouted, banged on the table, and cried out that he was there at the expressed wish of the President of the United States of America. I felt this was stretching it a bit; bluffing about the extent of President Reagan's involvement made me uncomfortable. Still, I didn't utter a peep as Peter eloquently waxed and raged. He just wouldn't yield. Even so, the unconstrained meeting adjourned without a deal. That would come later. Implausibly, considering the seemingly impenetrable blockade he'd come up against, Peter's bellicose bellowing had worked. An understanding was reached and a shaky détente went into effect. Still, the Russians issued strict provisos and we remained under constant scrutiny when we returned to Russia. Everywhere we went, the KGB was sure to go. Truly, my experiences with the Czech Secret Police were a walk in the park compared to the KGB's omni-sinister presence.

Armed with the go ahead, Peter arranged for the Columbia Broadcasting System (CBS) to air a special live edition of the CBS Sunday Morning Show from Moscow showing Horowitz's return as well as the recital, itself. The telecast, a co-production of CBS, the BBC, and CAMI

Video, would be transmitted live to the United States and throughout Europe. The Russian officials, however, made it quite clear that nothing would be shown in the Soviet Union. Further, Russian television would not service the telecast, in fact, they didn't want any part of it. Immediately, I chose Switzerland, a reliable neutral country, to provide my technical crew. The Russians felt they'd been coerced into the project and did their darnedest to keep a lid on it. Not a word about Horowitz's return appeared in *Pravda*, the official newspaper, nor was there any mention of the recital on radio or television. With no media coverage, Vladimir Horowitz would be the man who wasn't there. The Soviet officials, however, didn't reckon with the will of the people. Word got around. Russians knew the prodigal pianist was returning and excitement started to build.

Back in New York, Peter arranged for camera crews to begin shooting vignettes of the pianist as he prepared for the tour. They captured him practicing at his Manhattan home as well as conversing with family and friends about his impending trip. Although all appeared to be auspicious, the course of Horowitz in Moscow had many hitches to overcome. As if there weren't enough problems engendered by the host country, Mr Horowitz himself had a surfeit of personal whims to be indulged, including the need to play on his own piano, a need that had to be met. Thus, the film crew followed the departure of Horowitz's Steinway as it was lowered by a crane from his apartment window onto a lorry and then transported to a waiting cargo plane. The pianist's personal piano tuner met the instrument and accompanied it to Russia. Horowitz's own sound recording producer would be standing by to supervise the details of the live transmission. Technical problems fell into place but personal idiosyncrasies also had to be addressed, e.g., the pianist's dietary needs. A notoriously finicky eater, Horowitz ate the same dinner every evening. Dover sole with fresh asparagus or green beans. The American Embassy had to arrange for daily deliveries of fresh Dover sole and asparagus/green beans to be flown in from Western Europe. Further, at home Horowitz, an insomniac, watched recorded films all night until he fell asleep at dawn. He saw no reason to alter his viewing habits any more than to modify his diet. Consequently, his extensive luggage included a hand-picked collection of sci-fi and adventure films from which he could pluck selections to while away his wakefulness. Such indulgences for an ordinary mortal would be unlikely but Vladimir Horowitz was hardly ordinary.

I returned to Moscow in January of 1986 to survey the concert hall and select camera and lighting positions. Normally, directors choose to shoot recitals from the audience's point of view and put the cameras in the hall. I didn't want to do that; I wanted this concert to be different. I wanted to involve the audience but only as a background. I decided to put one camera in the back of the auditorium and two cameras, side-by-side, on the stage, both looking down, ninety degrees, onto the keyboard. One of those cameras had a close-up lens, the other a medium lens, which meant that when I shot the keyboard the camera positions would allow close-ups of Horowitz's hands and head and include his facial expressions, the audience would be seen in soft focus beyond his flying fingers. I'd used this technique at the BBC years before when Wilhelm Kempff played a recital and again for Vladimir Ashkenazy. The results had been amazingly intimate, exactly what I wanted for Horowitz. The details settled, I returned to New York. Late in March I made my third trip to Moscow in advance of the

Horowitz party which included his formidable wife, Wanda Toscanini Horowitz. The daughter of conductor, Arturo Toscanini, Mme Horowitz kept a sharp eye on her husband and a sharp tongue for anyone who got in the way of her spousal caretaking. Believe me, you did not want to cross swords with this lady. To give the dame her due, she held her fragile husband together. By ruling the roost, she allowed him to be affable, witty, and sweet. Not an enviable position for any woman but one the conductor's daughter stoically assumed and maintained.

The Horowitzes arrived in Moscow accompanied by Peter Gelb and the film crew. From the moment the pianist stepped off the plane, little was left unrecorded. Cameras followed him here, there, and everywhere, documenting every step from the American Embassy, where he stayed, to his strolls in the streets. Russian media ignored him, the people adored him. Despite all the efforts to keep his presence hush hush, crowds tailed the pianist from the moment he arrived and had to be held at bay by a special security force. (Members of that force themselves often stepped back to gawk at their charge.) Far from being upset by the mob scenes, Horowitz revelled in the attention. Grinning like the proverbial Cheshire Cat, he waved at everyone with childlike delight. A highlight came when he was taken to the home of his late friend, composer and pianist Alexander Scriabin where he was reunited with Scriabin's two daughters. The sisters still lived in the home the young pianist so often had visited. At one point, Horowitz sat down at the piano and, with the moist-eyed elderly ladies looking on, once again played their father's music on the composer's own instrument, an emotional experience for everyone present.

Meanwhile, would-be concert goers were lining up in front of the Moscow Conservatory hoping to buy tickets.

The vast majority would be disappointed. Apparently, though the concert hall has 1737 seats, only 400 went on public sale; the rest had been distributed to the powers that wanted to be there. In a touching show of devotion, crowds of disappointed potential concert goers stood outside the Conservatory for the length of the programme just to catch a glimpse of the pianist as he arrived and departed. While Horowitz had been shepherded around, I was left, more or less to my own devices, probably less, since I had no idea how many secret police were on my watch. Nonetheless, I was able to set up the cameras and to do the preparations as scrupulously as I wanted. We rehearsed and rehearsed, and then it was the 20th of April.

An hour before the broadcast, I sat in a control truck parked behind the Moscow Conservatory. Suddenly, the vehicle's doors flew open and a KGB crew barged in. Everybody was ordered out of the truck and for half an hour, along with the others, I stood in the open air, shivering, helpless, and furious, while agents searched every nook and cranny of the mobile unit. Politically speaking, because the sold-out concert hall was rife with leading officials, someone must have come up with the brilliant idea that a device might be planted to create a non-musical situation. The thinking was as screwy as everything else. Nothing was uncovered and about ten minutes before the concert we were allowed back into the truck. As I took my seat at the control desk, three KGB officers immediately planted themselves behind me and remained there for the entire concert. Imagine going into a live transmission with a trio of grim robots standing guard. (Robots, by the way, who would be the only Russians to view the actual broadcast and who showed no emotion, no reaction whatsoever during the entire performance.) Again, I turned my full attention to the monitors as the red light came on and Vladimir

Horowitz walked onto the stage where he had last appeared as an up-and-coming virtuoso. A roar arose from the audience, joined by deafening applause, and in the centre of the welcoming storm of approbation, his arms outstretched, stood the frail, smiling, 83-year-old expatriate.

In superb form, Horowitz played like a god. The programme included works by Scarlatti, Mozart, Rachmaninov, Scriabin, Liszt, Chopin, and Schumann. As the selections progressed, the audience became increasingly enthusiastic, shouting and cheering after each number. During Schumann's *Scenes from Childhood*, I spotted, as previously mentioned, a middle-aged gentleman with a single tear rolling down his cheek. An irresistible gift, I immediately cut away from Horowitz to show the weeping onlooker. That charged moment epitomized the emotional impact of the event and was remarked upon everywhere the programme was seen.

On stage, Horowitz was having the time of his life bathing in the power and the glory of his playing and absorbing all the adoration with genuine gratitude and pleasure. At the end of the recital, he returned to the platform six times and played three encores. As was his custom, he indicated the number of encores by holding up his right hand and showing three fingers. After playing the first encore, he held up his hand showing two fingers, played the second encore, and, after holding up a single finger, played the last. Then, he rose from the keyboard, turned to the audience and pressing his hands together leaned his right cheek into them signalling that he was ready to rest. Stopping briefly to pick up a single rose from one of the bouquets piled up on the front of the platform, Horowitz, absent-mindedly swinging the flower back and forth, left the stage. The concert was over but no one wanted to leave. A sublime spell demonstrating music's power to soothe, to unite, to excite and to inspire had been cast over all of us who, for the rest of our lives would say, "I was there."

Horowitz's *Return to Moscow* triumphed. No untoward incidents occurred, consequently sanctions eased and the rest of the Russian portion of the pianist's grand tour took place in a much-improved atmosphere of calm and understanding. Following Moscow, Peter had scheduled concerts in Leningrad and Kiev. From there the entourage would continue to Berlin, Hamburg, and Vienna, a long time for the elderly pianist to be travelling. But Horowitz soldiered on with his wife standing guard, his soul food nourishing him, his DVDs lulling him to sleep, and his fingers flashing over his own keyboard. My participation with the tour ended in Moscow and shortly after the recital I left for New York. Because the DVD wasn't due till August, I thought I'd have some welcome free time. I was wrong. I'd barely settled in when a call came from Peter Gelb. "I need you urgently", he barked into the phone. "You must come back to Europe right away. Horowitz is giving another concert in Vienna on 11 May and I've contacted Austrian television. It's going to be live. You must come back and do it." What could I say? I liked being ordered to do what I liked to do. I took the next flight to Vienna, happily reunited with old friends from Austrian TV, and had a day or so in which to prepare a different programme from the Moscow appearance. The selections changed but Horowitz again played superhumanly and the applause was unbelievable, surely one of the most rousing receptions Vienna ever witnessed. What a bonus for me to have participated in two outstanding musical events and, as if that weren't enough, Vladimir Horowitz turned out to be the gift that kept on giving. Both the Moscow and Vienna concerts had distinctive consequences for me.

Moscow had been a definite feather in my cap, so much so that Peter Gelb had called upon me again. Moscow begat Vienna and the latter telecast was viewed by the newly appointed general manager of the Vienna State Opera, Claus Helmut Drese. Impressed by my work, Herr Drese asked to meet with me. We hit it off. A keen music lover as well as administrator, Drese wanted to discuss ways in which to raise government consciousness on the importance of documenting the State Opera's presentations. "Your telecasts", he told me, "are a means of historical reference and reflect the quality of what's being presented on stage today." The way he spoke I knew he'd be seeking my services and indeed he did. Over the next five years, beginning with an old-fashioned *Ballo in Maschera* in September of 1986, I directed various productions for the State Opera including *Wozzeck, Khovanshchina, Lohengrin, Pique Dame, Il Viaggio a Reims*, and *Elektra*. The eclectic assortment was further enriched by some of the best singers of the day, Mirella Freni, Hildegard Behrens, Éva Marton, Plácido Domingo, and Vladimir Atlantov. Among other pleasures, the *Elektra* reunited me with the East German stage director, Harry Kupfer, protégé of the renowned Walter Felsenstein. Kupfer whom I met in Bayreuth when I videotaped his astounding *Flying Dutchman*, one of the most imaginative and fascinating productions I've ever seen, had been labelled an enfant terrible but this production was unpretentiously brilliant. The entire evening centred on Senta. Onstage throughout the performance, the story revolved around her struggle between a dream world and reality rather than the Dutchman's sombre tale. To further illustrate the protagonist's isolationist plight, Kupfer insisted that the Dutchman be portrayed by a Black singer thus giving the American bass-baritone Simon Estes a fitting showcase for his talent. That bit of casting really started opening doors for singers of colour. Pioneers such as Estes, George Shirley, Grace Bumbry, Shirley Verrett, Felicia Weathers, Leona Mitchell, Leontyne Price, and Martina Arroyo began chipping away at the solid block of prejudice that existed at the time. Kupfer and Götz Friedrich were among a dedicated band of directors who insisted upon casting based on ability.

31

The Elusive Maestro

In 1987, I'd been invited to direct a live telecast of Johann Strauss's *Die Fledermaus* from the Munich State Opera. I especially looked forward to this event because the legendary Austrian conductor Carlos Kleiber would be on the podium. Tall, handsome, shy when he wanted to be and outspoken when he didn't, Kleiber was a true original, possibly the greatest conductor of his generation. Save for five years with the Bavarian Opera, he never accepted a permanent post. Instead, he went where he was wanted, and he was wanted everywhere. Averse to the music "business" and the hoopla surrounding it, he never objected to making money and carefully selected his assignments. His demands included the highest fees, which he got and scuttlebutt had it that "he only agreed to conduct when his refrigerator was empty". (Like Luciano Pavarotti, he occasionally accepted payment in kind, preferring automobiles to horses.) Although Kleiber showed signs of musical talent as a youngster, his father, Erich, the world-famous conductor, did not want his son following in his footsteps and did nothing to encourage him—quite the opposite. Despite his parent's lack of support, after training in chemistry, Carlos embarked on his astonishing and idiosyncratic career. Notoriously temperamental, he often became extremely nervous before concerts. During rehearsals, if he didn't get what he wanted from the soloists and musicians, he'd throw temper tantrums and storm out of the pit. After a half-hour or so, he'd return, ask to be excused for his

Carlos Kleiber, "a riddle wrapped in a mystery
inside an enigma" and a brilliant conductor

immoderate conduct, pick up the baton, and continue the rehearsal. Most musicians considered his erratic behaviour worth enduring simply because of the opportunity to work with him. Preferring to conduct works that his father had conducted and often using his father's marked scores, Carlos free-lanced, going from opera houses to concert halls.

I had met Kleiber a few years prior to the Munich *Fledermaus*. A cat may look at a king but rarely, if ever, gets to know him and the prospects of my meeting the illustrious conductor didn't appear favourable, except for the "Czech factor". I somehow felt that Zdenka Podhajská's vast grid of acquaintances would include a friend of Kleiber's and asked her if she knew anyone who might provide an introduction. Ha. No middleman was necessary. Unbeknownst to me, Zdenka and Erich Kleiber had been friends at university in Prague and had remained close. Zdenka knew Carlos and his sister Veronika as youngsters, and called them by their family nicknames, Pie and Peaches. At my request, she immediately contacted "Pie" and told him that I, who was like a son to her, wanted to meet him. Open Sesame. Carlos and I got together and hit it off. We'd have lunch occasionally and our rendezvous always began in the same manner. After sitting down, he'd ask, "Are you taking me to lunch?" I would answer in the affirmative and Kleiber then would order his favourite dish, oysters—the priciest item on the menu. True to his frugal nature, he'd not have ordered them if he'd had to pay for them. I'm just mentioning this; believe me, I'd have paid anything to be in his presence. Bivalves aside, I liked him a lot and enjoyed his company and conversation, not to mention his music making. That's why the Munich invitation so appealed to me. I wasn't disappointed. *Die Fledermaus*, a delightful, opulent Otto Schenk production, fulfilled all my expectations. I relished my time with the soloists and the musicians and the inimitable Kleiber touch made the evening sparkle. I yearned to work with him again and though I had to wait, like all good things, it would happen.

In the late 1980s, I commuted between New York and Vienna, the latter had become a second home for me. Through my work with the State Opera, I made connections within the Vienna Philharmonic many of whose members played for the Staatsoper. I guess if I'd had a wish list at the time, filming that superb orchestra would have been near the top. I'd fallen under the Vienna Philharmonic's spell at the age of twelve when, like viewers all over the globe, tuning in to the televised New Year's Concert became a tradition. Riveted, my parents and I watched as the Vienna Philharmonic welcomed the new year. In those days Willi Boskovsky not only conducted but, following the original example set by Johann Strauss, led the orchestra while playing the violin. It was quite an act and I never forgot it. Dazzling memories of those New Year's Concerts abounded. Little wonder that I became euphoric when asked to direct the 1989 New Year's Concert. And, as if directing the broadcast wasn't exhilarating enough, Carlos Kleiber would be conducting. Blissed out, I returned to Vienna and began preparations.

During rehearsals for my first Vienna New Year's Concert, in accordance with tradition, a few days before the performance, an army of florists filed into the Musikverein and spent the nights creating a floral Garden of Eden. Crates of flowers were unpacked and positioned around the interior of the hall and behind the orchestra. Each day the perfume of the flowers grew stronger and stronger. The other prevailing scent was alcohol, a great deal of which was imbibed to get the florists through those long nights.

Blumen and *Schnaps* kept things rolling. The Musikverein became a luscious synthesis of sight, smell, and sound. Invited to join the florists' "drinking club", I entered willingly and happily.

At rehearsals, Kleiber handled the orchestra with complete aplomb. His presence was calming, his observations eloquent and, all the while, he conducted from memory. Demanding maximum concentration from the players, he'd joke and laugh with them while remaining fully in charge. Poetry in motion is a hackneyed expression but I can't think of a better way to describe the manner in which Carlos Kleiber conducted. Arms floating through the air, caressing the musical phrases with hand movements that seemed to touch the notes themselves, Kleiber used his tall slender body not like an acrobat à la Bernstein, but like a ballet dancer. I never before had seen such a totally expressive method of conducting nor, quite honestly, have I since. In order to do justice to his extraordinary performance at the New Year's Concert, I devised a variation on the camera angle I'd used for Stravinsky conducting his *Firebird*. Again, I positioned a small camera in the orchestra facing the podium. But rather than setting the camera eye-level to the conductor, I placed it down as low as it could go. Shooting up at Kleiber made it appear as though he were suspended in the air, an illusion heightened by his sinuous arm movements. That shot remains matchless; I never used it again. The concert itself reflected the essence of true musicianship, not a shallow or a pretentious note to be heard, just the illumination of the music itself. What a thrill to have my name associated with this magnificent event. Best of all, the producers asked me back for the next New Year's Concert, and the next, and the next.

Traditionally, each year a different conductor leads Vienna's New Year's Day performance. After Kleiber,

I worked with Zubin Mehta, and then Riccardo Muti. Leonard Bernstein was scheduled for the 1992 gala but when he died unexpectedly, Carlos Kleiber replaced him. Also on the programme, Rudolf Nureyev made his New Year's Concert debut. Nureyev choreographed an Arabian dance from Johann Strauss II's *A Thousand and One Nights*. Theoretically the principal dancer, Nureyev's performance consisted of a series of poses which he held while members of the Vienna State Opera Ballet whirled around him. Nureyev was a very sick man yet he insisted upon appearing. His colour ashen, he moved slowly and deliberately and his ability to hold those poses was a demonstration of sheer will. Despite his physical disabilities, he was a most cordial and pleasant gentleman, easy to get along with, charming. I recall how eager he was to meet Kleiber. After the concert the three of us had a pleasant, if subdued luncheon together with Nureyev hanging on Kleiber's every word. In little over a year, Rudolf Nureyev would die of complications from AIDS.

Notwithstanding both the death of Leonard Bernstein and Nureyev's desperate condition, I revelled in the opportunity to video Kleiber once again. Alas, this would be the last time we worked together. Thankfully, we continued to see each other on a social basis, most memorably, perhaps, in the mid-nineties.

I'd been engaged to do a live telecast of *Tristan and Isolde* from the Prinzregententheater in Munich conducted by Lorin Maazel, and invited Carlos Kleiber's son, Marko, to be my assistant. Marko, in turn, told his father who expressed interest in attending a performance. At the same time, Carlos, an inveterate private person, loathed and avoided public appearances. When Marko told me that his father wanted to be there but feared calling attention to himself, I instantly responded. "Tell your father not to worry. He doesn't have to sit in the auditorium. He can join me in the control wagon where he'll have complete anonymity. "But", I added, "he has to promise to just sit there and say nothing during the performance." Happily, Carlos accepted my invitation and gave his word that he'd keep quiet. What a coup! A once in a lifetime musical experience to watch one great conductor on the monitor with another seated behind me.

The day arrived. I stood outside the television truck as Kleiber drove up, parked the car, and stepped out. Shoulders hunched, head down, sunglasses covering his eyes, he hurried over to me. Honestly, he looked more like an MI-5 agent than a musician. We exchanged hellos and I took him into the truck, showed him to his seat, and took my place in front of him. The opera began. During the first act, although he stayed silent, I could hear him breathing heavily and occasionally grunting. Now and again, he'd blurt out, "No" or "Oh". I could feel his tension. At the intermission, Carlos got up, thanked me, and started out of the truck. I followed him as he rushed to his car. "What's the matter, Maestro?" I asked. "It's all too slow", he burst forth. "Slow, slow, slow! This is not the way to conduct *Tristan*. I can't bear to hear anymore." That said, he jumped into the vehicle and, wheels spinning, took off at top speed. I stood there with my mouth open; I couldn't fathom his ferocious reaction. Then again, Carlos might have been piqued that he hadn't been asked to conduct the *Tristan* himself. Who knows? Of course, I never told Lorin that Carlos had been there.

Carlos Kleiber's quixotic behaviour, one minute reservedly smiling, the next minute raging, could be difficult. Not surprisingly, his rants received more attention, and yet,

New Year's Concert in Vienna, 1992. I'm standing by
as Rudolf Nureyev and Carlos Kleiber greet each other.
Who is more pleased to meet whom is hard to say,
but Nureyev had long expressed his desire to meet
the conductor

many grace notes existed. I can think of one in particular
that sheds a softer light on him. When Zdenka died, Carlos
phoned me and we reminisced together, sharing stories of
our beloved friend. Before he rang off, he said, "I don't
know the financial situation, Brian, I only know that Zdenka never would accept any help. But, please, if there is any
problem, let me know. I will gladly cover all her expenses."
A princely gesture from a king of conductors.

32

Many Happy New Years

My association with the Vienna New Year's Concert covered some twenty years of traditional music and dance. That being said, a couple of breaks in "tradition" actually did occur, at least for me. In 2001, Nikolaus Harnoncourt conducted a New Year's Day programme of waltzes and polkas by the Strauss family, danced by members of the Vienna State Opera Ballet. Normally, the dance selections were filmed to prerecorded soundtracks months before the concert. I noticed that Harnoncourt's programme included Johann Strauss's *Vergnügungszug* Polka, "Pleasure Train Polka", the word "train" popped out. I decided to create, on tape, a specially filmed musical interlude involving actual trains and locomotives. Just outside Vienna, in Strasshof, the Heizhaus Railway Museum contains fifty early twentieth-century locomotives and steam trains. I found two of them from the 1930s, a large express locomotive and a small Prussian engine, both fuelled by coal, both able to send out volumes of smoke and steam. My idea was to film a three-minute race, the length of *Vergnügungszug,* for the two trains and their drivers. Could the little engine outrace the big one? You wouldn't think so since the latter had more power and energy. On the other hand, if you have a train that eats up fuel and runs out of coal, the little guy might overtake it. That, in a nutshell, was the story. I spent five wonderful days working with the camera crew and fulfilling childhood dreams. What kid doesn't want to be a train driver? I sure did. When the filming ended, I edited the material to match the rhythm and the structure of the polka and the visualization synchronized perfectly with the prerecorded sound. *The Pleasure Train Polka* pleased everyone. Viewers wanted more and the following year, I took on another off-beat subject.

The Euro was about to debut as both a coin and a bank note, and it struck me that the dissolving of the Austrian shilling and the evolving of its successor might make a tidy musical film interlude. I took my cameras into the Austrian Mint and filmed the story of how the new coins and notes were designed, printed, and minted. The resulting "ballet" was choreographed not for dancers but rather for print and pressing machines, and any moving image that would match the rhythms of Johann Strauss II's *Perpetual Motion Polka*. The mechanical ballet delighted audiences. We had another hit.

The next year, I again used the story-telling technique to show that making apple strudel could be turned into a very perky polka. We videoed people picking and collecting apples from the trees, peeling them in the kitchen, making the dough, and then baking the apples and dough together. Presto, in two and a half minutes a plate of delicious apple strudel took the spotlight. Although this musical vignette, like its predecessors, was well received, three times was enough for me and I returned to presenting classic ballet sequences.

Over a span of twenty years, I rarely had time to celebrate New Year's Eve myself, but I had the pleasure of bringing the happiest of New Year's Day entertainment to viewers all over the world. Only one three-year caesura interrupted my Vienna New Year's run. In the early 1990s, I spent more and more time with Claudio Abbado who served as *Generalmusikdirektor* of the Vienna State Opera. We weren't really friends, yet we had a very comfortable collaborative relationship. After four years of doing the New Year's Concerts with the Vienna Philharmonic, Abbado asked me if I'd like to take a Wien-break and accompany him to Berlin to document his New Year's Eve Concert with the Berlin Philharmonic, hoping it would become a holiday tradition. While I loved my Vienna New Year's gigs, the idea intrigued me. I accepted and advised the Vienna officials that I'd be in absentia. Aware of Vienna's New Year's dominance, Abbado wanted the Berlin concert to be something completely different. The Vienna programme featured music of the Strauss family, so Claudio devoted Berlin's 1993 New Year's Eve programme to Wagner, about as far as you can get from *die Familie Strauss*. I had a grand time working in the Berlin Philharmonic's magnificent concert hall, and with Abbado urging me on, decided to switch venues. I filmed New Year's Eve in Berlin for the next three years until the city of my dreams once again began calling me. I missed Vienna. In 1996, the prodigal son returned and thereafter videoed Vienna's New Year's Concert straight through 2011. At that point, I felt I'd done enough and gratefully ended my run.

It's been a while, but I still feel connected; I always will. I continue to take great pleasure in being a viewer of the Vienna New Year's Concert rather than a participant, especially since Michael Beyer, my colleague of many years, is now the director. I'd also like to acknowledge Haide Tenner, ORF's music chief, and producers Heidelinde Rudy and Karin Veitl who helped me to waltz through so many New Year's Concerts as well as Alexander Radulescu, who was my music assistant and associate director.

33.
A Harrowing Night at the Opera

The German soprano Hildegard Behrens made her Bayreuth debut as Brünnhilde in 1983. Although Peter Hall's production did not garner raves, Behrens did, and went on to become one of the outstanding Brünnhildes of her generation, a position she solidified with her appearance in the Metropolitan Opera's *Ring* cycle in 1989. Originally, the role of Brünnhilde had been offered to and accepted by the Hungarian soprano, Éva Marton. Unbeknownst to the Met, Marton, an EMI recording artist, previously had contracted to make a sound recording of the *Ring* with Bernard Haitink conducting. Meanwhile, the Met brokered a deal with Deutsche Grammophon to do a recording with James Levine conducting. The twain, EMI and DG, could never meet, and the Met had to let Marton go. She and her management went berserk. Lawyers appeared on the scene, squabbled, and somehow managed to settle the contractual monetary mess. Meanwhile, Brünnhilde was up for grabs and Behrens won the toss.

At the same time, the Met would be recording its *Ring*. Unitel planned to tape Harry Kupfer's 1988 Bayreuth version. Invited to direct that production, too, I had serious misgivings about becoming involved. Set in a post-nuclear world with high-tech laser and neon effects, I questioned how the apocalyptic-laced production, with its plastic see-through Valhalla and Chernobyl-styled Immolation, would work on the TV screen. To my way of thinking, it wouldn't. Also, as I've mentioned, both *Rings* occurred when my

Hildegard Behrens. A lawyer as well as a singer, Hildegard was no pushover. When it came to direction, she often danced to her own piper mother's health began to deteriorate and though I did the Met *Ring* at her urging, I withdrew from Bayreuth on my own advisement. I simply could not juggle two *Rings* at the same time. Understandably, Harry Kupfer was terribly disappointed. What had been an exceptional artistic relationship broke and more than twenty-three years passed before Harry could let bygones be bygones.

The Metropolitan Opera *Ring*, given in three cycles, occupied my time during February, March, and April of 1990. Besides Behrens, the cast included James Morris, the Met's fine-tuned Wotan, Jessye Norman, Siegfried Jerusalem, and Christa Ludwig. We recorded for a CD release as well as the PBS television broadcast and later a DG DVD. Unlike the Bayreuth recordings, which were taped in an empty theatre where cameras could be placed wherever I chose, the Met recordings took place during actual performances. Lighting and camera positions had to be carefully selected to minimize audience discomfort. Paying hundreds of dollars for a ticket only to have a camera sitting beside you or whizzing back and forth in front of you would justifiably outrage any ticket holder. I always wanted to get the best shot but not at the expense of a paying audience. We recorded the Met *Ring* in weekly performances. Very different from Bayreuth where we did *Götterdämmerung* one year, 1979, and the three others in 1980.

Rehearsals began at the end of March. In most international opera houses, principal roles for *Ring* cycles are normally double cast in order to safeguard against accident or illness. Behrens, who planned to sing Brünnhilde in all three cycles, would be covered by Gudrun Volkert. Siegfried Jerusalem, in his eponymous role, elected to sing only the first and the last performances. His cover,

William Johns would sing the second. Rehearsals went smoothly, although I did cross swords with one participant. Christa Ludwig sang Fricka in *Rheingold* and Waltraute in *Götterdämmerung* and when I asked her to rehearse for the camera she declared, "I have sung these roles many times. There is no need to rehearse." "Of course," I tried to explain, "I understand and admire your interpretations, but my camera team has never seen nor been part of a *Ring* production. In all fairness I need to brief them on your moves and how you'll play the role." "This is not my concern", retorted Ludwig. "You should have hired a crew that knows the *Ring*." That was that. Frankly, as great a singer as she was, I never did warm to her. Off stage, I found her to be a rather sour person.

Despite Ludwig's unhelpful attitude, everything went well until we came to the last scene in the second recording of *Götterdämmerung*, Brünnhilde's "Immolation" and the fall of the house of Wotan. Hildegard sang the final notes and was about to jump into the flames when a member of the stage crew miscued the instructions for Valhalla's collapse. The hydraulic lifts fell early and a beam knocked Hildegard unconscious. Severely injured, she was rushed to the hospital. Subsequently, she had to withdraw from the final *Götterdämmerung*. Gudrun Volkert stepped in, a disaster for us no matter how well she sang. Contractually committed to Deutsche Grammophon for a complete *Ring* with Behrens and Jerusalem, we no longer had Behrens. What to do? Myself beyond despair, happily I recalled that in the rehearsal tapes we had one with both Behrens and Jerusalem, and another with Behrens and William Johns. We'd be shooting the last performance with Volkert and Jerusalem and I saw no other solution than to play musical "shares" with the two Brünnhildes. In order to do so, Volkert had to be made up and costumed exactly as her predecessor. Fitted with Behrens's wig, dressed in identical costumes, and thoroughly coached in Behrens's every move, Gudrun Volkert stalwartly appeared in the last *Götterdämmerung*. However, I altered the camera script so that the ersatz Brünnhilde would rarely, if ever, be seen on camera. Having taken care of the physical appearance, we now faced the vocal challenge. Jerusalem's singing came from the first rehearsal and the last recording, Behrens's vocals had to come from the first rehearsal and the second recording. And, every note Gudrun Volkert sang in the third performance had to be replaced. Opera recordings are peppered with incidents where actual notes are electronically made louder, longer, sweeter or even outsourced e.g., the young Schwarzkopf hitting the high C for the aging Flagstad in a *Tristan* recording. But our *Götterdämmerung* required both physical and vocal prestidigitation. What we had was a nightmare of editing.

Probably the biggest challenge came in the Immolation scene when Brünnhilde is about to get on her horse and ride into the flames. The only tape we could use came from the first rehearsal, not the second performance which showed the beam hitting Behrens on the head. Alfred Muller, video editor of Nexus Production, took that rehearsal bit, put it in and masterfully wove a patchwork quilt into a unified whole. Everything in that *Götterdämmerung*, including the finale, looks and sounds absolutely authentic. Over the years I've viewed the recording many times and though I know the lead tenor and the lead soprano never appeared together in the final recording even I can't pinpoint the edits. We never declared publicly what we had done because we never were asked to, and no one ever voiced a complaint.

IV

ACT

34.
Crossroads

In October of 1987 PBS Great Performances planned to videotape Houston Opera's opening night production of *Aida* and, a few days later, the world premiere of John Adams's *Nixon in China*. In preparation for the latter, I went to Texas in September to learn Adams's demanding score and to meet with Peter Sellars, the director. A whirlwind of activity, Peter seemed to be everywhere at once, re-thinking this, re-thinking that, and constantly changing his mind. The situation became tense and voices often got loud but it was an important premiere. Fortunately, if nobody else knew where Sellars was going, they followed along and everything eventually came together. Rehearsals for the *Aida* were better organized. Pier Luigi Pizzi, the director, also designed the décor, traditional for the most part, but the "Triumphal March" had a new twist. A pair of mobile, life size, model elephants combined with the dancers in a clever manner which made for exciting television pictures. All things considered, my Met camera crew and I had a grand time with both operas. In addition, the hard work had been nicely balanced by the pleasure of being in the company of Mirella Freni and Nicolai Ghiaurov who were appearing in the *Aida*. We'd not seen each other since the Met *Don Carlo* and renewing acquaintances made the Houston stay an exceptionally gladsome one. In fact, that Houston visit proved to be more serendipitously eventful than I ever could have imagined.

A few days before the opening night, I received a hand-written note at my hotel. The message read "I look forward to joining you at table 41 at the after *Aida* party" and was signed "Jack Mastroianni". I had no idea who this was but that was irrelevant since no one in the television contingent, including me, had been invited to the party. With so many sponsors and benefactors to take care of, TV crews usually don't appear on the opening night gala's most wanted list. Obviously, a case of mistaken identity. I had no way to contact the man, so I tossed the note into the wastebasket and thought no more about it. *Aida* opened and during the days following, the Great Performance contingent was kept busy with taping. After the third performance of *Aida,* a matinee, I went backstage to congratulate Nicolai and Mirella, stopping first in his dressing room and then going next door to see Mirella. I knocked and entered. She was not alone, a tall, bearded man stood next to her. "Brian, come in, come in. This is Jack Mastroianni, Jack this is Brian Large. I want you to know each other." Jack Mastroianni? The name had a familiar ring. Aha, I remembered, the mystery note sender. We shook hands and exchanged a few words during which I discovered that Jack, an American, was Mirella's manager. I mentioned, of course, that I'd received his note, adding apologetically that since I didn't recognize the name and hadn't been invited to the party, I'd let it go. "Not to worry", Jack smiled, going on to explain that Mirella, assuming I'd be there, had suggested he contact me. The three of us nattered on until Jack checked his watch. "I really have to leave, I've got a plane to catch." He embraced Mirella, shook my hand, gave me a business card on which he carefully wrote his home telephone number, and left for the airport.

"Nice man, no?" Mirella said smiling broadly when the door closed. "Very", I agreed, admitting to myself, but not to Mirella, that I felt an affinity towards the young American. I returned to New York and soon began viewing the *Aida* tapes. On impulse, I called Jack Mastroianni and when he didn't answer, left a message telling him that I was editing the *Aida* tapes and wondered if he'd like to come over to the studio and watch them. A half-hour later Jack called back and accepted my invitation. He arrived at the studio and we viewed the tapes together; I was impressed by his knowledge of opera. As he was leaving, I mentioned that I'd be returning to Houston to continue the *Nixon in China* taping. Jack then proposed that we arrange a celebratory dinner in Houston with Mirella and Nicola and watch the PBS *Aida* telecast, together. I quickly agreed.

At dinner with Mirella and Nicolai, I remember observing how easily Jack fit in and how genuinely solicitous he was of Mirella. During our tête-a-tête, I learned that, after the *Aida* finished, Mirella would return to Italy where she had a run of *Bohèmes* in Florence. Nicolai would remain in the States for his next engagement. While they often appeared together, they also maintained separate schedules. Jack mentioned that he would be accompanying Mirella to Florence. At that point, she turned to me saying, "Brian, are you very busy right now?" I thought a moment and answered, "Well, I've got the *Nixon* to finish but that's nearly done and after that I'm free for a few weeks." "Good," exclaimed Mirella, "if you are not busy then you must join me and Jack in Florence. We'll have a good time."

I returned to New York, finished my work and then did, indeed, join Mirella and Jack in Florence. The three of us had fun exploring the city together. We trekked everywhere, back and forth across the Ponte Vecchio, shopping, dining, visiting the museums and galleries, enjoying both sides of the Arno. And then, I had to return to London. Jack offered to drive me to the airport in Milan and I accepted.

During the ride, I wanted to make my position clear. I spoke openly about my feelings towards him and hoped that he felt similarly about me. Unexpectedly, I found myself asking him if he might consider a relationship. For a while, saying not a word, Jack didn't take his eyes off the road. Then, very gently, he declined my offer telling me that he'd recently started a new job at Columbia Artists and could not consider any personal commitment for at least three years. A new job? Three years? What was he talking about? I turned to look at him and, in that moment, all became clear. Jack was over a decade younger than I, still on the way up in his career, still eager to seize the world, much as I had been at his age. The feelings may have been there, the timing was off. Quickly, I changed the subject and our talk, albeit slightly more guarded, continued until we reached the airport. As I got out of the car, Jack turned to me, said something about staying in touch, and smiled warmly. I smiled back. "Goodbye for now", I said, and gently closed the car door.

Some weeks later, I returned to New York and once again contacted Jack, only to discover that the poor fellow had a whopping case of the flu. I went over and for the next week or so journeyed back and forth to look after him until he regained his health. During the course of his recovery, our friendship flourished. We lived separately but our lives began to mesh. I've said it before and it's worth repeating. I believe that some fate, some force, intermittently stepped in and completely altered my existence. My mother putting me on her lap and inspiring me to music; Stanley Spratt encouraging me to continue on a musical path; the way I got my job at the BBC by answering an advert in the *Telegraph*; my great luck at having Tony Craxton and John Culshaw as mentors; John Dexter getting me to the Met, and now,

Jack Mastroianni who would not just contribute to my life, but actually save it. And, here's how that happened.

We'd been seeing each other for a while when, in March of 1988, I mentioned to Jack that my "stomach" had been bothering me and I didn't know why. With hindsight, I realize I had issued a cry for help. I tended to ignore physical concerns whereas Jack stayed on top of his which included regular medical check-ups. I, aside from a few emergencies, hadn't been inside a doctor's office, ever. He suggested that I go for a check-up and recommended his physician. Ordinarily, I'd have pooh-poohed the idea but I really felt poorly and when Jack became insistent, I made an appointment. A week later, I had a complete check-up. Following the examination, I sat across the desk from the doctor. Calmly, he told me that he'd seen something which needed a follow up. "I'd like to recommend a specialist but before I give you his name, may I ask you a question?" "Of course", I answered. "Very well then …", he cleared his throat and continued … "would you mind being seen by an African-American doctor?" I looked at him, incredulously. "Doctor, I'm interested in getting into the best of hands and I don't care whether they're pink, green, or striped. My only question would be, is he the best doctor for me?" The doctor smiled, "I understand, and I'm truly sorry to have to pose such a question but there are people who would feel uncomfortable and I have to ask." I shook my head. "Frankly, Doctor, it's a sad commentary on our times that such a question is even raised."

The referral was given, and I made an appointment to see Dr Kenneth Forde, a pioneer in colon cancer screening. Dr Forde examined me, discovered that I had colon cancer(!!) and needed immediate surgery. After the initial shock, I put myself in his hands. Surgery was scheduled for 1 April 1988. I cancelled all upcoming engagements for the rest of the year, except for one. The doctor allowed me to complete a live Met matinee of *Ariadne auf Naxos* on 31 March. How did I get through the next couple of weeks? I put everything other than *Ariadne* out of my head and on the last day of March, directed an exceptionally fine telecast. At least, I thought to myself, if I don't make it, I'll go out on top.

On April Fool's Day 1988, Jack took me to Columbia Presbyterian Hospital where I was admitted, prepped, wheeled into the operating room, knocked out, and sliced. Dr Forde had taken pains to make sure I was prepared for the procedure; in fact, he actually "scored" it. Asked what music I'd like to go to sleep to, I quickly replied, "Frankly, Doctor, I'm more interested in what music I'd like to wake up to." He got a kick out of my response. After nine hours of surgery, by the grace of God and the skill of Dr Forde's hands, I awoke to the strains of Mozart's *Piano Concerto No. 24*. How great the sound I cannot tell you.

Ten days later, I returned to my Central Park West apartment. Everything had happened so quickly I almost didn't have time to be terrified. Almost. Facing months of painful recovery, I couldn't make any decisions for myself. I didn't have to; Jack took care of everything. I don't wish to dwell any longer on my brush with mortality, only to say I learned much from it. One thing's for sure, had any link in the chain of events not connected, had Jack not pushed me to see his doctor for a routine check-up, had not his doctor sent me on to the specialist, and had I not undergone surgery, I would not be here today. Everything was set in motion by Jack Mastroianni. He saved my life and in so doing became part of it.

Returning to work after a life-threatening interlude took time. I don't think I'm cautious by nature but I didn't want to begin with the gruelling schedule of directing full operas, I thought it wiser to stick my toe in the water by accepting the Met's invitation to direct a "simple recital" (their words) on the opera house stage on 18 September 1988. The recital turned out to be Luciano Pavarotti with James Levine accompanying him on the piano. That combination, while light years from "simple", wasn't a full-scale opera and thus less demanding to direct. And, oh, what an incredible evening it was. Luciano, white bandana unfurled, sang Mozart, Rossini, Bellini, Respighi, and Puccini arias gloriously. But for me the most fascinating aspect was the opportunity to watch Levine at the piano. A consummate musician, his accompaniment perfectly complimented the composer's intent and the tenor's interpretations. I couldn't have chosen a better way to get back to business.

Having taken the initial step, I cautiously began to accept more engagements. The first from a local San Francisco television station, KQED, to direct a concert in Golden Gate Park with Kurt Adler conducting the San Francisco Opera Orchestra and soloists. I particularly chose this event because it was strictly local, no national or international relays. If I didn't have the energy to completely pull it off, the audience would be small and save me from major embarrassment. All went well. I could feel my energy and strength returning. At the SFO's request I stayed on to direct productions of Meyerbeer's *L'Africaine* with Shirley Verrett and Vivaldi's *Orlando Furioso*, the latter reuniting me with Marilyn Horne. With one recital, one local broadcast, and two national telecasts under my belt, I slipped back into my normal schedule, if indeed my schedule ever could be judged normal.

With Johnny Walker and Jack Mastroianni
at the Sony BMG Masterworks reception in New York City, 2007

35.
Dealing with Divas

In September of 1983, the Metropolitan Opera opened its centennial season with a spectacular production of Berlioz's *The Trojans*. The all-out presentation of the five-hour epic included thirty-three scene changes, a chorus of one hundred and thirty singers, sixty dancers, twenty acrobats, an eighty-piece orchestra, three huge offstage bands, and some three thousand costumes. Fabrizio Milano, a young Italian director, worked with designer Peter Wexler to create a visual masterpiece capturing the heroic classical work; the arrival of the Trojan Horse was especially rousing. I had worked with big Berlioz pieces before, including his *Te Deum* in Liverpool Cathedral that, apart from everything else, called for twelve harps, and his *Requiem* in London's St Paul's featuring four brass bands at the four points of the compass. But I'd never ever done anything as titanic as *The Trojans*. This really was exciting. Immediately, I increased the number of cameras from the normal six to eleven and carefully positioned them to fully capture the splendid staging.

Along with the sets and costumes, a big buzz accompanied this production because of its leading singers, Plácido Domingo, Tatiana Troyanos, and Jessye Norman. The role of Aeneas lies unusually high and Domingo had expressed concern that he might not be able to do it. For a while it was touch and go as to whether or not he'd stay the course. At the last minute, he found his groove asking only that the tessitura be lowered a step or so in a few places. Domingo

Jessye Norman. The incredible planes of her
mythic visage are awesome

375

gave a fine performance, Troyanos sang a lovely, convincing, and moving Dido, but along with the production itself, the dignified gravitas that Jessye Norman brought to the role of Cassandra garnered the most accolades.

Jessye and I were long-time friends. I'd met her in 1972 when she sang Elizabeth in *Tannhäuser* at Covent Garden. London became the American singer's home base for five years, during which time we became well acquainted. Jessye was at the peak of her career when she sang Cassandra. Still relatively unspoiled, she was excited to be making her Met debut. We taped the two rehearsals that preceded the live recording and I invited her to come to my office and look at the tapes. I always did this as a courtesy for any artist who wanted to take advantage of my expertise. I used meaningful close-ups for Jessye, in other words, I concentrated on the sculptural planes of her magnificent countenance. I didn't want to get so close that you saw her tonsils, but I did want to have the camera revel in the beauty of her visage, the astounding cheekbones and those glorious eyes. Truly, her face was a work of art. Knowing that I would do everything to enhance her performance, she felt comfortable with me and appreciated my efforts.

On the night of the live taping, everything went well until twenty-five minutes before the end when, without warning, every light in the control truck switched off and every picture on all the monitors faded to black. My first thought was, "Have I died? Is this the end?" I'd never before experienced anything like this. Along with Michael Bronson, the TV producer, and the rest of the technical crew, I staggered out of the mobile unit and into the street. Obviously, there had been a power failure. Immediately, Bronson sprinted from the mobile unit on Amsterdam Avenue into the stage door of the opera house. Miraculously, the power failure had not occurred inside the Met and the opera was nearing its end. Quickly, Bronson got word to Levine in the pit explaining the circumstances. Since we'd not been able to record the last twenty-five minutes, Bronson requested that, when the auditorium emptied, we go into overtime to recreate the last half hour. Considering the healthy overtime paychecks, the crews and the stagehands were quite willing to stay on; Tatiana Troyanos, who'd finished the opera singing Dido's farewell, was not, and with good reason. She'd given her all and had no voice left to repeat her gruelling scena in the wee hours. Despair was in the air. We all stood around, helpless. We'd failed. Suddenly, I remembered that I had a VHS copy of the dress rehearsal in my office. "Let's see if the quality is good enough technically and musically to use it", I proposed. The tape was retrieved. James Levine reviewed it musically, I reviewed it visually, and Troyanos assessed the quality of her performance. In the end, the three of us agreed and Levine declared the rehearsal tape absolutely acceptable. A collaborative sigh of relief filled the opera house and everyone went home. When the broadcast was aired and the DVD was released, except for those of us directly involved, no one realized that the video contained the finale from the rehearsal and not the performance.

Another unforgettable Jessye/Met experience occurred in January of 1989 when I returned to the Met for a daring double bill of two twentieth century masterpieces, Schönberg's *Erwartung* and Bartók's *Bluebeard's Castle,* both of which had been chosen to showcase Jessye. The former is an atonal drama in four scenes for solo soprano and lasts about half an hour. In it, The Woman (she has no name) wanders through a moonlit forest looking for her lover. She finds his blood-stained body and the opera ends. The Freud-soaked, 1909 piece is eerily gripping and Jessye handled the singing and the acting with infinite assurance. Samuel Ramey joined her in *Bluebeard's Castle*, another operatic nod to Freud, this time about a man who brings his bride home to his castle where, unbeknownst to his new wife, he's stockpiled his previous brides. Sam Ramey matched Jessye, note for note, singing and acting superbly. The two of them made the most of the material allowing plenty of opportunities for me to present them in a series of striking dramatic poses and close-ups.

Great artist that she was, when it came to temperament, Jessye Norman was no angel. A complicated person, she could be difficult, sometimes very difficult, particularly after she achieved stardom. There were two sides to her and I saw and heard both of them. Depending on her mood, one minute she could be speaking with a nuanced English accent, a remnant of her five-year sojourn in London, and in the next breath she could switch to the strident. Volatile, always. Even so, I got along with her. I respected her and I believe she felt well-disposed towards me.

The majority of Jessye's operatic work happened at the Met and included the previously discussed roles as well as Ariadne in *Ariadne auf Naxos*, Sieglinde in *Valkyrie*, and Emilia Marty in Janáček's *Makropulos Case*. Among the projects we did together outside of the Metropolitan, *The Magic of Spirituals*, a Carnegie Hall presentation in March of 1990 with Jessye and Kathleen Battle singing and James Levine conducting the Metropolitan Opera Orchestra, stands out. Although I'd videoed a Met production of *The Marriage of Figaro* in which "Kathy" Battle sang Susanna, I didn't know her well. A talented and attractive performer, Ms Battle had a lovely voice, but the eponymously named diva also possessed a fierce disposition. Generally speaking, she wasn't a team player. In 1994, she ran afoul of the Met's general manager, Joseph Volpe, who fired her from a production of Donizetti's, *The Daughter of the Regiment* for alleged "unprofessional" actions towards her fellow artists. During rehearsals Ms Battle apparently arrived late, left early, and sometimes didn't show up at all. When she did appear, she spent most of her time complaining about everyone from stage hands to singers. Her behaviour became so disruptive, Volpe felt he had no other recourse than to take her out of the picture. Such a shame, really.

There's an old saying, "When Greek meets Greek then comes a tug of war with no quarter given", which easily could have been applied to the meeting of the two divas in Carnegie Hall. Jessye, three years Kathy Battle's senior, and a more established artist, expected her due. Ms Battle had other ideas. Always late to rehearsals, she'd spend precious time making sure her hair and make-up was precisely as she wanted. Kathy primped while Jessye fumed. The underlying battle between the two singers caused an ongoing atmospheric tension. But they were pros, and the night of the performance, they came together, went on stage, and put on a magnificent show. The evening honoured Marian Anderson, who was in the audience, which might have contributed to the singers' cease fire. Whatever the reason, the concert was splendid.

Spirituals and gospel songs were not in my area of expertise and I had to do quite a bit of research in order to do justice to the music, probably more for that hour and a half than for many a full-length opera at the Met. I needed to know the essence of the style that Battle, Norman, and Levine were trying to create. Stepping out of my comfortable music zone always excited me, both for the challenge of learning something new and then executing it. I came away with a deep respect and appreciation of the American Spiritual songs born from those held in bondage.

I lost contact with Jessye for a long while until one evening, in the spring of 2009, I bumped into her at Carnegie Hall. We hugged and chatted and then she said, "You know Brian, I still remember that wonderful spiritual concert we did together here. It's been ten years and I'd really like to do one more big show with you. If the opportunity ever arose, would you be willing?" "Willing? Of course, Jessye. I'd be honoured." "Oh, that's grand. I'm going to get on it and I'll contact you when something comes up." Frankly, I didn't think anything would come of it, but within the year she phoned. "Brian, I've found the perfect place for us to do a concert together." "Wonderful", I answered. "Where is it?" "Well, ever since I did that televised Christmas concert in Notre Dame Cathedral back in '92, I've thought about doing a concert of religious music in a religious setting. Not a Christmas concert, I've done enough of those. Anyway, I found this fabulous church, the Basilica Mariä Geburt in Mariazell, Austria. It's a breathtaking building with a great acoustic and Mariazell is an important pilgrimage destination. Catholics from all over Austria come there." "Sounds good to me," I answered, "but I have to admit I don't know that church." "Why don't you take a look at it and then we can talk further. Honestly, once you see it, you'll understand why I'm so eager to do this."

Jessye's enthusiasm got to me. I decided to make my own pilgrimage to Mariazell and drove there when I returned to Vienna. One look and I knew Jessye was right, the basilica was a spectacular architectural shrine. I wandered around thinking about the multitude of camera angles it offered. Ever since my early days with the BBC I'd always loved working in cathedrals; they give extra visual perspectives, so much more interesting than in concert halls. The idea of being in a majestic temple pleased me. The only drawback, Mariazell was in the mountains and it would be difficult to drive the technical trucks around the narrow, up-and-down streets. But I could deal with that and, knowing Jessye's resoluteness, so could she.

The recital was scheduled for 16 May 2012 when the weather in Mariazell would be warm and sunny. Jessye, accompanied by her pianist, Mark Markham, would sing Schubert lieder, Beethoven arias, spirituals, and a gospel version of "The Lord's Prayer". Then, using a microphone, she'd perform a few Duke Ellington songs transcribed by a composer named "Edward Kennedy". (That's when I found out that Duke Ellington had been born Edward Kennedy.) Austrian television, and Unitel, had agreed to record the concert and transmit it at Christmastime. Word soon got around that Jessye Norman was returning and a lot of buzz began to build. She hadn't been on an Austrian stage for a while and her public missed her.

On a sunny, warm day in May, everything came together. Jessye, herself, was in sunny, warm form. "How maaahvelous to see you, dear Brian!" she exclaimed when we caught sight of each other (kisskisskiss, hughughug). We talked through the programme, dined together, and then each retired for the night. The next morning, I awoke, shivering. I went to the window, threw open the sash, and came face to face with winter. Overnight, the temperature had plummeted, snow had fallen, and a foot and a half of it covered the ground. Worse, ice lurked beneath the snow. The phone rang. I knew who was calling. "Brian," gasped Jessye, "I don't know how I'm going to get to the cathedral." "Don't worry, we'll get you there", I assured her. "But, more important," she continued, "I simply can't sing in this weather. It's too cold. If I take a breath, I'll choke. Please call whosoever is in charge and tell them I want the heat turned on in the cathedral to a minimum of twenty degrees." This was ten o'clock in the morning, the concert started at seven o'clock in the evening. My first thought? How could you possibly heat up a baroque basilica to twenty degrees in eight hours? "Jessye, excuse me, but I'm here to document your performance. I can't be responsible for the heat in the cathedral." Pause. "Well, then ...", she responded in tones as frigid as the temperature, "... find out who's in charge because unless I get twenty degrees, I will not sing." And she hung up.

Dressing quickly, I trudged through the snow to the church where I managed to find the sexton. I explained the situation, ending with Jessye's ultimatum. He looked at me quizzically. "Tell your singer that if we had turned on the heat a week ago, it would have taken till now for Mariä Geburt to heat up. And, I might add, you think you have problems? We've sold 1,600 tickets at 200 Euros each. It's a sold-out house. What's more, the President of the Republic and his wife are the guests of honour and they're coming with a whole bunch of government officials. Please inform Frau Norman that no matter what the temperature, she has to sing." I smiled at this innocent request. Oh yes, I'm going to tell Jessye Norman what to do. The sexton, perhaps abashed by his outburst, added, "Look, would an electric heater help?" "Anything would help," I sighed, "but it would be asking a lot of one heater." "Okay," said the sexton, "I'll see how many I can get a hold of." I thanked him and then phoned Jessye. "I'm at the cathedral and it's not as cold as you'd think. I'll be over to pick you up." Long pause, and then Jessye purred, "What about the twenty degrees, my dear Brian?" "Well, I've spoken to the sexton and he's focusing on it." "He'd better be." I understood Jessye's concern and totally sympathized, but I had a recording to worry about.

Returning to the hotel I found her seated in the lobby, bundled up in one of the hotel's eiderdown quilts, with plastic bags wrapped around her sandalled feet. "You've done something about the heat, right?" she greeted me. "Yes, yes, the sexton is looking into the matter." She gave me a half-smile that read half-frown. We got into the car and drove down the hill to the cathedral where a path had been cleared at the entrance. I helped her out of the car. Clutching the quilt around her, and holding on to my arm, she walked gingerly down the path into the basilica. She took her time, as well she should have, one little slip and kaboom. The cathedral was cold. Two small electric heaters had been placed on either side of a piano positioned in the apse. Jessye eyed the heaters suspiciously. "Is that it?" she queried. "Just for the present, my dear, just for the present." "Okay, okay", she muttered. We next turned to the programme. She told me that she'd talk through it but she would not sing till the actual recital. I replied that she had to sing at least one aria because the cathedral was full of echoes and I needed a sound check in order to balance her voice. "No, no, no," she cried, "I'm not staying in this place. It's going to be too cold; I know it." She stopped talking, took a look around, and suddenly announced, "That does it! I'm not going to perform." "Okay, okay, but may I just tell you one thing?" I implored. Begrudgingly, she nodded her head and I went into an impromptu spiel frantically making things up as I went along. "Tonight has been advertised as a great event. More than 1,600 people, probably 2,000 will be here. Fans and friends of yours have come into the mountains just to see you. They've paid 200 Euros a ticket and what's more, the President of the Republic and his wife will be here." "I don't care. I'm going to cancel." "This is not professional, Jessye", I grumbled. She sneered. "What do you mean not professional? I cannot perform under these conditions." "And what am I supposed to tell the people who've bought tickets. They're going to want their money back." "My dear Brian, that is not my problem." "Okay, so you want to cancel?" "YES! And let me tell you something else, this is the first time in my entire career that I've ever cancelled anything. The people will understand." Overlooking the fact that I'd been around long enough to have witnessed a few Norman cancellations, I had a sudden vision of a cathedral chock-a-block full of fans with me announcing, "Sorry folks, there's no concert. Thanks for coming." This was serious; I had to think of something. And then it came to me, I knew what I had to do and I was ashamed at myself for doing it, but the show had to go on.

"Jessye," I said, softly, "I hear you. I respect you. I will do what you ask, I'll apologize for you and tell the audience that you are indisposed and with greatest regret, have to disappoint them. I'll do it, but it's going to be very difficult for one particular reason." "What reason?" she snapped. "Well, I wasn't supposed to let you know but I'm going to anyway. I believe you're aware that the President of Austria and his wife and members of the government will be here ..." "I know, I know." "Ah, but you don't know everything and there's a particular reason I'm finding this so difficult to do." "What's that?" she said exasperatedly. "Well, I wasn't supposed to, but I'm going to tell you." "Tell me what?" she barked. I sighed, "I was sworn to secrecy and it means breaking my word." "Break it fast!" Jessye ordered. "Well, they're come to honour you and at the end of the recital the President intends to give you a very important medal." Silence. I knew what she was thinking,

... a recital, ... on television, ... a presidential medal ... in front of thousands of viewers. "Oh well," said Jessye, in dulcet tones, "that's different, that's very different. My dear Brian, why didn't you tell me this before?" "It was meant to be a surprise." "Well, well, a medal, eh? Hmm, that throws a special light on the situation. Very well. Despite the temperature and everything else, I will try my hardest to sing. But let me look at the programme." I handed it to her and she glanced at the list. "It's too cold to sing this, and it's too cold to sing that", said she while poking the page with her index finger. "I don't think I can sing this one either, but maybe I can do that one." By the time she looked up, she'd eliminated a half dozen numbers. Still, she was going to sing. "Oh Jessye," I cried, "you're the best. I won't tell anyone and I won't make any announcements, you just sing what you want." "Well, I don't want to disappoint the President, do I?" She was absolutely gob-smacked at the idea of getting the medal as I knew she would be. As for me, I was utterly wasted. God forgive me, in my zeal to make sure the recital happened, I made up the presidential medal story. I dared not think of the outcome.

Jessye never left the cathedral but waited out the time in a small chamber near where the priests and acolytes changed into their robes. A heater glowed in the centre of the room and Jessye, still wrapped in the hotel quilt, sat in a large chair with visions of medals dancing in her head. The hour arrived, the audience entered, and soon the basilica bulged with hardy souls who'd braved the errant elements to see their star shine once again. Jessye, sans the eiderdown quilt and resplendent in her concert attire, entered, followed by her accompanist. To rapturous applause she took her place next to the piano well with the brave little heaters flanking her. Recognizing the President and his wife in the front row, she nodded grandly to them. Unrehearsed, the recital and the recording began. We hadn't done an audio test so the first piece was sacrificed because we had to use it to balance her voice. As for the singing, what can I say? Her voice was not in its prime but she used every vocal resource in her extensive repertoire. Such was the excitement at seeing and hearing her, she could have sung scales and the audience would have shouted huzzahs. Using a microphone, she sang the Duke Ellington songs and raised the roof; people leapt from their seats. At the end of the recital, she stepped forward and bowed graciously. As she did, the President of the Republic and his wife arose and walked towards her. Jessye was smiling from ear to ear; she knew this was the medal moment. Except of course, it wasn't. The President congratulated her, shook her hand, as did his wife, and after a brief exchange of words, they turned and left. A look flashed across Jessye's face. I knew that at that moment she realized she'd been hoodwinked. Her face frozen in a strained smile, Jessye continued to receive select persons. Finally, she turned and stomped off to her dressing room. As was my wont, I went to congratulate her and knocked on the door. "GO AWAY!" she shouted. I paid no heed, opened the door, and walked in. "What do you want?" she demanded. "I've come to thank you for the recital." "I was not in good voice." "You were fine, the audience loved it." She sneered at me saying, "Before anything else happens, I want you to send me a copy of the tape." I said I would, thanked her again, and left. She never mentioned the medal.

I returned to Vienna and immediately heard from Jessye's secretary, Brenda Robinson, a lovely lady who handled the nitty-gritty of the singer's life. "Jessye feels she wasn't in good voice", Brenda advised me, "... and before anything can happen, she wanted to review her performance before giving approval." I said I'd get right on it and soon sent a copy of the edited tape. A couple of weeks later, Brenda called again. "Jessye's reviewed the tape and, with regret, says she cannot allow it to be televised or issued as a DVD." I knew that the "with regret" came from Brenda rather than Jessye. "I understand", I answered. "Please tell her I tried my best, but the weather conditions were beyond my control. I appreciate her unwillingness to approve of the tape and assure her that I'll pass on the information to ORF and Unitel." For my part, I had done my best (and worst) to make the concert happen and no longer felt compelled to do anything further. As far as I was concerned, Jessye had every right to reject the tape, it was her property. I informed Unitel and ORF, and was assured they'd take care of everything. At least I'd been able to follow Jessye's wishes not to release the tape and I hoped that might make up, somewhat, for my indiscretion.

On Christmas Eve 2012, my hopes were dashed. Jessye Norman's Mariazell Basilica concert was transmitted, and rebroadcast the following day. What's more, Japanese television also aired it. My goose was permanently cooked. Jessye called her lawyer and brought legal action against me, Unitel, and ORF for releasing the recital against her expressed wishes. Alas poor Jessye, the law suits came to next-to-naught because her wishes had been expressed *verbally* and did not appear on the signed contract. Unitel and ORF were within their rights to broadcast the programme. I believe they were sued for $700,000 and that Jessye settled for a token payment of $35,000. I neither received anything nor wanted anything. I remained abashed, aghast at what had happened. For the first time in my professional life, if only to save the day, I had fabricated a story. The day may have been saved but my friendship with the intractable Jessye Norman was over.

Divas can force you into doing what you'd never think of doing, in this instance, concocting a cock-and-bull fable to save a performance. I did it knowing full well Jessye's imperious nature couldn't tolerate such treatment. Still, I'm convinced the medal story was the only way to get her to sing and that, after all, was my job. In conclusion, I cannot stress enough the importance of a mutual exchange of confidence between artist and director. Artists trusted me to show them to their best advantage and for the most part, I think I succeeded. That one time, to my undying regret, I did not. The bottom line? Dealing with divas is not for sissies.

Jessye Norman and I in happier times. The song ended but the melody lingers on

36.

An Incomparable Prima Donna

Of the many singers I have known over the years, there is one for whom I hold a special affinity, one whose humanity was as much a hallmark of her persona as her lovely voice. Mirella Freni served as catalyst for my reconciliation with Leonard Bernstein, was indispensable as a singing partner and disciplinarian for Luciano Pavarotti, and most significantly, she played matchmaker for Jack and me, our own Dolly Levi.

We met in 1977 when Nicolai Ghiaurov brought her to the recording studio for BBC2's opera production of *Macbeth.* Smitten then, I remained under her spell. I wasn't the only one. All prima donnas are idolized by their fans but in each generation only a handful are beloved; Mirella Freni belonged to those few. Lovely in visage as well as voice, admired for her "vocal allure" and her "spirited personality", she became the darling of opera audiences, everywhere. Her gift, the ability to blend the sublime and the everyday, created a diverse diva, one who walked among us, an accessible star.

Her first appearance on stage, Micaela in *Carmen,* took place in her hometown of Modena in 1955. Ten years later she made her Metropolitan Opera debut as Mimi and appeared with the company for the next four years until, after a much-praised appearance in Gounod's *Roméo et Juliette* with Franco Corelli in 1969, she disappeared and did not return to the Met for thirteen long years. During that time, her career flourished in Europe where she

Mirella Freni, the hand that made her fair
also made her good

reigned at La Scala earning the soubriquet, "the last of the prima donnas". At La Scala, Herbert von Karajan, not my favourite maestro, but still Herbert von Karajan, conducted her in Franco Zeffirelli's legendary production of *La Bohème* in 1963. After the performance, the Emperor of Salzburg announced that he'd found his "ideal Mimi and a kindred artistic spirit". For the next twenty years, the two of them often collaborated. Gradually, she began adding heavier roles to her repertoire, always judiciously. Mirella knew what suited her voice and would not step outside the boundaries. She never sang *Butterfly* on stage. She even refused von Karajan's invitation to sing Leonora in Verdi's *Il Trovatore* and the title role in Puccini's *Turandot* because she believed they would "destroy" her voice. Whatever she sang—light or heavy, Mimi remained her signature role.

The years passed; Mirella came to the US to sing in Chicago and San Francisco but did not return to the Metropolitan Opera until 1983 when she appeared in the magnificent *Don Carlos* that I recorded. After that, Mirella's Met performances became sporadic. Without doubt, in doling out roles, the Met always favoured Scotto whose repertoire, in many instances, matched Mirella's. What could have been a prickly situation, however, settled into a mutually beneficial détente. Scotto preferred being in America and singing at the Met while Mirella fancied Europe and La Scala. Until Scotto retired in 1987, Mirella continued occasional appearances in New York where her fan base remained strong. In 1991, the Met held a gala to celebrate her twenty-five years with the company. Then, on 27 April 1997, between the acts of Giordano's *Fedora*, which I was videotaping, Mirella received the key to New York City from the mayor. The one and only time such an event ever occurred on that stage. (Mirella usually avoided any large-scale ceremonial events and only agreed to this one because her grandson was very impressed by his *nonna*'s accomplishment. If I remember correctly, she promised to give the key to him—which I'm sure she did.) In 2005, the Metropolitan Opera celebrated the fortieth anniversary of her Met debut and her fiftieth anniversary on stage with a gala concert conducted by James Levine.

Mirella possessed an invincible spirit and I still smile at delightful memories of her both on and off the stage. One that really tickled her happened in 2004 when a show horse was named in her honour. The bay mare, however, had a far less stellar career than her namesake. Out of thirty-seven jumping contests, the four-legged Mirella Freni only won one. The one and only Mirella won scores of rewards, including our hearts.

I admired Mirella not only for what she achieved but for what she maintained over her incredibly active half-century career. She was full of fun but there was no nonsense about her. Gifted with a beautiful voice and a natural talent, she never coasted on the given. Quite the contrary, she realized from the start that to get to where she got, the top, she had to work on her technique. And oh, did she work. She wanted things just so and to attain that goal, she laboured every single day. When we were working together, I'd occasionally hear her revisiting a particular passage. I couldn't suggest that I'd *heard* something; that would have been going too far. Instead, I'd say, "Mirella, you don't *look* happy, is something troubling you?" thereby leaving it up to her to talk if she wanted. Often the problem might be a single note or a bothersome phrase. I can't tell you how many times she would shut her dressing room door and practice that one fragment over and over again until she got what she wanted. She practiced every single day to keep the supporting breath secure and her voice fresh and vibrant. She never took anything for granted but continued to refine her art and that's why she was able to perform into her mid-sixties. Typically, Mirella herself critiqued the fixed aspects of her late career. "Who wants to see and hear a sixty-year-old grandmother singing Mimi?" she'd laugh. Well, a lot of people did. Even so, when I videoed those performances, she'd gently ask that I respect her with the camera. "Don't forget, Brian, I'm a *nonna*." I took the hint. But even as she grew older, her voice remained fresh and mobile simply because she took care of it. And in the final years of her career, she mastered the Russian language and vocal line, and moved into the Russian repertoire. All this at a time when most prima donnas are putting their tried-and-true portrayals on parade. First came Tatiana in Tchaikovsky's *Eugene Onegin*. Six years later she added *Pique Dame* to her Scala repertoire, recording it with the Vienna State Opera on Austrian television. In 2002, she premiered Tchaikovsky's *Joan of Arc*, a nineteen-year-old, in Torino which she brought to Washington Opera in 2005, to end her illustrious career.

Another endearing quality, despite her celebrity, Mirella retained the virtues of her upbringing in Modena and remained bright, warm, caring, and modest. A generous hostess, we'd often talk things over in her kitchen as she'd prepare lunch or dinner. As down to earth as anyone could get, she liked being a housewife. She wasn't a pushover, though, and when she didn't like something, she'd let you know in no uncertain terms. As mentioned, she was one of the few, if not the only person, who could put Pavarotti in his place. And finally, while she enjoyed singing, she was equally satisfied being wife, mother, and *nonna*. She was a woman first, and then a singer.

Mirella died in Modena on 9 February 2020. The funeral took place in the Modena Cathedral. More and more,

I've been mourning lost friends. I find some solace in remembering them in their prime and rejoice in the many
events that brought us together. Mirella's irrepressible
spirit remains. I'm honoured to have documented her
Mimi, Alice Ford, Adriana, Marguerite, Aida, Elizabeth
in *Don Carlos*, and last but by no means least, that ever
fascinating Fedora. I am equally grateful for all those warm
exchanges and the simple good times.

Mirella and I
preparing *Faust* in Chicago

37.

How a Star Was Born

In the mid-80s, Christopher Raeburn, a fellow Londoner and a senior recording producer for Decca Records, invited Jack and me to hear a tape he'd made of a twenty-two-year-old mezzo from Rome. Daniel Barenboim and Herbert von Karajan, he informed us, had heard the singer on a TV broadcast celebrating Maria Callas and each had urged Christopher to "give a listen". He did and was so captivated he test recorded her. Intrigued, Jack and I popped over to Christopher's and listened to the tape; Jack immediately wanted to hear more. Raeburn proposed an in-person impromptu audition in Pesaro. And so, in mid-August, following a visit to Salzburg, Jack and I drove off to Rossini's birthplace on the Adriatic coast and arrived during a molten heat wave.

The audition had been scheduled at noon in an elementary schoolhouse which we found without much fuss. The custodian let us in and took us to a classroom, "oven" would be the better word. Heat choked the place. A lonely little fan had been placed on a table and intrepidly did its back-and-forth business but with near zero cooling effect. Jack and I sat down near the machine and waited … and waited. After nearly half an hour had passed, we began to think we'd been stood up. And then a distant clatter of shoes on the pavement outside broke the silence. Clip-clop, clip-clop, the rattle grew louder and louder till the door of the classroom flew open and a lovely young lady burst into the room followed by an older woman and a young man

Brilliant singer,
compassionate friend,
Cecilia Bartoli

carrying music books. Apologizing profusely for being late, hot, sweaty, and out of breath, the singer introduced the two companions, her mother and her accompanist. Pulling the latter along with her, she then went to an upright piano standing against the wall. The mother smiled and slipped into a chair next to Jack. Quickly helping the accompanist set up the music, the young artist took control of the room and announced, "I am going to sing 'Cruda sorte' from *L'Italiana in Algeri*. Jack looked at me and I looked back at him. At that time, the pyrotechnics of the chosen Rossini aria were just about the exclusive property of Marilyn Horne. Singing "Cruda sorte" (roughly translated, "Bad Luck") at an audition would be tantamount to playing Russian roulette with six real bullets, sheer nerve. Nonetheless, the singer nodded to her accompanist and, leaning over, he began pounding away on the defenceless piano. Obviously sight reading, and clueless as to what he was playing, the result bordered on excruciating. Nonetheless, the young woman got through it easily, smiling all the while even as her accompanist floundered in a tidal wave of black and white keys. The second the aria ended, the singer leaned over and profusely and sincerely thanked the pianist and then politely showed him to the door. Her calm handling of his expulsion allowed him to leave with minimal damage to his ego. Before Jack could say a word, the singer begged our forgiveness for mistakenly believing that she had hired a competent musician. "I will sing for you now Mozart's 'Voi che sapete'", said she and without further ado, sat down at the piano and, accompanying herself, sang. It was as though a bottle of vintage champagne had popped open. The voice was fresh, bubbling, rich, both mellow and brilliant. She had a virtuosity and a clarity that glistened. And, as if her vocalizing weren't enough, her piano playing was equally impressive. This was our introduction to Cecilia Bartoli, a phenomenal musician and as we later would learn, a beautiful human being.

Following the audition, Jack and I took Cecilia and her mother for a coffee. We learned that both her parents, Silvana and Pietro, sang in the Rome Opera Chorus. Moreover, Silvana had been her daughter's only teacher. Jack wanted to sign Cecilia on the spot but she already had a few agents vying for her. Jack called Ronald Wilford, head of Columbia Artists Management, and apprised him of the situation. Wilford advised him to drop it since other agencies already were involved. But Jack was determined, and a determined Jack usually got what he wanted. It took a year, and I don't know how he did it, but he finally signed Cecilia for CAMI. She became one of his shining stars and a dear friend and colleague to both of us.

As Jack skilfully guided Cecilia's career, I had the pleasure of doing many projects with her. Speaking of guiding careers, I don't think the general public has any idea of what it took to get an artist's name known before the Internet and social media took over. In those days, "overnight sensation" meant years of struggle and planning. Then, Facebook, X/Twitter, Instagram, TikTok, et al. ran up the celebrity clock and unknowns burst onto the international scene in a matter of days rather than years. The results weren't always beneficial to the singers. Too much, too soon, so to speak. Jack took his time presenting Cecilia. He believed in her a million per cent and promoted her with enormous energy, concentrating, at first, on concert appearances. She established herself in Europe and then made her North American debut in Quebec in 1990. From there she came down to New York and that summer made her NYC debut in a *Mostly Mozart* concert at Lincoln

Center. Other appearances followed including one with the Chicago Symphony and by 1992, Jack managed to open the door to Carnegie Hall for an all-Rossini programme conducted by Charles Dutoit. That performance, by the bye, was voted one of the ten best concerts of the year. Cecilia was on her way.

During the summer of 1993, my dad's health deteriorated. Over the years, he'd kept himself busy carving violins while smoking cigarette after cigarette. Eventually, he suffered from acute emphysema. Increasingly, he experienced difficulty in getting around. I could look after him when I was home but I had to make sure he was well cared for when I travelled. My family always came first and I needed to know my dad was safe in order to carry on with my work. To that end, I found a nearby care facility where he stayed when I went on assignments. In 1993, barely finished with a recording of *Turandot* in San Francisco, I received a call from the nursing home. My dad had contracted pneumonia and was in critical condition. I flew back to England and spent a few days with him before he passed. Jack came in from New York and helped with the funeral preparations. Cecilia flew in from Rome, came to my home, and took over the chores—cooking, cleaning, and doing anything else that made life easier. One evening, she asked what music would be played at the services, I explained I'd be inviting students from the Royal Academy to sing at the funeral. "Why would you do that?" Cecilia asked, "I'm here. I will sing for your father. I will sing for you." I could not hold back my tears. Raised as an only child, I now knew what it meant to have a sister. And so that angel sang my father to his rest with Schubert's "Ave Maria" and Mozart's "Exultate Jubilate", the perfect musical farewell for John James Robert Large. Cecilia's singing touched everyone. Indeed, the Vicar who conducted the service was so impressed he asked Cecilia, since she was there already, might she consider giving a recital to benefit the church's organ fund? I couldn't blame him for asking, neither could I blame Cecilia for politely declining. Enough is enough. Her presence and participation overwhelmed me. I owed her much and within a year an opportunity to properly thank her presented itself.

Jack had arranged for Cecilia to appear on opening night at Carnegie Hall in September of 1994 performing Bellini and Mozart arias accompanied by Neville Marriner and the Orchestra of St Martin in the Fields. PBS, scheduled to televise the event, asked me to direct. I was overjoyed to be working at Carnegie Hall along with Cecilia and eager to bring out the best from the best. She was in top form; the beauty of her tone, coupled with her masterful technique were extraordinary, especially in the Bellini. She had a natural stage presence and brought the same warmth and joy that lit her personal life to her public appearances. I loved exploiting her talent through the camera. As always, her performance was not only a gift to the audience, but to me and my camera crew, as well. After the Carnegie event, Jack began promoting Cecilia on the operatic stage.

Along with Judy Flannery, a San Francisco producer, he set up an independent video company, NBSC, specifically to give Cecilia a wider international presence; she needed it. Cecilia had a profound fear of travelling, especially on airplanes. The NBSC videos would do the travelling for her. (In case you're wondering, NBSC stands for New Broom Sweeps Clean. Jack always had a bit of the reformer in him.) Once NBSC got rolling, projects began to take shape. I remember one in particular because it took an incredible amount of planning and had stunning results.

Cecilia wanted to video *La Cenerentola,* Rossini's sparkling version of *Cinderella,* but we needed to find a location. Because of Cecilia's Roman roots, we thought it would be fitting to look for a venue in her hometown. First, we tried the Teatro Argentina where Rossini's *Barber of Seville* had its premiere in 1816. What a disappointment. The theatre had been totally modernized and, in the process, stripped of its original atmosphere. We quickly moved on to the Teatro Valle where *La Cenerentola* had premiered in 1817. Unlike the reinvented Argentina, the Valle was in its original exquisite shape, the ideal setting to turn into a television studio. The only problem lay outside the theatre. The Valle sat on an extremely narrow street barely three metres across; no way could mobile television trucks drive, let alone park, on it. We had to find somewhere nearby to put the vans and, at the same time, run a cable to the theatre. Luckily, we discovered the perfect spot, a parking lot around the corner. The lot was run by a group of squatters who'd occupied it for so long it had become their property. They agreed to let us park the vehicles for free but they had to "safeguard" them and for that we had to pay. If you didn't pay you could kiss your equipment goodbye; they'd steal it right out of the trucks. Oh well, when in Rome, etc. We settled on a price, and everything fell into place. The Bologna Opera House agreed to loan us their *Cenerentola* production and to transport the scenery and the costumes. The sound crew came from London, and I brought my camera crews from New York and San Francisco. Everything was at the ready when came the awful news that Cecilia's elder brother, Gabriele, a talented violist, had been diagnosed with a brain tumour. Cecilia immediately left to be with her family. The recording and all other arrangements had to be cancelled. The repercussions were predictable, the international crew had to be laid off and compensated, the Teatro Valle sued, a deal had to be made with the airlines, and on and on. What a sad state of affairs. Still, Cecilia did not give up the idea of recording *La Cenerentola*, and neither did her manager.

A year or so later, Jack contacted David Gockley, general manager of the Houston Opera, and before the clock struck twelve, *Cenerentola* had found a new home. The Houston Opera production was recorded by Decca and shown on PBS in April of 1996. Decca later issued a DVD. We had a ball recording it. In my opinion, this opera is Rossini's happiest creation; the music bounces along and quite honestly, I prefer it to *The Barber of Seville*. Cecilia sang with incredible vigour and rose to the music's every challenge. The entire production bubbled, and based on its success, Jack proposed a second video for NBSC, a recital by Cecilia who, at this point in her career, wanted to widen her repertoire, especially in the Baroque repertoire. Cecilia always had shown great interest in the eighteenth-century Venetian composer Antonio Vivaldi. She planned to include him in her programme and felt that Venice would provide the perfect setting. I concurred as did the rest of the principals. Ergo, Judy, Jack, and I flew to Venice to find the right spot. For various reasons we passed on the obvious choices, La Fenice and the Teatro Malibran, opting instead for a non-theatrical setting. Setting our sights on the San Marco Basilica, we spoke with the church authorities. They presented us with a few daunting concerns, e.g. the basilica often flooded at high tide, and the gondolas bearing our equipment might not be able to pass under the low bridges along canals bordering the basilica. It took only one meeting with the San Marco representatives to realize that we'd be better off looking elsewhere. The next potential haven, a building which in Vivaldi's day had been a music school for orphans, particularly appealed to

Cecilia. Alas, like San Marco, it, too, came equipped with too many hitches. Turning back to churches, we hopped over to Santa Maria della Salute. Santa Maria is positioned between the Grand Canal and the Giudecca and the open canal would have made transporting the equipment a breeze. That was the plus side. On the minus side, the enormous church would have swallowed up an intimate recital and Santa Maria joined San Marco in the rejection bin.

Jack and I had nearly run out of location ideas when, along with Judy Flannery, we were invited for dinner at the Venetian residence of an American friend, Marilyn Perry, Chairman of the World Monuments Fund. Marilyn served *bigoli in salsa*, a Venetian speciality of thick long pasta in a white wine, anchovy, and onion sauce. Delicious. Among other topics, we discussed the vicissitudes of finding a proper location for Cecilia's video. "Do you know the Teatro Olimpico in Vicenza?" Marilyn asked. The three of us looked blank. "You must go there", she insisted. Having said that, she arranged for us to have a private viewing of Andrea Palladio's final design, a small theatre gem built in the late 1580s and finished after the architect's death. The Olimpico was, and still is, the oldest serving theatre of its kind in Italy and famed for its stage and *trompe-l'oeil* scenery designed by Vittorio Scamozzi. Made of wood, the theatre itself had the liveliest and most brilliant acoustics imaginable. The Olimpico was the perfect location proving, once again, any problem can be solved over a plate of good pasta.

In June of 1998, we began work on "Live in Italy" within Palladio's petite theatre. The programme included arias by Bellini, Donizetti, Handel, and Mozart and Baroque arias by Vivaldi and Caccini. For the arias, Cecilia handpicked the Sonatori de la Gioiosa Marca, a Baroque musical ensemble, to accompany her; the rest of the programme, she'd be accompanied by the redoubtable French pianist, Jean-Yves Thibaudet. Her cheery uplifting presence set the tone for the entire broadcast. Cecilia is a natural, one of those special performers who presents herself in a secure, smiling manner, no phony-baloney. But like all great artists, she'd had much with which to contend. She herself told me that as easy-going as she appeared, she'd had to overcome difficulties in order to present herself in an assured manner. She cited a particular stumbling block that plagued her in the early years of her career; each time she did a trill or ran a scale, her eyelids began fluttering. She had no control over this, indeed, wasn't even aware of it. Once apprised of the situation, she addressed it and with intensive practice managed to defuse the trill-trigger effect.

And so, Cecilia Bartoli's career flourished, albeit in Europe rather than the United States. Smaller European opera houses, not vast American auditoriums, better suited her voice. Moreover, Cecilia's appearances in the States were constrained by her paralyzing fear of flying. Not surprisingly, she eventually chose to remain in her comfort zone. In my opinion, given Cecilia Bartoli's work ethic and natural gifts, what distinguishes her singing is her unrestrained joy—there's that word again!—and for me nothing demonstrates that ecstasy more than the *Viva Vivaldi* DVD we taped in Paris in 2000 which absolutely embodies her rare combination of artistry and virtuosity.

Today, while she still occasionally performs, Cecilia has moved into administrative roles; in 2012 she was named artistic director of the Salzburg Whitsun Festival and in 2023 she became the director of the Opera de Monte-Carlo, the first woman to hold that position. It's a sure bet that whatever she does in the future will be done brilliantly and, of course, with joy.

The overwhelming
interior of Vicenza's
Teatro Olimpico.
Andrea Palladio's
last design and Italy's
oldest working theatre

Gergiev seated at my right with camera and
sound crew in the Czar's Box at Mariinsky
Theatre, St Petersburg, Russia, 1992

38.

Happy Birthday, Peter Ilyich

In 1989, I returned to the Soviet Union at the invitation of Valery Gergiev, chief conductor of the Kirov Opera. At that time, I happened to be doing the lion's share of directing operas in Europe. Gergiev, under exclusive contract with Phillips Records, recognized the value of documenting performances for worldwide distribution and was bound and determined to have his company keep in step with the times. He hired me to record Tchaikovsky's *Pique Dame* and Mussorgsky's *Khovanshchina* from the legendary Mariinsky Theatre. (While the Kirov embraced the possibilities of documenting its repertoire, the Bolshoi, still adhering to strict party lines, did not. I worked at the Bolshoi only once, to record Tchaikovsky's opera, *The Maid of Orleans*.)

My Met camera crew and I arrived in Leningrad and checked into the historic Astoria Hotel. Then, we walked over to the Mariinsky Theatre and, after pausing to admire the magnificent façade, entered a realm of gold. I've been in theatres and concert halls all over the world but never had I seen anything to match the glorious, gilded Mariinsky. For over two hundred years this historic theatre premiered Russian operas, from Glinka's *A Life for the Tsar* to Mussorgsky's *Boris Godunov* and Tchaikovsky's *The Queen of Spades*. Here, also, Petipa and Fokine choreographed Tchaikovsky's *Sleeping Beauty*. Unrivalled in the richness of its décor and in its performance history, the Mariinsky is a unique sanctuary of culture. That being said, the Kirov productions were traditional, aka old. Costumes were lovely but faded. The soloists, chorus, and orchestra dazzled. The company bent over backwards to give us what we wanted. Sessions were easily organized with extra lighting, camera, and music rehearsals available. We recorded the two operas in two weeks and at the end, Gergiev made it known that he wanted us to return on a yearly basis. We did so for several years, recording *Sadko, Mazeppa, The Fiery Angel, Ivan the Terrible* and Verdi's first version of *Forza*. And then, the requests for our services ended.

By this time, I'd become intrigued with working in Russia and continued to look for projects that would allow me to return. Fortunately, Peter Gelb was looking, too, and in 1990, he found one—the 150th anniversary of Tchaikovsky's birth. Gelb called and asked me to join with him in creating a celebration. I eagerly agreed and a concert was scheduled in Leningrad's Philharmonic Hall. Preparations got underway, everything fell into place and suddenly, we were there.

Moscow, Russia's historic capital city, had been impressive but Leningrad, formerly St Petersburg, then Petrograd, and soon to return to its original name, was an architectural dream. Palace Square, the Nevsky Prospect, Palace Bridge, St Isaac's Cathedral, and the Hermitage, all astonished. The scenic views were magnificent but times remained hard in the Soviet Union; not the least of the difficulties was a food shortage. I remember watching scores of Russians fishing with rod and string through holes in the frozen Neva, not for sport but for sustenance.

Despite the grim realities of everyday life, the city's beauty overwhelmed me. Eager to sightsee, I found an interpreter/guide and rushed around with him trying to absorb all I could. In my enthusiasm, I lost my footing on the ice, tripped, and fell on my face. My sunglasses cracked apart, nicking my right eye. The guide hurriedly took me to a nearby clinic. I was petrified as we'd all been cautioned "Whatever happens, do not go to a Russian hospital." What else could I do? The guide banged on the door of the clinic and called for someone to come to my aid all the while advising the staff inside that I was *Amerikanski*. At last, a voice cried out from behind the door. "Does he have a credit card?" Assured that I did, the door opened and I was rushed into a consulting room. The doctor who attended me spoke a little English, enough to express his concern that glass splinters might have got into the eye. Happily, none was found. I was given painkillers and told to come back the following day. Sporting a patch, I returned to the Astoria Hotel, exhausted and thankful. Next day, I returned to the clinic and my eye, though sore, had improved. I had to wear the patch for a few days and admit to finding it rather dashing.

The morning of the concert, I went to pay my respects to Tchaikovsky in the house where he had lived and died. I walked through the rooms carrying on a whimsical discourse in my mind, thanking the composer for his rich legacy and advising him that he was in for a very special treat that evening. As I left the Tchaikovsky residence, on a sudden impulse, I took a taxi to Tikhvin Cemetery where Tchaikovsky is interred along with Glinka, Borodin, Mussorgsky, Glazunov, Rimsky-Korsakov and other Russian musical giants. Profoundly moved by the experience, I resolved to return. (Twenty years later, it happened. I came back with Renée Fleming and Dmitri Hvorostovsky to film *Odyssey of St Petersburg*, a musical journey through the art and history of the "Venice of the North". In one memorable sequence, Renée softly singing a musical phrase from *Onegin*, placed flowers on

Tchaikovsky's tomb. Tears filled the eyes of all who witnessed that tender homage.)

Time to prepare for the Birthday Concert. I left the cemetery and soon arrived at Philharmonic Hall. What an incredible structure. Built around a series of twenty-four floor-to-ceiling creamy beige marble columns and topped by a ceiling-full of a dozen crystal chandeliers; the hall also happens to be an acoustical gem.

The Tchaikovsky Concert featured the Leningrad Philharmonic Orchestra led by Yuri Temirkanov with soloists, Jessye Norman, Yo-Yo Ma, Itzhak Perlman, and Boris Berezovsky, a Russian pianist, a monster celebration calling for a huge fourteen camera setup. The musical offerings that evening included Perlman playing two Tchaikovsky Serenades, Berezovsky playing the final movement of Tchaikovsky's *Piano Concert No. 1*, Jessye singing three Tchaikovsky songs in French, and Yo-Yo performing the composer's *Rococo Variations*. The celebration ended with a spectacular rendition of the *1812 Overture* by the one-hundred-member orchestra and two military brass bands inside the hall. Outside, we'd arranged for the Leningrad military to bring over twelve large cannons to be exploded at the *Overture's* climax. At the same moment a huge fireworks display would be set off over Philharmonic Hall and all the church bells in nearby cathedrals would ring. An astounding event to pull off and quite an ordeal as I had to direct with only one eye. Thanks to the crew, everything went perfectly. Unlike the Horowitz recital, this programme aired on Russian TV. The climate had been changing in Eastern Europe; within a few months the Berlin Wall would come tumbling down.

I continued to hop between the USA and Europe and, gradually, Berlin became a frequent stop. The local TV station, SFB, invited me to work with the Berlin

Philharmonic. Then, in May of 1991, Euro Arts, the video company, based in the German capital, initiated its series of May Day Concerts for European TV stations. May Day is an official holiday in most countries, and each year the concerts were performed in a different city. The inaugural programme took place in Prague which allowed me to return to my former home away from home for a Mozart concert. Mozart loved Prague as much as I did, or maybe I should say I loved Prague as much as Mozart did. Howsoever I phrase it, Prague was a magical place for Mozart and me, not to mention the millions of tourists who've been coming there for centuries.

I spent the next six years celebrating the 1st of May all over Europe. From Prague (twice), to London, to Meiningen, to Florence, to Leningrad. Also in 1991, Euro Arts began a series of open-air concerts in the Berlin Waldbühne, a 22,290-seat arena built for the 1936 Olympics located just outside the city. Like the arena in Verona, the Waldbühne is a *gemütlich* venue for bringing together those who love music and enjoy listening to it while picnicking, drinking wine, and seeing friends. The programmes always ended with the crowd singing "Berliner Luft", a signature tune from Paul Lincke's operetta, *Frau Luna*, as they gathered their belongings, said farewell to friends, and went off to their homes. The warmth and comradery of the Waldbühne gatherings really got to me. Thus, when the Met asked me to do various galas, including the one celebrating the 25th anniversary of the Met at Lincoln Center, I tried to capture Waldbühne's sparkling spirit. By the way, the Met gala marked the first time anywhere that Plácido Domingo and Luciano Pavarotti sang together on stage. They closed the evening and brought down the house with the duet from Act IV of *La Bohème*. Soon, the two of them would be joined by another stellar tenor and, together, the three of them would make history.

LEFT:
The Mariinsky Theatre
and its lush interior

RIGHT:
The grave of Peter Ilyich
Tchaikovsky, Tikhvin
Cemetery, Alexander
Nevsky Monastery,
St Petersburg, Russia

BELOW:
With Valery Gergiev

39.

Three Musketeers

My schedule for the spring and summer of 1990 was full. March through mid-May, I'd be at the Metropolitan Opera to complete their *Ring* cycle. Otto Schenk's magical production had no peer and working on it would be a pleasure. I also would be taping Harry Kupfer's Bayreuth *Ring*. Kupfer's gloomy take on Wagner's heroic fairy-tale didn't appeal to me as much as Schenk's, but I had committed to both. C'est la vie.

My mother had been feeling unwell when I left London for New York in March, and I was uneasy about leaving her. She said she'd be fine and insisted that I go. On my return, her condition had worsened. When I told her I would withdraw from Bayreuth, she wouldn't hear of it. "You have professional obligations to fulfil, Brian. That's what you should be doing, not hanging around me." This time I didn't listen to her and informed Bayreuth of my decision. Saying "no" to Harry Kupfer was difficult, I never would have done so had not my mother's health been so precarious. Sadly, her condition continued to deteriorate and surgery had to be scheduled. Despite her intense discomfort, my mother steadfastly expressed more concern for my father's and my wellbeing than for her own. My father coped as best he could and I tried to manage things for them both as best as I could. Nothing to do but wait and hope.

Those three: The Athos, Aramis, and Porthos of Song:
Domingo, Carreras, and Pavarotti

The days passed slowly and then in mid-June, I received a surprising phone call from Ray Minshull, John Culshaw's successor at Decca. Minshull and Mario Dradi, an Italian impresario and artists rep, were planning a concert in Rome and they wanted me to direct. I certainly wasn't looking for work but the event, as described, appealed to me on several levels. The concert, a ring-around-the-rosie lark rather than a weighty *Ring*, would be a welcome change from heavy duty dealings with Wagner. Moreover, it was a one-off that would take no more than ten day's work. Regarding family concerns, Rome was a two-and-a-half-hour flight; if needed, I could get back fast. The event sounded exciting and challenging, and most important, doable. I accepted Ray's invitation. And that is how I became involved with *The Three Tenors*, a once in a lifetime global phenomenon which became an iconic moment in television history and "changed classical music forever".

The story of that extraordinary evening begins with the popular Spanish tenor José Carreras who, in July 1987, had been diagnosed with a rare, deadly, leukaemia and given a one-in-ten chance of survival. Those crushing odds hovering over him, Carreras entered the Fred Hutchinson Cancer Center in Seattle, Washington, to undergo extensive and gruelling treatment. Two years later he emerged cancer-free, eager to resume his career. To celebrate the occasion, Carreras's manager, Mario Dradi, proposed an open-air concert with all profits going to the tenor's Leukaemia Foundation. Carreras had done benefit shows before but this time he felt less equipped to carry an entire programme alone; he wanted "backup". Dradi devised a plan, a variant of Dame Myra Hess's "two pianists for the price of one" hypothesis. To wit, wouldn't the comeback be even more extraordinary if it featured not only Carreras but another tenor. Wait, why only one other tenor? How about two other tenors, and not just run-of-the-mill tenors, either. How about two from the top of the heap, namely Plácido Domingo and the *tenore* du jour, Luciano Pavarotti. How about that?

Although the idea of putting together Carreras, Domingo, and Pavarotti had been bandied about for years, their calendars, especially Pavarotti's, never could be synchronized. This time the gods smiled and by-the-same-token, a very special date became available. Dradi brilliantly scheduled the performance for 9 July 1990, the eve of the FIFA World Cup Final in Rome's Olympic Stadium. He scored another coup by presenting the show in the *Terme di Caracalla*, the ruins of an ancient bath house and a popular summer venue for open-air performances. Once the concert was announced, the eyes of the world focused on Italy including those of the three tenors. Devoted soccer fans, they were tickled to be a part of the championship celebrations. Decca Records company put together the entire package and retained all recording rights. When Decca officially hired me to direct the world telecast, I promptly invited the Swiss crew from Polivideo to join me in Rome. Four years prior, we'd worked together, beautifully, on *Horowitz Returns to Moscow*; I knew they'd be more than up to the challenge.

Early in January of 1990, Dradi managed to get the three principals together to discuss the programme. Zubin Mehta joined them and was given equal billing, CARRERAS/DOMINGO/PAVAROTTI/MEHTA read all the posters and advertisements. Mehta would lead an orchestra of nearly two hundred musicians gleaned from the Rome Opera Orchestra and the Maggio Musicale of Florence. While they would play one orchestral selection, the Sinfonia from Verdi's *I Vespri Siciliani*, their appointed task lay in accompanying the tenors in arias from the works of Verdi, Puccini, Meyerbeer, Cilea, and Giordano and Neapolitan songs, all chosen by Dradi and the artists. And yet, despite the splendid setting, the illustrious singers, the incredible orchestra, and a programme bulging with surefire show-stoppers, Mehta felt the evening needed even more pizzazz, something to knock everyone's socks off. To that end, he suggested closing the concert with a potpourri of well-known international songs. The others quickly agreed. Mehta then contacted composer/arranger Lalo Schifrin, best known for his cinema and television scores *(Bullitt, Mission Impossible, The Three Musketeers,* etc.) and invited him to prepare a medley. Schifrin accepted and was flown over to join the meeting where he guided the singers in creating a universal hit parade. The result, a dazzling col-lection of songs from around the world, including Broad-way numbers, "Maria" and "Tonight" from *West Side Story* and "Memories" from *Cats*, plus a galaxy of worldwide favourites including "Ochi Tchornye" (Dark Eyes), "La Vie en Rose", "Matinatta", "Wien, Wien nur du allein", and "Amapola". The eclectic selection allowed the singers to show off their expertise in English, Russian, French, Italian, German, and Spanish. Mehta further enhanced the evening's distinctiveness by having Schifrin arrange "Nessun dorma" for three voices as an encore. Already chosen as a solo number, Puccini's *Turandot* aria would make its second appearance as a "trio", thereby ending the entire evening in a triumphant, triumvirate burst of blended vocal glory.

A week before the concert I arrived in Rome and my first stop was Caracalla to set the stage. I knew I had to create an atmosphere of intimacy among the performers while providing a sense of the venue's hugeness. The task didn't faze me; I'd already directed numerous operas in the Verona Arena, the largest open-air amphitheatre in the world. Aware that some hundred thousand fans attempted to buy tickets (Caracalla could accommodate six thousand), I began by choosing camera positions that would afford television viewers the best "seats" in the house. Looked at from that perspective, we had a potential TV audience of ninety-four thousand to satisfy. I positioned cameras all over the arena, cameras on cranes, cameras on the stage, cameras in the audience, and handheld cameras in the orchestra. In total, there were fourteen of them, a good healthy number. Once the cameras were set, I got together with Corrado Bartolini, the lighting director, and explained that I wanted to do more than simply illuminate the arena. I wanted to paint the entire scene with light, to suffuse the ruins with a subtle glow and to gently lead viewers from the outside into the baths themselves. The performers on stage, the audience in the arena, and the viewers at home needed to *feel* the light. Caracalla is surrounded by the pine trees so identified with Rome and we arranged to backlight them in a manner that gave a sense of shape, atmosphere, and architecture. Lights were placed at the foot of the trees causing the branches hanging above to glow like sculptured ivory arms. On the stage itself, rim-lit arches and spaces were awash in an otherworldly luminescence. Corrado and his crew did a masterful job. Honestly, if I do say so myself, the lighting was breathtaking. Primed and ready, Caracalla awaited.

Piano rehearsals began in the Rome Opera House. The tenors were cordial to one another, still, you could feel an underlying tautness. The world of singers' egos is combustible, anything can happen. That Pavarotti was the leader of the pack was a given, and jealousy, both professional and personal, existed between him and Domingo. Beneath the *gemütlich* surface, lay an intense rivalry. The fact that Pavarotti consistently received the lion's share of publicity especially rankled Domingo. Little wonder. A publicity magnet, Pavarotti willingly did anything that called attention to his well-padded being. New York, home to the Metropolitan Opera, was his city and he set records there as a participant in Fifth Avenue's fabled parades. Whether a parade marched for Columbus or St Patrick, whomever or whatever, the "Day" belonged to Luciano Pavarotti. Standing on a float, seated in a car, or even astride a horse, he'd ride along Fifth Avenue waving and smiling, leaving an indelible impression on the hordes of onlookers who only knew about opera because of him. He truly was "larger than life", and there wasn't much Domingo could do about that. Pavarotti himself always remained conscious of his "numero uno" status, at the same time, he realized that he was the odd man out in this situation. Carreras and Domingo were buddies; whenever they put their heads together and began speaking in Spanish, Pavarotti eyed them suspiciously. I believe he was uneasy about the other two potentially ganging up on him and usurping his prime position. Fat chance. He ruled the roost. Of the three, Carreras showed the most equanimity. Whatever his mood, as the linchpin of the occasion, he wisely kept his feelings to himself. Their rivalry notwithstanding, Domingo and Pavarotti were united in a genuine desire to bring Carreras back into the fold. Further, they were gratified to support not only his Leukemia Foundation but their own favourite charities in the bargain. Carreras's entire fee went to his foundation, Domingo turned over his pay to earthquake relief in Mexico, and Pavarotti earmarked his cut for medical care in Italy. While all profits would go to charity, money, money, money was a separate entity and brought its share of conflict. For example, each of the artists supposedly received an equal amount. Pavarotti, however, happened to be an exclusive Decca recording artist and talk arose of an under the table deal that brought more cash to its star. Bert Chappell, Decca's producer, actually told me that he had travelled to Rome with a suitcase full of American money in order to keep Luciano "sweet".

Back to the piano rehearsals at the Rome Opera House, where questions remained to be answered. At the January meeting, the big issue was who would sing what. Each of them could have sung any of the chosen arias and each of them wanted to sing certain ones. Consequently, with Zubin Mehta as ringmaster, except for one aria, nitpicking over individual numbers had taken up a lot of time. No surprise, Pavarotti, already closely identified with the *Turandot* show stopper, received "Nessun dorma". Not to be outdone, Carreras and Domingo would take their turns at Puccini's lush aria during the encore. The music assigned; the big question now became what would be the batting order? Who would start the evening? Who would follow? And who'd be number three? After interminable discussion, Mehta again assumed the role of number one problem solver. "Why not do it alphabetically? C, D, P, Carreras, Domingo, Pavarotti." Domingo and Pavarotti really couldn't argue about Carreras topping the list as he was the reason for the concert in the first place. The arias already chosen and assigned, the batting order now set, the atmosphere quickly improved and piano rehearsals ended on a positive note. Finally, the two orchestras assembled, blended, and prepared the arias and songs; special effort went into learning the only stranger in the woodpile, Lalo Schifrin's Medley. At last, everyone was bused over to Caracalla where all participants united as a single force. Gradually, the atmosphere had changed from apprehensive to festive during the rehearsal period. Clearly, this was going to be something special. Here and there, a minor hitch arose, but in the main, the egos had landed and adjusted.

Everybody was a winner that balmy summer night before the World Cup, and no one delighted in the occasion more than the tenors themselves. However, not everything went as smoothly as anticipated; the evening scheduled to end with a bang, started off with an unexpected jolt. Dradi wisely had contacted Rome's airports to arrange for flights to be diverted from the arena during the performance. Man plans, the gods laugh. Carreras came onstage and opened the evening with "Il Lamento di Federico" from Cilea's *L'Arlesiana*. As he neared the end of the powerful, plaintive first verse, an airplane suddenly soared over Caracalla. The sound was audible. Carreras looked up, followed the plane's arc, and, breaking into a big smile, raised his hand to his lips, blew a kiss to the heavens, and went on singing. The glitch did nothing to lessen the evening's impact, rather, the incident highlighted Carreras's composure and, while we couldn't erase the noise, we managed to reduce the engine's roar in the final edit. The rest of the performance proceeded smoothly. The singing was grand, the banter and cavorting light-hearted, if occasionally school boyish, and the joy the performers evinced was irresistible and infectious. The applause at the end of the medley was so intense, Mehta made a spontaneous decision to repeat the entire number which was greeted with a wall of cheers and applause from the audience and a dropped jaw by me. Here's why.

I always worked from a bound score in front of me and simply flipped over the pages as the evening progressed.

That evening, I was handed an unbound score which meant I had to find another method of getting the separate pages out of the way. Never thinking I'd have need of them again, I cavalierly began tossing the loose sheets over my shoulder. When Mehta announced the repeat, I dropped to the floor, frantically gathered up the scattered pages of the medley and put them back in order. Luckily, a little on-stage by-play by the tenors took up time and I was at the ready when Mehta again raised his baton. Although the final number was performed twice, only the attendees at Caracalla experienced the double-dip. Because the second version of the medley seemed a little more polished than the original, I chose to use it in the edited video. And then came the "Nessun dorma" encore. At the end of the aria, as they approached the final three cries of *vincerò* (I will win), the tenors huddled together and began pointing to one another, seemingly determining who would tackle it first. A lot of supposedly impromptu horseplay had gone on throughout the evening but to my knowledge, that moment was the sole completely extemporaneous exchange among the tenors. The decision was reached and this time D preceded C. Domingo began the *Vincerò*, then was joined by Carreras and, finally, Pavarotti. Having the programme conclude with a resounding "Vincerò, Vincerò, Vincerò" was absolute perfection.

The tallies for the evening exceeded every prediction. The number of television viewers? Forget the estimated ninety-four thousand, *The Three Tenors* was seen by one billion. The live album of *Carreras Domingo Pavarotti in Concert* sold ten million copies, won the Grammy Award for Best Classical Vocal Performance and remains the best-selling classical album of all time. "Nessun dorma", the unofficial theme song of both the concert and the World Cup, became opera's international anthem. That

July evening in the ancient ruins of Rome's Terme di Caracalla defined "a night to remember".

All good things supposedly end but, in this instance, an essentially good thing that should have ended, went rogue. Although the Caracalla concert was meant to be a one-nighter, its success had been so overwhelming, the idea of doing a repeat inspired all manner of entrepreneurs eager to jump on the bandwagon. Among them loomed a would-be P.T. Barnum by the name of Tibor Rudas. The Hungarian born Rudas was a colourful man. In his youth he'd formed an acrobatic act with his brother and the two of them travelled around Europe performing with local circuses. When World War II broke out, the brothers, who were Jewish, wound up in the Bergen-Belsen Concentration Camp. Somehow, they managed to survive. After the war, they resettled in Australia, set up a dance studio and began producing popular musical shows in Melbourne. By 1963, they'd made their way to Las Vegas where they created their own thriving entertainment company producing girlie shows in various casinos. At the time of the Caracalla concert, Rudas already had his foot in the door as a proper presenter having organized a successful series of orchestral concerts featuring the ubiquitous Pavarotti. For many years, the tenor had been appearing throughout the United States in (large) theatres, casinos, and sports arenas. Rudas may have missed the boat with the original *Three Tenors* but after its phenomenal success, he was ready to take over. Consequently, when Mario Dradi turned his mind to a repeat performance, he was stunned to learn that the three tenors already had been signed for a second go by Tibor Rudas. The spotlight quickly switched to the erstwhile Vegas showman who was immediately approached by the press. Questioned as to what his credentials might be as a presenter of a musical event of such magnitude, Rudas answered, "I was a boy soprano in the Budapest State Opera." This dubious qualification remained the only one he ever offered.

Rudas put the singers' second round, now officially entitled *The Three Tenors*, into Los Angeles's Dodger Stadium. Once again it would take place on the eve of the FIFA World Cup Final (1994) to be held in nearby Pasadena. One huge difference between the first two outings is worth noting. This time each of the tenors received a million dollars, an unheard of and unimaginable amount for a classical performer. Asked to comment on their munificent wages, Pavarotti matter-of-factly responded, "We make the money we deserve." Although Dodger Stadium was, aesthetically, a long way from the Baths of Caracalla, Rudas's vision was to create a new Rome in the fifty-six thousand seat stadium. At great expense he filled the place with all manner of plastic odds and sods, including rocks, pillars, and statuary, and adding waterfalls and streams to fill any empty spaces. The glitzy result was far more Hollywood than Eternal City, not my cup of tea, for sure. Still, I was invited to direct. I hesitated. Musicality aside, I simply loathed the setup. Plastic pillars instead of real pine trees? Artificial waterfalls and running streams? Nevertheless, the show must go on, and it did, but without me.

Even though some reviewers were sharp enough to comment on the drop in natural elegance and the rise of artificial scenery as well as an increase in forced high jinks the second concert scored an enormous success. The redoubtable Rudas found his groove in Los Angeles and shook off the limitation of waiting four years for the next World Cup Finals. *The Three Tenors* could stand on its own and from that appearance on Tibor Rudas would shepherd the three-tenor franchise into the entertainment stratosphere.

For nearly two decades, from New York to London, from Vienna to São Paulo, from Paris to Beijing (in the Forbidden City, no less), from Tokyo to Seoul, Tibor Rudas presented *The Three Tenors* in amphitheatres and stadiums world-wide for a grand total of thirty-three appearances. And, whether true or not, the singers received their "set" fee, each time they appeared together. You do the math. For a long time, I was repeatedly asked to direct, each time I politely said no. Many friends told me I was making a big mistake but I couldn't do it, and I haven't regretted my decision. Rome had been exceptional. I knew the show never would be as good again. Nothing could match or equal the success of that initial concert. Nothing did. Nonetheless, for a good long while, the singing triumvirate remained immensely popular and spawned countless imitators in varying ranges from soprano to baritone.

As for the original threesome, by 2003 their performances had become routine rather than original. The same banter, the same jokes, the same stories, and the music itself remained more or less the same. Here and there they'd come up with something different. When Frank Sinatra attended the Los Angeles performance, C, D, and P sang "My Way" in a touching tribute to "Ol' Blue Eyes", a charming moment, but only a moment. Basically, the shows were repeats and often under-rehearsed. A million dollars or not, the participants were phoning it in and eventually went on automatic pilot. Even so, they continued to roll merrily along until the public no longer showed up. The joyride had ended. To be fair, whatever else is said, in its heyday *The Three Tenors* touched millions, and turned

Conductor
Zubin Mehta
joins The
Three
Musketeers

many of them on to classical music—and it's still going. In June of 2023, St Paul's Cathedral in Rome presented a Three Tenors Concert. The tenors? Emil Alekperov, Carlo Napoletani, and Gian Carlo Polizzy who may be fine singers but are hardly household names. Whatever else, *The Three Tenors* remains a genuine marvel.

As a result of my own single brush with that musical meteor, even I had a rather astounding personal experience. A few months after the Rome spectacle, I received a phone call from a gentleman who introduced himself as Frank Zappa's Production Assistant. Mr Zappa, I was informed, wanted to meet with me. Frank Zappa wanted to meet with me? I knew of the guitar-playing jazz, rock/pop idol by reputation. Who didn't? He and his band, The Mothers of Invention, were a headlines constant. Why would such a mega pop star want to talk to me? My curiosity piqued, I agreed to a luncheon date. Meeting Frank Zappa turned out to be quite a jolt. He was the untidiest man I'd ever seen. Wild, seemingly unwashed, black hair surrounded his black mustachioed-goateed face, and his piercing black eyes looked right through you. Although his dress, tee shirt, and distressed jeans, politely might have been termed casual, scruffy was a better fit. Overall, he presented a grungy picture. Zappa got right to the point. "That *Three Tenors* was a hell of a show, very impressive. Started me thinking. I'm envisioning a psychedelic sound and light show for me and my band similar to, but kind of different from *The Three Tenors*. What I want to know is, would you be interested in working with me?" Having declared his lopsided intention and without waiting for my answer, Zappa's ideas poured forth like lava from a volcano. "We'll have to find a venue sort of like the Baths of Caracalla ... but not the Baths of Caracalla, of course, it's been done. There's the Colosseum in Rome, the Acropolis in Athens, the Taj Mahal in India ..." Stopping short of proposing a crater on the moon, Zappa concluded with, "We have to think big; don't you agree?" Indeed, I thought to myself, why not think big? I found myself totally confused but rather intrigued as to where Zappa's zany ideas might lead. Still, I was out of my depths. My work was with the world's foremost conductors and soloists in sedate concert halls and opera houses. What could I bring to a psychedelic free-for-all in the Taj Mahal? I advised Zappa that I probably wasn't the best choice to direct a rock production. "I'm a classically trained musician", I explained. "What's the big deal? I'm a trained musician, too!" hollered Zappa, who then launched into a litany of credits. Improbably, they were impressive. Zappa claimed as a mentor, Edgar Varèse, the French-born American composer known as the Father of Electronic Music, and announced that he, Zappa, had personally rescored and recorded rock versions of Mozart's *Symphony No. 40* and Holst's *The Planets*. Moreover, he'd collaborated with Zubin Mehta and the Los Angeles Philharmonic; Kent Nagano and the London Symphony Orchestra had recorded two of his CDs, and Pierre Boulez and the Ensemble intercontemporain (EIC) had performed his music in Paris. "Why don't you speak to Zubin and Kent and Pierre and hear first-hand how much they learned from working with me? And, by the way, you should speak to the members of the London Royal Philharmonic Orchestra, too. They played the soundtrack for my *200 Motels* film." The second I heard the words *"200 Motels"*, something clicked. In case you don't remember Zappa's cinematic opus, let me enlighten you.

200 Motels is a satirical rock opera, juxtaposing elaborate dance sequences with scenes of various sexual encounters, both straight and gay, that members of the band experienced on their road trips. Tony Palmer, my erstwhile office-mate, directed the film version and what transpired became the stuff of legend. I won't burden you with details, suffice it to say that after the live show was banned on obscenity grounds from the Royal Albert Hall, Tony arranged to have *200 Motels* remounted and filmed at Pinewood Studios. In the process, production costs exploded and, predictably, *200 Motels* flopped. When I gently reminded Zappa of his film's fate, he quickly assured me that what he had in mind now was on a "totally different planet" from *200 Motels*. Which planet that might be made me a little apprehensive but I agreed to "think about it". Suggesting that we take time to seriously consider how to proceed, I assured him I'd don my thinking cap and would have a few ideas to share at our next meeting. We shook hands and said goodbye.

I did give his galactic project some thought and prepared a few notes for our future get together. It never happened. Early in 1991 Frank Zappa was diagnosed with advanced prostate cancer. Realizing that he'd never have the strength for his super concert, he dropped his plan. Within two years, he was gone. Would I have collaborated with Zappa had he not been stricken? Put it this way, I might have considered it. One thing's for sure, I would not have had the possibility of doing it had it not been for *The Three Tenors* concert. Without doubt, my brief encounter with Frank Zappa occurred only because of my association with C, D, and P.

Over the years, I continued to work, individually, with the three tenors and, in the main, got along with all of them. Regarding the quality of their singing, Carreras possessed a sweet lyrical voice which, alas, never quite returned to its original shimmer. Domingo was blessed with an amazing, heroic, dramatic voice and fully realized his potential. Pavarotti was blessed, too, with the voice of a god. As for their personas, Carreras was a true gentleman. Whenever and wherever I and my crew were working with him, at the end of every performance he would come from the stage door to the TV truck to personally thank us. He did it every time. Domingo did it many times, too. Pavarotti? Never. Pavarotti's thank you came from hearing him sing.

A final thought on *The Three Tenors*. Deservedly or not, I've had to live with the consequences of my contribution to that epic evening in Rome, a subject which, after all these years inevitably rears its controversial head. To illustrate: I've collaborated on numerous concerts and operas with conductor Franz Welser-Möst, former director of the Vienna State Opera and, presently, music director of the Cleveland Symphony Orchestra. On one of those occasions, we discussed *The Three Tenors*. I admitted that while the Caracalla presentation highlighted my professional life, I remained haunted by varying degrees of regret for aiding and abetting what amounted to the dumbing down of opera. *The Three Tenors* was a distinctive child of its time but so much changed because of that concert. Audiences began to view opera as a sort of circus and arias became high-wire acts. Circus or opera, each discipline has its own merits and a little interchange is always acceptable. However, thanks to the combined forces of the three tenors, belting popular tunes along with operatic arias became an accepted practice and the line between classical music and pop/rock was bent out of shape, permanently.

In his 2021 autobiography, *From Silence: Finding Calm in a Dissonant World* (pub: Clearview), Franz Welser-Möst quoted my final assessment of the first Three Tenors Concert: "We created on that day a monster which could not be tamed. It was a monster and there was no way back." Once more, I plead guilty. In my defence I only can say I had the best of intentions. Then again, so did Dr Frankenstein.

40.

Tremava Tutta Roma

I was directing a gala in Vienna when Andrea Andermann, an Italian actor, author, and producer, phoned one morning, introduced himself, said he had a "very special project", which he wanted to discuss, and asked me to meet with him that afternoon. Ordinarily, I didn't leap into such situations without doing a bit of background checking, but something about this man's enthusiastic approach prompted me to say okay. We met in the Bristol Hotel bar that afternoon and said our hellos, whereupon Andermann immediately got to the point. He'd been obsessed by a dream project for ten years which would soon come to fruition. "I'm doing a live telecast of *Tosca* on location in Rome with each of the acts set in Puccini's original settings. Act I in the church of Sant'Andrea della Valle, Act II in the Palazzo Farnese, and Act III at the Castel Sant'Angelo. And, again according to the libretto, each act will take place at the exact time of day—noon, sunset, and dawn of the following morning. Would you be interested in doing it with me?" Dazzled by his project and eager to find out more I said yes. After a few additional words, we made plans to meet in the Eternal City, shook hands, and wished each other well. I couldn't stop thinking about this project—what a fabulous concoction.

The Vienna Gala ended and all roads led to Rome where I met Andrea in the lobby of my hotel. "Before we do anything else, I want to show you the *Tosca* sites. Are you

Catherine Malfitano and Plácido Domingo
turning up the heat in Rome, *Tosca*, 1992

435

ready to go?" "You bet", I enthused. We went outside and, expecting him to ask the doorman for a taxi, I stopped at the entrance. Andrea continued walking, turned and waved me on. We reached a rack of mopeds and Andrea unlocked one of them along with a pair of safety helmets. He put his helmet on quickly, waited as I fumbled to attach mine, assisted me onto the back of the motor scooter, sat down in front, and before you could say *La Dolce Vita*, we were off. I knew my way around Italy's capital city but this was the first time I'd seen it from a moped. Andrea's zeal was infectious. As we slithered through the crowded streets, he shouted over the traffic roar, pointing out various places of interest until we reached Sant'Andrea.

As we walked around the imposing baroque basilica, Andermann showed me where the action would take place. Then, it was back onto our chariot and over to the Palazzo Farnese, an important high Renaissance building. (When the designer Antonio da Sangallo died, Pope Paul III, a member of the Farnese family, appointed Michelangelo to complete it.) We stood in front of the staircase Tosca ascends to make her entrance into Scarpia's chamber. (When she catches her breath, she sings "Vissi d'Arte".) Next, we were off to the Castel Sant'Angelo on the banks of the Tiber where we climbed to the battlement from which Tosca leaps to her death. All the time we were site-seeing, I'd been caught up in Andrea's enthusiasm. Now, as I stood on the parapet looking down at the river, I couldn't help thinking, "How the hell is he going to pull this off?" We returned to our chariot and zipped down the road to a trattoria overlooking the Tiber. As we sipped our aperitifs, I asked, as casually as I could, "So, how do you envision doing all this?" Andrea smiled. "The point is, Brian, I don't want to simply televise a stage production. I want to visualize *Tosca* in film terms." "What do you mean by film terms?" "Well, basically, I want to create a live spectacle, something that has the look, the quality of a live film not a television relay." "But, Andrea, in practical terms, how do you see it?" "Put it this way, I want to break through the fourth wall of the opera house, and expand the audience of a couple of thousand into a million who'll be watching the action and hearing the music in the actual locations Puccini designated." When I asked who was going to bring all this to fruition, Andrea said RAI, the Italian national TV service, had become involved and he currently was negotiating with Giuseppe Patroni Griffi, a well-regarded Neapolitan stage director, playwright, as well as film maker Vittorio Storaro, a cinematographer who'd worked on films such as *Apocalypse Now* and *The Last Emperor.* Griffi would stage the action, Storaro would handle the cinematography, "… and", said Andrea, "I hope that you will translate everything into a live television film." Wow. This was something really spectacular, really innovative. I'd never heard of such a project before and, to my chagrin, had never thought of anything like it myself. The recording of this event would be incredibly complex and time consuming, but no way could I turn down such a dynamic experience. I had to do it.

On a clear July Saturday in Rome, 1992, with Catherine Malfitano in the title role, Plácido Domingo as Cavaradossi, Ruggero Raimondi as Scarpia, and Zubin Mehta conducting the RAI Orchestra and Chorus, a conglomeration of singers, scene builders, lighting and camera crews, and and all manner of technicians, gathered together and began to make Andrea Andermann's dream project come true. The first "set", Sant'Andrea della Valle, consisted of various built-up levels in the church's nave and apse to provide raised areas for intimate scenes between Tosca and Cavaradossi. Wider space had been created where the processional would take place and Scarpia would enter. Everywhere you looked scaffolding, rigged with lights, loomed and included huge spotlights such as are used in major cinema shoots. Question: Where was the orchestra? Answer: The orchestra and the chorus were in the RAI studios a good three kilometres from the church. In order to synchronize the two components, the sound would be relayed through loudspeakers hidden away in each of the three locations. Along with the speakers, television monitors also were concealed in various sections of the church, the palace, and the castle. Monitors would relay Zubin Mehta's baton to the singers. The soloists, themselves, would be wired with body mikes either in their hair or in their costumes. If the TV monitors somehow failed, assistant conductors, relaying Mehta's beat to the singers, were positioned in each location. Mehta, himself, would hear the singers through headphones. In all, there were three mobile control trucks—one for each of the location sites, and twenty-seven cameras, including several steady handheld ones. These were mounted on the camera operator's body in such a way that the operator could follow the action from one situation to the next and keep everything fluid. If it sounds complicated, you may take my word, it was.

My main objective was visual "fluidity", I didn't want to shoot any of the action as if it were coming from a stationary camera at the back of the auditorium, that is, shooting on a ninety-degree axis. I wanted the cameras to have the flexibility to cover one hundred eighty degrees. For example, if you're shooting ninety degrees on an apple, you're shooting one half of it. If you're shooting one hundred eighty degrees, you're shooting all around it, circling, circling. I believed this motion would create something filmic and alive. Adding to the technical legerdemain,

Andermann wanted each act performed in the correct time sequence specified in the libretto. Act I began at 11 a.m., Act II at 9 p.m., and Act III at 6 a.m. the next morning. The first two acts were interior locations thus the weather was inconsequential. But Act III takes place outside and weather definitely mattered. "Give us the sun" became our rallying cry.

Before the live transmissions, we had two run-throughs, not only as a safeguard, but also because of the complexity in synchronizing vision and sound over the three kilometres between the orchestra and the soloists. Everything went well and we were ready for the live transmissions. Act I began and proceeded smoothly and then the unexpected happened. Just before her entrance, Tosca called to Cavaradossi from offstage. Domingo raced over to greet her and bring her into the church. He'd navigated easily through the various structures we'd erected but halfway to his goal, Domingo tripped and fell on his rump. Unhurt, he picked himself up. No big deal, we would edit out the pratfall later. One potential hazard did hang over the production, the Act III finale. Not only were we concerned about the weather, we had qualms about Tosca's leap from the Castel Sant'Angelo tower into the Tiber. A huge basket had been suspended over the side of the battlement which hung two meters below the parapet. Malfitano had to run up a set of steps and then, with her final cry of "O Scarpia, avanti a Dio!" hurl herself over the parapet and into the river aka the basket. We made everything as safe as possible. Still, I have to give Malfitano great credit. With nerves of steel, she ran up those steps and hurled herself over the parapet for the two run-throughs and the actual performance. Any miscalculation and she'd have been singing Tosca with a heavenly choir.

Chatting with Plácido

The morning of the live transmission, everyone gathered on the Castel Sant'Angelo battlements. We watched as a glorious dawn spread over the Vatican. The weather had cooperated, now only Tosca's leap concerned us. All went smoothly, from the opening song of the shepherd boy to the moment before Tosca's leap. Malfitano rose from beside Cavaradossi's corpse, ran to the steps, looked back at the pursuing soldiers, turned, raced up the steps, cried out her last words, threw her arms open, and leapt over the wall executing a perfect slam dunk into the basket. An incredible shot for a fantastic climax. (With all the precautions taken on set today, I'm not sure this bravura scene would be allowed.)

The reviews for *Tosca* were as spectacular as the actual programme which was shown all over the world. Andrea Andermann realized his dream and, in the process, made himself a very famous man. He hoped to follow *Tosca in Rome* with *Traviata in Paris*. The set-up would be similar: first act in a private residence, the second act, scene 1 in a country home, scene 2 in the salon of a 7th arrondissement mansion, and the third act in an attic atop a house on the Isle Saint-Louis. It took him another eight years to create that production and, though asked, I chose not to be a part of it. I wasn't as enthusiastic about the *Traviata* project as I had been for the *Tosca*. For me the settings could not equal the grandeur and magnificence of the Roman locations. Andermann went ahead and the production scored in ratings and revenue. Pleased, he made plans to do yet another film, this time *Rigoletto* in Mantua. I admired what Andermann was doing but no longer wanted to be involved.

In *The Innocents Abroad,* Mark Twain wrote, "From the dome of St Peter's one can see every notable object in Rome ... a panorama that is varied, extensive, beautiful to the eye, and more illustrious in history than any other in Europe." Twain was right, the Eternal City stands alone. I did not need to repeat myself.

41.

An Exception to the Rule

Dealing with divas is not for sissies has been established. That being said, I've been gratified to serve artists who, to varying degrees, not only valued my suggestions but utilized them. Among others, Birgit Nilsson did it with Elektra, Marilyn Horne did it with Isabella, and Hildegard Behrens with Brünnhilde. Hildegard, however, had been trained as a lawyer and her legal mind sometimes got in the way of going with the flow. Whenever I said, "Catch the light", she'd answer, "Why?" and then, begrudgingly, comply. Thus, I cannot count Hildegard as a complete convert but she was a powerful Brünnhilde, nonetheless. So, too, was Gwyneth Jones, Bayreuth's Centennial Brünnhilde. Unlike Hildegard, Gwyneth welcomed counsel. Of all those performers with whom I shared my thoughts and experience, there is one who not only "got it", but actually went on to expand and incorporate it into her own set of procedure.

About to appear as Desdemona in a new Elijah Moshinsky production of *Otello* at the Met, a rising young soprano asked to speak privately with me during taping sessions. I invited her to come to my office. After thanking me for my time, she explained that she was quite concerned about her appearance on the TV screen. She'd given birth to her second daughter a few weeks before and now suffered the attendant after-birth woes of excess weight, lack of sleep, and keeping her energy up. All of which she informed me and at the end of which she pleaded with

Renée Fleming as the Marschallin in
Der Rosenkavalier, Royal Opera House,
Covent Garden, London, 2016

me. "Please, Brian, will you show me the rehearsal tape? I want to work on everything and get it right for the opening." Accordingly, I ran selections for her on the VHS machine. I cannot tell you how intently she watched that screen, nothing escaped her. She observed every facial reaction and every movement of her body, questioning as she watched. "I'm bloated, Brian. My face is puffy. I'm carrying too much weight and I'll come across as clumsy. What do I do?" "All you have to do, is think in terms of the TV screen", I advised. "Find the light and then angle your face and your body to it." We went over the basics together, finding those angles, tilting the head, twisting the body one way or another, all depending on where the light fell. As I spoke, she continued to scrutinize the tape, absorbing and processing everything. We finished, she thanked me, and left. I really felt that I'd helped her. On opening night, she created a lovely Desdemona. She'd observed, critiqued, and learned how to do things right, right for her, not anyone else. Two years later, she appeared as a breathtaking Manon which, to my way of thinking, took opera to another level. Today, some thirty years on, Renée Fleming is internationally renowned, still singing, still learning, and coming into her own as an author and administrator.

Renée Fleming's story is a good example of how-not-to-be-a-diva and yet, become one. Aptly nicknamed "the-diva-next-door", her relaxed, natural demeanour is suited to that epithet; she's far more friendly than frosty. Although equipped with the big three components of stardom—looks, brains, and talent—she did not spring forth fully-formed. A small-town girl with a big-time voice, she had to hone her persona as well as her art. Several years after she won the prestigious Richard Tucker Award, she hired a publicist who immediately counselled her on her image, advising her to have her hair styled, and to develop a new wardrobe. (Full disclosure: that same publicist wrote the Introduction to this book.) Renée's formal studies included winning scholarships from the Eastman School of Music and The Juilliard School, as well as a Fulbright to study in Germany. And of course, she has that God-given voice.

Both Renée's parents were music teachers in Rochester, New York. Her grandparents had come from Czechoslovakia and those Slavic roots enabled her to sing in perfect Czech and Russian. She's an accomplished jazz artist, too. While still studying, she performed in nightclubs to earn tuition money. At one point, she turned down a request from jazz saxophonist Illinois Jacquet, to tour with his group of musicians and stuck to her studies. Yet, along the classical way, she managed to indulge her love for all musical theatre, eventually starring in *Carousel* on Broadway and *The Light in the Piazza* in London's West End and Los Angeles. Renée also became the first classical singer to perform at the Super Bowl and in December of 2023 received a Kennedy Center Honor for lifetime achievement.

I followed Fleming's career with great interest. For me, the defining moment occurred when Renée sang Strauss's *Four Last Songs* at Carnegie Hall's Opening Night Gala in 2004. I was fortunate to direct that telecast. Quite frankly, I went barmy over her sumptuous singing of Strauss's soaring music. Musically speaking, Fleming and Strauss were made for each other. I made up my mind, then, that I would move heaven and earth to record as many Fleming/Strauss concerts as I could, especially the operas—*Rosenkavalier, Arabella, Ariadne auf Naxos*, and *Capriccio*. When I presented my idea to Renée, she agreed.

Our collaboration began with a *Rosenkavalier* at the 2009 Baden-Baden Easter Festival with Christian Thielemann conducting. A few years later, in 2012, Thielemann conducted *Ariadne auf Naxos* at the Baden-Baden Festival. In 2013, we recorded *Capriccio* at the Vienna State Opera with conductor Christoph Eschenbach, and, in 2014, at the Salzburg Easter Festival with Thielemann conducting, Renée sang *Arabella*. Thus, at the peak of her singing, Renée's interpretations became available in four DVDs, a legacy made possible through video technology.

Renée continues to augment her legacy. She penned her own story, *The Inner Voice: The Making of a Singer*, in which she shared her personal process of learning to sing and the challenges of building her career. Most recently, she created and edited *Music and Mind: Harnessing the Arts for Health and Wellness*, a compilation of essays examining how music and performance affects and influences the brain. An artistic advisor and consultant at many performing arts companies, she is a World Health Organization Goodwill Ambassador for Arts and Health. I could go on and on but, let's just say, how many opera singers do you know who've been interviewed by the Harvard Business Review? (*HBS Magazine*, March-April 2024.)

Renée Fleming is one of an elite few female singers who've gone beyond mere warbling. Mary Garden, the Scotch-American superstar in the early decades of the twentieth century, probably is the most well-known. Garden both sang for and ran the Chicago Opera Association. In the latter role, she was responsible for presenting the world premiere of Prokofiev's *Love for Three Oranges*. Women simply didn't do things like that, then. They really don't do it that much now, but Renée Fleming is doing it. She passionately believes in using her celebrity to benefit and forward humanity and her dedication is unwavering.

Looks, brains, talent, Renée Fleming has it all!

42.

Ave Atque Vale /
California, Here I Come

My employment at the Metropolitan Opera ended in January of 2010, definitely with a bang rather than a whimper. The last assignment, a live international telecast of *Boris Godunov*, had reached the Act I Coronation Scene when, without warning, the audio went dead. I had no sound therefore no control over the transmission. Faced with a bona fide broadcasting disaster, I had to think fast. Generally speaking, I'm either fluent or familiar with most of the languages in which operas are written. However, except for *spasibo*, I am neither fluent nor familiar with Russian. By the grace of God, as part of my preparation for *Boris*, I had learned the Russian text phonetically in order to follow along with a sense of what was happening. When the audio conked out, within a split second I instinctively began to sing the words at the top of my lungs. By lip reading, I stayed in sync with the singers on stage and kept the transmission going. After some seven minutes of caterwauling, the audio returned and my solo ended. At which point the sound truck technicians burst into a generous round of applause. And by heaven I deserved it. Personally, I thought it a fitting finale to my three decades of Met service. I saved the day because I'd remained faithful to my tried-and-true methodology. To wit, no matter what happens always "follow the music and the words". That adherence to my particular style allowed me to leave the Metropolitan Opera on a high note and I remain ever grateful for the privilege of working

The Dorothy Chandler Pavilion, one of the USA's largest performing arts centres, and a cultural anchor in Los Angeles County at that legendary house during golden years of glorious singing and superb productions.

I did not remain opera-houseless for long. Even before my departure from the Met, Lady Luck embraced me yet again. My leave-taking from Lincoln Center coincided with an offer from another American company. Edgar Baitzel, Los Angeles Opera's chief operating officer asked if I'd be interested in doing my thing way out west. My thought? Why not? I flew to Los Angeles for my first visit. What a geographical challenge that city is, I never did figure it out, although I did manage to learn my way around the Dorothy Chandler Pavilion and the Disney Concert Hall. Still, Los Angeles is a long way from being *die Stadt meiner Träume*—i.e., a pleasant enough place to work but not somewhere I could settle down, permanently.

At our initial meeting, Edgar Baitzel offered me two works to document, a new production of Berlioz's *The Damnation of Faust*, and *Nicholas and Alexandra* by Deborah Drattell, a world premiere commissioned by the company. The Berlioz was under the direction of Achim Freyer, a German artist/stage designer/director who trained with Brecht and thereby enjoyed an exalted reputation. I'd met Freyer, briefly, in the early seventies during my BBC days when, with a taping in the offing, the Stuttgart Opera invited me to come and view Freyer's production of *Der Freischütz*. I flew to Stuttgart to check out the potential. Upon entering the opera house, I came face to face with a most bizarre scene. Freyer had set up a display in the foyer as a harbinger of the opera's woodlands setting. The tableau consisted of clumps of tree trunks, boulders, giant mushrooms and flowers, all clustered together. I drew closer and caught sight of a handful of assorted youngsters, dressed in bunny rabbit costumes, hopping around inside the artificial glen. Apparently, this bucolic balderdash was meant to set the tone for the entire production. Well, a tone definitely was set for me, one which impelled me out of the whole deal. I declined the job explaining I didn't think I could do the production justice. Now, here I was in Los Angeles making my way in a Met-less world and again presented with a project about which I had serious misgivings. I had doubts about *Damnation*, too. I particularly questioned Freyer's saddling the cast with huge headpieces and masks, about as anti-singing as you can get. Still, I had agreed to work with the LA Opera. So into the breach I went and taped the bobble-headed production as best I could.

When the *Damnation* recording finished, I then tackled *Nicholas and Alexandra*, a production one critic deemed "the biggest tsarist disaster of all time". I did not disagree. Mind you, it's not that I have anything against new works. As much as I love Wagner, Verdi, Mozart, Puccini, Strauss, et al., beginning with Britten and *Owen Wingrave*, I've been pleased to work with contemporary composers, including Carlisle Floyd, Aribert Reimann, Wolfgang Rihm, John Corigliano, Tan Dun, Mark Adamo, and Hans Werner Henze. I've always supported current composers and have given them the same consideration and care as I did to the "old boys".

On the subject of televising new operas, beginning with *Willie Stark* I learned from experience that finding someone to pay for a TV premiere of a new work poses a Herculean challenge to any opera company. For example, the Met Opera's Sybil Harrington would underwrite *Aida* at the drop of a hat and throw in her own for any opera Franco Zeffirelli cared to produce. Why? She loved *Aida;* and, apropos Zeffirelli, she once told me that whatever Franco wanted, he got; her check for him was ever at the ready. That's the way most sponsors react to re-quests—they give to what or to whom they like and tend to be trepidatious of works that are outside their comfort zone. A good example of "to-air-or-not-to-air" occurred in 1992 when the Met commissioned Philip Glass to compose an opera commemorating the 500th Anniversary of Columbus's discovery of America. The Met had poured oceans of money into the production and, hoping that a donor eventually would subsidize a telecast, asked me to prepare the video. I looked over Glass's *The Voyage* and, intrigued by the English, Spanish, and Latin libretto as well as the score, agreed to do it. Please note that I was *asked*, not *contracted* to do it, which meant I'd be working on spec. Institutions only contracted you when the project was funded. But that was fine with me. By choice, I had become a free-lancer after I left the BBC. I didn't want to be on staff at the Met or anywhere else and continued to sign a contract for every production I videoed. Over the next two months I prepared *The Voyage*, from laying out the score on the piano to recording a performance. The Met attempted to interest sponsors in the finished product but no one would pick up the tab. In its premiere season, Philip Glass's *The Voyage* was performed six times on the Met stage and never again. As far as my monetary reward for preparing it, I received none. No contract meant no cash. But, that's all part of the job—win a few, lose a few.

Whatever their production merits, neither *Nicholas and Alexandra* nor *The Damnation of Faust* ever saw the light of a TV screen. To this day those video recordings remain stowed away in the LA Opera archives, completed, edited, and shunned. Indeed, of the eight or so operas I recorded for the company, only two ever were broadcast, Renée Fleming in *La Traviata* and Plácido Domingo in *Il*

Postino, a new work by Mexican composer Daniel Catán. (In December of 2023, Catán's melodious and fanciful *La Florenzia en el Amazones* became the first Spanish language opera presented by the Metropolitan Opera.)

When I began working with the LA Opera, I'd been made aware of a "hidden agenda" regarding my hiring. Ostensibly, LA wanted me to tape new productions. Specifically, LA Opera longed to present and record a certain quartet of German operas and thus become a viable contender in the heavyweight arena of *Ring* videos. One afternoon as I sat in the office of LA's General Manager, Plácido Domingo, he let the cat out of the bag. "You've done the *Ring* in Bayreuth and at the Metropolitan, Brian, and now you're going to do it here!" My ears perked up as Domingo continued. "James Conlon will conduct and Achim Freyer will direct. He'll stage it, design it, do the lighting and the costumes, everything, himself. By the way, you should know that Freyer requested you." "I don't think I'm the right person to direct this *Ring*", I quickly responded. "What does that mean?" asked Domingo. I fumbled for an honest answer and came up with, "I'm not sure I'm on the same wave length as Mr Freyer." My wave length was brushed aside.

Pre-production work began on the *Ring* and everything that I feared would happen, happened. Just as he'd covered the heads of *The Damnation of Faust* cast, Freyer outfitted Wotan and his cohorts in overpowering masks. Yes, the masks had eye slits and an opening over the mouth, but why make singers spend seventeen hours straining to be heard and not being seen? Ludicrous. Predictably, the reviews vindicated my views. Management soon realized that the cost of filming this *Ring* could, and likely would bankrupt the company. The project was abandoned.

Lest I sound too negative, I had some good times in Los Angeles not only with the opera company but, also, with the LA Philharmonic. In 2009, I taped the orchestra's new music director, Gustavo Dudamel, conducting his opening concert, Mahler's *Symphony No. 1*. Dudamel, an energetic young Venezuelan, followed the Bernstein jump-up-and-down-on-the-podium school of conducting and quickly ingratiated himself with LA audiences. A year later I returned to video his second opening concert and two productions (Handel's *Tamerlano* and Massenet's *Thaïs*) for the LA Opera. By this time, I had reached yet another "been there, done that" milestone and decided to call it a day. I bade farewell to Los Angeles and headed eastward, making video whistle-stops along the way. One highlight, a concert of Mahler's *Seventh* with Boulez conducting the Chicago Symphony, brought me back to the "City of the Big Shoulders". I'd been there when Georg Solti commanded the podium and still have great fondness for Chicago and its excellent orchestra.

Back in Europe, I continued to pick up assignments here and there, one notable opportunity came from Jonas Kaufmann. I'd met Jonas when he sang the Italian Tenor in Renée Fleming's recording of *Der Rosenkavalier* in 2009. Since that time, he'd crashed through the Pavarotti-Domingo-Carreras ceiling and had taken his place among the premier tenors of the day. His repertoire encompassed an amazing breadth of roles from lyric and spinto to dramatic. In June of 2015, Jonas planned to sing an evening of Puccini arias at La Scala, and asked me to direct. I did and had a ball. Among other adventures, I went to the Puccini Museum in Lucca and found rare original footage of Puccini himself at home. The museum kindly let me use clips of the composer playing the piano, walking in his garden, and sailing his boat all of which were incorporated into Kaufmann's programme. Between the visuals and Kaufmann's singing, the audience sat mesmerized. Some months later I recorded Kaufmann's *Cavalleria Rusticana* and *Pagliacci* at Salzburg's 2015 Easter Festival. Singing both leading roles in those two operas on the same evening was a feat accomplished by only one other tenor of the day, Plácido Domingo. While I enjoyed these assignments, I no longer felt the need to "be there or do that". Pressure off, I had more time to take a deeper look at where I'd been and catch up with old friends. And then, a fortuitous encounter set me on my present path.

I always kept in touch with Valerie Solti, Sir Georg's widow, either at her home in London or as guest at her villa in Castiglione della Pescaia in Southern Italy. We originally met in Munich in 1969 when Solti invited me to direct a Bartók concert for ZDF, the second German television channel. Thereafter, Valerie and I maintained a friendship that lasted fifty years. Formerly, a prominent BBC television presenter, in 1964, Valerie had been sent to interview Solti in his hotel room. From all reports, a classic *coup de foudre* occurred. Valerie, married at the time, divorced her husband, wed Solti and they were together until his death in 1997. An energetic patron of the arts, Valerie established the Solti Foundation for young musicians and kept a close eye on it. The two of us often got together in London and talked at great length about Georg and his brilliant career. Valerie expressed regret that, although her husband had penned his memoirs, his accomplishments had not been fully explored and chronicled. "I'm sad," she said, "I'm the only one who knows the whole story and if I don't do something, so much will be lost." "Well then, do something!" I proposed. We talked more about the prospect and when we parted, she said, "You know, Brian, if anyone should be writing his own story it's you! How about this? I'll write Georg's, if you'll write yours." I laughed and answered, "It's a deal." I didn't give it too much thought until the pandemic hit the world and all life, musical and otherwise, suddenly went on hold. With unaccustomed time on my hands, I took Valerie's advice and began to fashion my own story. Sadly, before Valerie was able to realize her part of our bargain, her health declined exponentially and she died at home in London in March 2021.

The formal end to my career turned out to be something of a double header and took place in October and December of 2017. For some time, Plácido Domingo had been alternating his singing roles with appearances on the podium. He'd been engaged to conduct *Don Giovanni* in the Estates Theatre, the very theatre where the opera premiered, and asked me to direct the video. I didn't hesitate. To return to my beloved Prague and to work in that historic theatre, what a fitting way to end my career. Who could ask for anything more?

And then, just when I thought I was out, they pulled me back in. Following the *Don Giovanni* recording, Jonas Kaufmann asked me to direct *Andrea Chénier* at the Bavarian State Opera; yet another offer I could not resist. Hence, the conclusion to my life's work as a director came full-circle not in Prague but in Munich where it all began fifty years before.

Anja Harteros as Maddalena, Jonas Kaufmann as Andrea Chénier
at the Bavarian State Opera, Munich, 2017. My farewell to opera

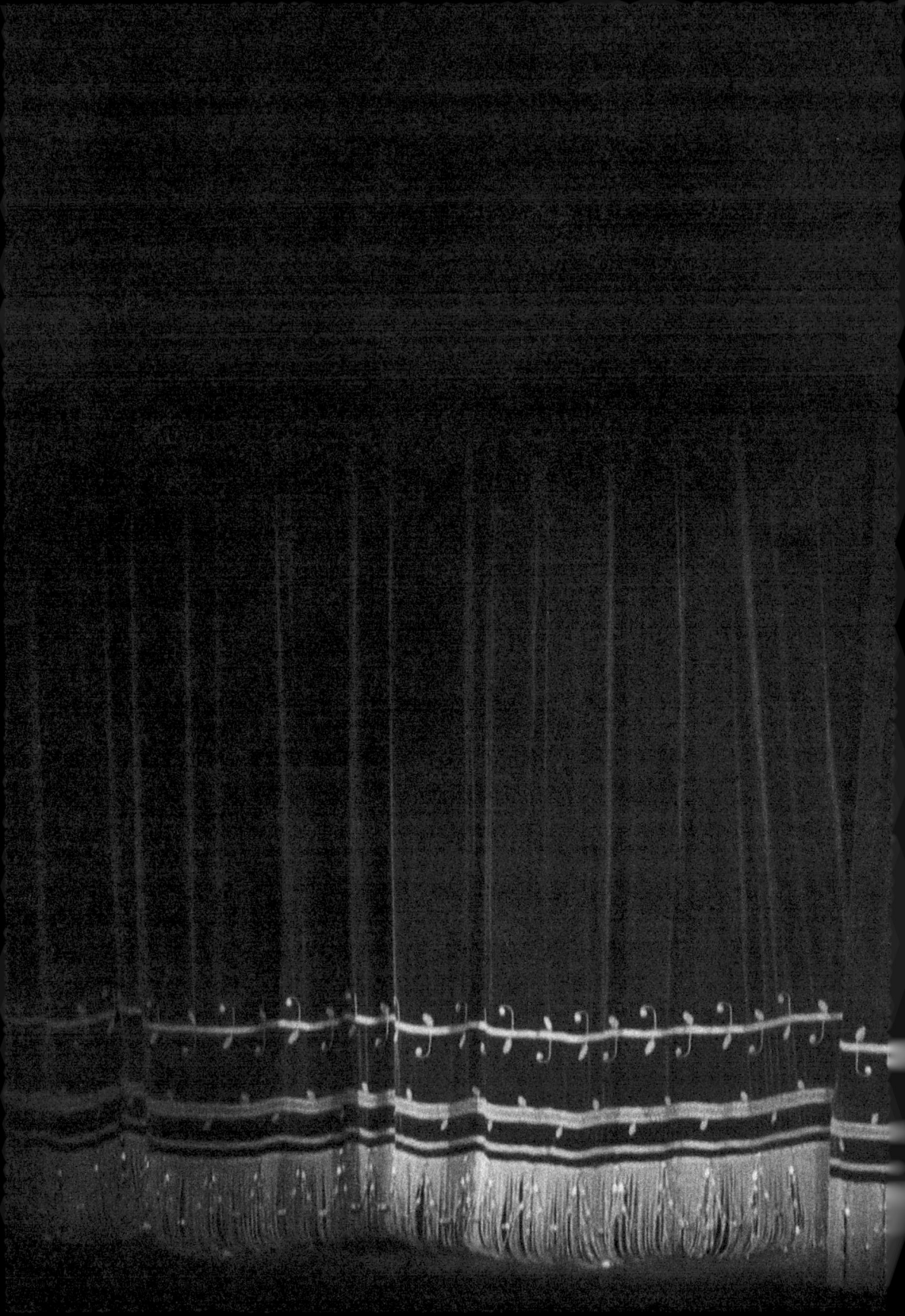

CURTAIN CALLS

43.
Et Alia

Statistics say that by the age of 72, the average person meets approximately 80,000 people in his/her lifetime. Further, that same average person winds up actually knowing some 600 persons. Considering the nature of my work, the extent of my travels, as well as the number of years I've been around, I can't even imagine what my numbers might be. And while I've done my utmost to include the most relevant personages in this book, I have a surfeit of significant others. I don't want to present a "laundry list", but at the same time, I cannot conclude my memoirs without acknowledging a few more associates and colleagues who have enriched and influenced my life. I'll begin with Van Cliburn, a musician whom I greatly admired and very much wanted to record.

In April of 1958, with the Cold War freezing relationships between Russia and the United States, a musical miracle occurred in Moscow. Van Cliburn, a 23-year-old, 6'4" pianist from Texas, won the inaugural International Tchaikovsky Piano Competition, a contest which had been specifically created to display the Soviet Union's cultural superiority. The gangly American played Tchaikovsky's *Piano Concerto No. 1* and Rachmaninov's *Piano Concerto No. 3* and received an eight-minute standing ovation. An engaging fellow, Cliburn became an international celebrity, even the Russians adored him. He actually maintained a friendship with the Soviet leader, Nikita Khrushchev, for many years. Here was a young man, just a couple of years older than I, and he'd conquered the world. Van Cliburn became an idol of mine, someone I wanted very much to meet. It took a while, but it did happen. Moreover, opera proved to be the catalyst for our eventual meeting.

Cliburn was an opera fanatic, he once commented that he hated touring because it robbed him of opportunities to attend opera performances. When in New York, he always went to the Metropolitan Opera House, and when not there in person, faithfully watched the opera relays I did for PBS. He told friends how much he admired my work. I knew nothing of this. Then, in 1993, long after his retirement in 1978, Cliburn visited New York. While in the city he heard that I was editing at the Nexus Studio on West 41st Street. Just like that, he took a cab to the studio, went to the reception desk, and asked to see me. Did he have an appointment, the receptionist asked? "No," replied the pianist, "I only want to say hello and compliment Mr Large on his PBS transmissions." Apprised of his presence, I was knocked for a loop and rushed over to the front desk. We met and he couldn't have been more enthusiastic about my work which, he said, gave him "great pleasure". I was equally effusive about listening to his recordings. Nonplussed at his sudden appearance, but "on the job", I invited him to watch me do some editing which he eagerly accepted. By the end of the session, I'd made up my mind to grab this God-given opportunity to do something I'd dreamed of doing but never thought possible. "You've paid me such an enormous compliment by coming here", I said to Cliburn. "I'd like to do something special for you in return. Could you ... would you... consider doing a video remake of any of your previous recordings? We could get a location, orchestra, or conductor of your choice just to document you with modern technical means." He looked at me somewhat quizzically, and then said, "You know, that's an interesting idea, Brian. Let's think about it and stay in touch. I'll get back to you." He took my phone number. What a coup this would be. I really got excited at the thought of recording him. A couple of weeks later, he called. "Brian, I can't thank you enough for the offer. I was so moved that you wanted to work with me and I really would like to do it, but I'm afraid it's too late. I can't do it. I don't have the nerve and I don't have the facility to bring my playing back to life. But thanks so much for thinking of me. I'm very grateful." I, of course, was crushed, but fully understood his decision. Out of practice for so long, he'd have had to spend long hours trying to get back in "fighting" form. Basically, it was too much to ask of anyone but I still can't help wondering what it might have been like to record him. For me, Van Cliburn always will be, "the one that got away".

Now, I'll continue with conductors and singers, the ones who didn't get away.

Part musical virtuoso, part spectacular showman, *Leopold Stokowski* brought pizzazz to the podium. Like everyone else, I knew of Stokowski because he conducted the soundtrack of Walt Disney's *Fantasia* (1941). He also appeared in the film and through the magic of cinema technology appeared to shake hands with Mickey Mouse. That quick clasp made him the most famous conductor of his day. Born in London to an Irish mother and Polish father, he'd been an organist and pianist before he took up the baton. In 1905, he emigrated to the United States, where he became a naturalized citizen. Engaged to conduct the Cincinnati Symphony Orchestra, he left after a few years to take over the Philadelphia Orchestra and turned that slightly under the radar group into one of the world's premiere musical ensembles. Our paths crossed when, about to turn ninety, he returned to England to conduct the London Symphony Orchestra in a series of concerts. BBC2 assigned me to direct two of them and I began my preparations. Among Stokowski's plenteous accomplishments, he arranged his own versions of classical works, such as transcribing Bach's organ pieces for full orchestra and reorchestrating Tchaikovsky ballets into suites. Indeed, one of the London concerts featured both the Bach and ballet works. Unfortunately, the LSO library only had the original scores and I couldn't fully research and prepare without seeing Stokowski's arrangements. When he arrived in London, I received his versions and crammed my brain with his notes. The manner in which he transcribed the music while honouring the source, provided insight into his musicality. Another Stokowski innovation actually transformed the layout of the symphony orchestra as we know it. After much consideration, he changed the Philadelphia Orchestra's seating plan by switching the violins to the left and the cellos and double basses to the right, an alteration that became standard. Along with re-working scores and flipping the orchestra seating, Stokowski stopped using a baton and adopted a "free hand conducting style". Sometimes his arms were outstretched one hundred eighty degrees on each side, sometimes he stuck them straight out at ninety degrees. Lifting his right hand high above his head and holding it there, he'd drop the left hand almost to his waist, and thus positioned, limned the music with his fingers, shaping the whole into a shimmering aural rainbow. Totally unorthodox, but oh, the sumptuous sounds he elicited. Watching Leopold Stokowski conduct provided me with a lasting memory. Just a memory, though, I never met the man. He did no socializing during the BBC tapings and I only viewed him on the TV monitor.

Alas, I was denied the pleasure of shaking the hand that shook the hand of Mickey Mouse.

I didn't hear anything like the Stokowski sound until years later when I worked with *Pierre Boulez*. Boulez, whom I've mentioned in connection with the Bayreuth *Ring,* also conducted sans baton, but his style was more mathematical than Stokowski's lyrical turns. Boulez's arm movements were limited and creative clarity was expressed through the exceptional independence between his left and right hands. I had the honour of taping Boulez conducting the Vienna Philharmonic in a performance of Bruckner's *Ninth Symphony* from the St Florian Monastery Church in St Florian, Upper Austria. Anton Bruckner had been the organist in St Florian's, had composed his nine symphonies there, and is buried in the Monastery crypt, all of which might have inspired Boulez. It certainly inspired me. So much so that in the slow movement of the *Ninth*, I took the camera down to the crypt and allowed it to linger on Bruckner's tomb. I felt that this sombre yet inspiring shot might touch viewers. It certainly had touched me.

Stokowski's and Boulez's conducting methods, one emotional, the other mathematical, differed, but, whether I was recording Stokowski's sumptuousness or Boulez's clarity, each was a treat to hear and document.

For the BBC2 series, International Concert Hall, I directed three orchestral programmes by visiting orchestras from abroad, beginning with Karel Ančerl and the Czech Philharmonic, followed by Bernard Haitink leading Amsterdam's Concertgebouw Orchestra, and concluding with the Toronto Symphony Orchestra and its young Japanese conductor *Seiji Ozawa*. One knew what to expect from the first two conductors, both established maestros, but the relatively unknown Ozawa completely astounded the audience and viewers. Disarmingly attired in a turtle neck pull-over complete with love beads dangling from around his neck, Ozawa led a white-hot rendition of Tchaikovsky's *Fifth Symphony*. His outlandish garb (maestros still favoured white or black tie) and his fervid conducting took the audience by storm. Ozawa obviously had great gifts and a natural talent for western music. Looking back, I feel safe in calling him the first "hippy" maestro. Not long after that appearance, Ozawa was appointed chief conductor of the San Francisco Symphony Orchestra. Later, he became music director of the sacrosanct Boston Symphony Orchestra, a post he held for twenty-nine years. While I never worked with him in either of those venues, I did have the opportunity to direct a very special concert with Ozawa and the BSO and soloists Yo-Yo Ma, Itzhak Perlman, Rudolf Firkušný, and Frederica von Stade. In December of 1983, Peter Gelb invited me to record a *Dvořák in Prague* concert on the 100th anniversary of the world premiere of the *New World Symphony*. Excited to be back on Czech soil, it was equally gratifying to be a part of a once in a lifetime event. Nine years later, I again met Ozawa on yet another auspicious occasion when the Vienna Philharmonic invited him to conduct the 2002 New Year's Concert. Asked to direct the telecast, I was delighted to see him again. Despite the years, Seiji had kept his boyish demeanour and his boundless energy. This concert marked the first appearance of an Asian conductor at the venerable New Year's event, and, leave it to Seiji, not only did one tradition yield, he scheduled a piece by Austrian composer, Joseph Hellmesberger, Sr, marking the first time a composer other than a Strauss was played. Seiji left the BSO in 2002 to take over as music director of the Vienna State Opera. He began his tenure by conducting Janáček's *Jenůfa* and we again worked together on the *Pique Dame* that featured Mirella Freni, Vladimir Atlantov, and Martha Mödl in her soul-stirring portrayal as the Old Countess. That recording alone, is a fitting testimony to Ozawa's legacy.

As I've previously noted, of all the conductors I came across, *Adrian Boult* had to be the most gentlemanly. He used a very long baton and his hand movements were a model of clarity. At the opposite end of the scale, *Valery Gergiev* employed a toothpick-sized baton and conducted in a herky-jerky manner. Using his fingers as if playing a tremolo on a keyboard, his beat was often unclear. Gergiev never wanted to be regarded as a "Russian" conductor and considered himself a western orchestra leader, a "von Karajan of the Steppes". From the mid-1980s to 2014, he actively conducted in Western Europe, the UK, and the USA. Of late, in the existing tensions between Russia and the West, "the von Karajan of the Steppes" remains close to those Steppes and apart from managing the Kirov Opera, is now the boss of the Bolshoi in Moscow.

Regarding Russian conductors, I preferred the stern-faced *Yevgeny Mravinsky*, principal conductor of the Leningrad Philharmonic Orchestra and a disciplinarian of incredible strength. The antithesis of Gergiev, Mravinsky's traditional three/four beat was so sharp, you could have sliced bread with it. I also admired another exemplary Russian conductor, *Yuri Temirkanov*. He and I recorded the Tchaikovsky 150th Anniversary Gala together in St Petersburg. Temirkanov succeeded Mravinsky as chief conductor of the Leningrad Philharmonic and was director of the Kirov Opera before Gergiev. Temirkanov, like Mravinsky, came from a different world. An old school Soviet thinker, he'd known Prokofiev and Shostakovich personally and himself enjoyed cult status as a champion of works by Glinka, Borodin, Tchaikovsky, and Rachmaninov. Surprisingly shy, Temirkanov was a phenomenal musician and a dedicated artist. Of note, he conducted without baton, a departure from his strictly classic background.

I first encountered the Venetian born *Giuseppe Sinopoli* in Berlin in 1987 when I directed a Deutsche Oper production of Verdi's *Macbeth*. Putting it simply, Sinopoli had the most brilliant intellect of any person I ever met. Considering the 80,000+ I'm supposed to have met, that's quite a statement to make—and I mean it. Trained as a doctor and qualified in medicine, Sinopoli collected ancient Greek relics, became an expert on Greek vases, and published a book documenting his vast collection of Greek ceramics. Crazy as it sounds, he also was an expert in criminal anthropology. Devoted to the music of Mahler, Richard Strauss, and Richard Wagner, Sinopoli's insights into their scores were as brilliant as they were ardent. When he heard that Leonard Bernstein was video recording all of Mahler's Symphonies with the Vienna Philharmonic, he aspired to do the same with the Philharmonia Orchestra in London, and asked me to work with him. I grabbed the opportunity and approached the Philharmonia's manager, David Wheaton. David liked the idea, but the money couldn't be raised and the plan had to be shelved. Sinopoli never realized his dream project. Too bad, it would have been extraordinary. Sinopoli's passion was matched by his intellect and he brought a clarity to Mahler inherited from his studies of Webern, Schönberg, and Berg, the second Viennese School. In 2001, he suffered a heart attack while conducting *Aida* in Berlin and died a few days later at the age of fifty-four. An incalculable loss.

Sinopoli wasn't the only conductor who wanted to record the complete Mahler symphonies. *Lorin Maazel* yearned to do them, too. A child prodigy gifted with perfect pitch and a photographic memory, Maazel was born to American parents in Neuilly-sur-Seine, and raised in Pittsburgh, PA. His conducting career began in Los Angeles when, at the age of eight, he led the University of Idaho Orchestra in Schubert's *Unfinished Symphony.* A virtuoso violinist, he made his instrumental debut at the age of fifteen. In Salzburg, I documented a performance of him playing his own violin concerto and conducting with his bow. Earlier in these pages, I recalled the time Carlos Kleiber balked and walked at Maazel's slow reading of *Tristan.* Indeed, some of Lorin's performances could seem emotionally distant. And yet, he could turn around and offer others that were fiery and intensely personalized. Lorin was a loner and, since I'm one myself, I was drawn to that aspect of his personality. Self-assured, brilliant, fastidious, Maazel's list of accomplishments astonishes. Along with the standard repertoire, his prodigious repertory included Wagner operas, Mahler symphonies, and Strauss tone poems. And don't forget he had them all in his head. Among other appointments, he served as music director of The Cleveland Orchestra, the Pittsburgh Symphony Orchestra, the Orchestre National de France, the Bavarian Radio Symphony Orchestra, the New York Philharmonic, and the Munich Philharmonic. In 1960, Maazel became the first American to conduct at the Bayreuth Festival. Incredibly prolific, he led more than 7,000 concerts and made more than 300 recordings. Simply put, Lorin Maazel was all over the place. We met during his tenure with Munich's Bavarian Radio Symphony Orchestra. Aware of my work, he called and asked if I would collaborate with him and his orchestra on a series of live Sunday morning concerts. I accepted.

We joined forces and continued to work together on many occasions. More than that, Lorin and I became good friends and to my delight, I soon found myself part of his Munich inner circle. I still treasure the memories of those glorious "at home" evenings at the Maazel's where we broke bread together, joked, laughed, and talked about all things musical. Like Lorin, two outstanding members of the group, the Bolshoi Ballet's Maya Plisetskaya and her composer husband, Rodin Shchedrin, maintained a residence in Munich. Maya was special, a prima ballerina assoluta, and a genuine hoot. In hesitant English, Maya talked openly about her Soviet years in the Bolshoi, how she fought to come to terms with the regime and why, unlike many of her colleagues, she never defected to the West in her prime. Outspoken about the standards of present-day dance, she deplored the fact that young performers found it hard to combine technical virtuosity with dramatic acting. Strong, almost tough, and never without a cigarette, but when she danced, she was divine.

When he served as general manager of the Vienna State Opera, a post held in the past by both Mahler and Richard Strauss, Lorin fell under Gustav Mahler's spell and when Sinopoli died, Lorin tried to take on Mahler's complete symphonies with the Philharmonia Orchestra. Lorin had a "twist", he wanted to perform each symphony in a different basilica in a different European city. He called to ask if I wanted to participate. I readily agreed and again contacted the Philharmonia's David Wheaton. The project failed. As had happened previously, money, the root of all projects, couldn't be raised.

At the age of seventy Lorin accepted the music directorship of the New York Philharmonic. And, in the latter part of his career took more time for composing. In 2005, he wrote an opera based on George Orwell's *1984* which had its world premiere at the Royal Opera House. He invited me to direct the DVD of that performance, a singular honour. Indeed, he constantly threw opportunities my way. For example, in 2007 Sheikha Mozah, wife of the Emir of Qatar, decided that her country should have its own symphony orchestra. After a world-wide search, one hundred musicians and their families were brought to Doha to form the Qatar Philharmonic. Maazel conducted the inaugural concert in October 2008 and insisted that I accompany him and record the performance. Thus, I had the unique opportunity to visit a new part of the world and to discover a new culture as well as new music. Lorin turned those young musicians into an orchestra of international standing and gave me the privilege of recording a historic event. Little wonder that I so prized our friendship. For me, Munich was never the same after Lorin's death in 2014. And when Plisetskaya passed a year later, I knew it was time to hang up my hat and move on.

I often worked with *Claudio Abbado*. Abbado, a fine musician, wanted to appear easy going and always wore a "genial" mask. My guess is he needed to cover up a basic insecurity. He didn't trust others easily; everyone was suspect and out to make him feel less great than he wanted to be. Nevertheless, he could get everything into motion and did some of his best work in the operatic canon at La Scala and the Vienna State Opera. Like Sinopoli and Maazel, Abbado sought to document Mahler's entire symphonic oeuvre but only recorded a handful with different orchestras—the Chicago Symphony Orchestra, the Berliner Philharmoniker, the Vienna Philharmonic, and the Lucerne Festival Orchestra.

Sinopoli, Maazel, Abbado all tried their best but, in the end, the only conductor who could charm the money out of the backers' pockets and make the Mahler project a reality was Leonard Bernstein. And, while Georg Solti and his Chicago Symphony Orchestra did document a complete audio account, Bernstein's recording with the Vienna Philharmonic remains the one and only video version of the entire Mahler cycle.

An Austrian aristocrat with an impressive lineage, *Nikolaus Harnoncourt*, a cellist turned conductor, was obsessed with the need to create historically correct performances. His legendary attention to detail included the use of period instruments and extreme tempi which, for my ear, often were too fast or too slow. All things considered, he was at his best with Haydn, Mozart, Bach, and Monteverdi. He did a splendid video of Haydn's *Orfeo ed Eurydice*, with Cecilia Bartoli which I happily directed in Vienna. We worked together harmoniously on two New Year's Concerts and the Vienna Philharmonic played brilliantly for him, but again, in my opinion something was missing. Still, it was a happier experience than a production of *Die Fledermaus* which I recorded at the Theater an der Wien. Harnoncourt managed to make Strauss's buoyant masterpiece of musical froth, boring. I respected the man but never became a fan. He didn't need me, he had plenty of them.

In 2003, *Mariss Jansons* replaced Lorin Maazel as music director of the Bayrisches Rundfunk Orchestra. A Latvian by birth and an outstanding conductor of his time, Jansons, like Gergiev, did not want to be pegged as a "Russian" conductor. To that end he specialized in Mahler, Strauss, and the classical symphonies of Beethoven and Brahms. Old habits are hard to break, though, and having been brought up in the Soviet system, he never lost the Soviet mentality and remained forever wary. His musicianship could not be faulted. Like his conductor father, Arvīds Jansons, and his teacher, Yevgeny Mravinsky, he knew exactly what he wanted and how to get it. And he loved his players and would do anything for them, campaigning vigorously for the repertoire and petitioning for a new concert hall in Munich. But he wasn't good at handling administrators and when it came to personal decisions, he'd do anything to avoid conflict or confrontation. In other words, he wanted to be Mr Nice Guy and always was, except when he could not support you as you might have wanted.

Jansons and I worked together for the ten years while he led Munich's Bavarian Radio Symphony Orchestra and I greatly admired his musicianship. I also grew fond of Munich. A truly musical municipality, Munich supported three great symphony orchestras. Jansons conducted the Rundfunks, *Christian Thielemann* steered the Munich Philharmonic Orchestra, and *Zubin Mehta* led the Bavarian State Opera Orchestra. Although primarily involved with Jansons, (we did forty-five concerts together) I worked with them all.

On one memorable occasion, I went with Thielemann and the Philharmonic to Vatican City where they presented a programme of religious music in the presence of Pope Benedict XVI—a significant coup. Not to be outdone, the Rundfunks quickly began negotiations with the Vatican. A year later, Jansons and his orchestra appeared before the Pope to perform Beethoven's *Ninth*. I went along, too. The concert was not transmitted live but rather recorded for later transmission, a blessing as it turned out. Jansons conducted with such zeal, he somehow jabbed the baton into his nose. Blood began dripping and he could do nothing except try to wipe it away with the back of his left hand. I couldn't do anything about it, either, until the editing. After hours of painstaking effort, we were able to electronically paint out the crimson stains on the maestro's face frame by frame—a miracle of editing, for sure.

Another, rather phantasmagoric Munich event comes to mind. City officials decided that all three orchestras should play together at the same time! Accordingly, Thielemann, Jansons, Mehta, their respective musical ensembles and over fifty thousand Münchners gathered together in the Munich Olympic Stadium and after doing their individual orchestral bits, the three ensembles united. Mehta's orchestra began playing Wagner's "Ride of the Valkyries", Thielemann's group joined in, followed by Jansons's, and in the end all three orchestras, some two hundred players, were joined in sound. Personally, I found the result contrived, but the audience gobbled it up.

At the age of thirty-three, *James Levine* became music director and chief conductor of the Metropolitan Opera in 1976. I met him three years later when I first came to the Met. Ninety per cent of the productions I directed were conducted by him, yet our paths barely crossed. Passionate about Verdi, Puccini, and Alban Berg, Levine's repertoire covered a vast range from Mozart to Wagner and beyond. An amazing musician and a first-rate pianist, singers appreciated the way he "breathed with them" in performance. Apart from daily rehearsals he'd conduct from one to three performances a week, a practice criticized by some who accused him of hogging the rostrum to keep out other talented conductors. He loved his musicians and, like Mariss Jansons, he wanted to be the "good guy" for his orchestra. Beyond his Met duties, Levine maintained a busy schedule as a symphonic conductor, appearing regularly with orchestras in the States and Europe. In 2004, he became music director of the Boston Symphony Orchestra. I never was asked to direct any of his BSO performances and as far as I know, few, if any, were taped. Regarding the Met productions, Levine and I rarely met to discuss upcoming tapings or to review past tapes. I got the distinct impression that Levine really didn't like to see himself on screen. In sum, our professional dealings were minimal and I never knew him socially. Although his Met tenure ended tragically, without question James Levine fortified the house by building a world class orchestra.

Considering all the maestros I've come across, the most unusual had to be an Englishman with whom I worked only once, but the occasion was unforgettable. At the Royal Festival Hall in November of 1971, *Edward George Heath* led the London Symphony Orchestra in a performance of Elgar's *Cockaigne Overture*. BBC2 covered the event and I directed. At the time of the concert, Mr Heath happened to be the Prime Minister of the United Kingdom. Although Heath had been "coached" by no less than André Previn, some members of the public decried the PM's efforts as "amateur". His presence, however, gave this concert a real sense of occasion and was, in the main, a triumph. Mr Heath loved music as much as, if not more than, politics and admirably bore himself on the podium. So much so that following the PM's London appearance, Herbert von Karajan invited him to guest conduct the Berlin Philharmonic Orchestra in Berlin. The die having been cast, orchestras in Chicago, Philadelphia, Cleveland, and Minneapolis followed suit. Without doubt, the BBC's TV coverage had unforeseen benefits for the Prime Minister. In 1974, Heath retired from both politics and conducting. Margaret Thatcher took his place in the Houses of Parliament, but made no attempt to usurp his podium. Here endeth the conductor portion. Now, to the singers.

After World War II, a trio of great Brünnhildes, *Astrid Varnay, Martha Mödl,* and *Birgit Nilsson,* dominated the Wagnerian scene. I had the honour to serve all three of the former Three Bs and though well along in their careers, each made an indelible impression. What artistry! I've already shared my experience with Nilsson, so let me tell you about the other two vintage Valkyries who, when I met with them, had long since hung up their horned helmets.

Astrid Varnay participated in the Met's *Mahagonny* premiere. Still a grand-looking woman, make-up turned her into a hag and she gave a thoroughly convincing portrayal of the avaricious, mean-spirited Widow Begbick. Off stage, Varney was the complete opposite, a thoroughly delightful lady. I worked with her on another occasion when Götz Friedrich, by then the all-powerful super director of the Deutsche Oper, had made his company the flagship of German opera houses. Friedrich had the brilliant idea of taking Wagner's sombre *Götterdämmerung* and superimposing it on Offenbach's lighthearted *Orpheus in the Underworld.* To play the Olympians, Friedrich engaged a number of very distinguished, elderly, Wagnerian singers, including Astrid Varnay. The result was a delightful musical romp with all sorts of inside jokes going on. Varnay and the other seniors had a ball doing it as did I recording it. That cheeky production was a huge hit.

I met with Martha Mödl for the first time at the Vienna State Opera where she sang the Old Countess in *Pique Dame.* As far as "old", at eighty years of age, she certainly filled the bill. Unofficially retired, she occasionally returned to the stage for a visit with the Old Countess, a role which she sang in both Russian and German. The voice had greatly weathered but, by God, what a character she created. At our first meeting I told her how special it was for me to work with her. "Ach," she sighed, "I'm afraid I'm too old to do television. I don't know anything about it. I don't even have a television set. What do I have to do? Tell me what you are looking for, Brian, and how I can help you to help me." I told her not to be afraid and to put her trust in me, and we went to work. I had her sit down in front of her dressing room mirror and speak the words in Russian, I particularly wanted her to go over the death scene. "You're in your nightdress sitting in a chair in your bedroom. You're snoozing when Hermann comes in. You wake to see him hovering over you. He demands that you tell him the secret of the three cards. You're shocked, terrified, and you suffer a fatal heart attack. The question is, how do you die?" "How do you want me to die? I can die anyway you like, with a scream or a whimper, whatever." "In my opinion there's only one way. You have to die silently, with your eyes wide open while we work the camera to capture the shock of a heart attack within your eyes." "Okay", she said, and facing the mirror, she ran through her death scene a few times. When finished, she turned and asked, "How is it?" "Well, you've died, but it's got to be stronger." "Stronger? How can it be stronger?" "You've got to make your eyes wider with no blinking, and no breathing, and you've got to hold the pose for one minute because I'm going to make a big close-up of your face." Each time that we shot the scene that wonderful woman did it as close to a minute as she could. In between takes, I'd go into her dressing room and there she sat in front of the mirror, dying over and over again. The result was petrifying and, as usual, you don't have to take my word for it, it's on YouTube. "Martha Mödl's creepy Countess is the central feature in this *Queen of Spades*", wrote one reviewer and I couldn't have agreed with him more.

In 1961, the American mezzo, *Grace Bumbry,* made a spectacular Bayreuth debut when Wieland Wagner cast her as Venus in *Tannhäuser.* The choice set off a racist firestorm. Bumbry, the first person of colour invited to participate in the festival, was attacked by the conservative German press and public. They weren't subtle about their complaint. Declaring a "*schwarze Venus*" (*black Venus*) unacceptable, they demanded she be replaced. Wieland Wagner shrugged off the detractors averring that he didn't care what colour she was, Bumbry would sing, period. And sing she did, so gloriously that she completely conquered the house. The audience applauded for a full half hour of curtain calls, forty-two of them to be exact. Not only did she triumph in the Festspielhaus, from then on Grace Bumbry became known worldwide as *Die Schwarze Venus*— not pejoratively, but adoringly. Friends of Jacqueline Kennedy who'd attended the performance wrote to tell the First Lady of the sensational debut they'd witnessed. In turn, Mrs Kennedy invited Grace to sing at a White House state dinner. Concurrently, impresario Sol Hurok put her under contract, and a dazzling career followed.

During her heydays, Grace lived the life of a diva— clothes, jewels, and fast cars, including a Maserati which she drove at Ben Britten speed. Always good copy for the press, she once leaked word that in an upcoming London production of *Salome* she planned to peel off all seven veils and present herself wearing only her "jewels and perfume". And strip down to her baubles and scent, she did. The gems, however, were placed in strategic areas and were large enough to cover the terrain. According to the singer herself, Covent Garden never sold so many binoculars, before or since. Extravagant, gorgeous, immensely talented, vivacious, and sultry, Grace Bumbry defined the words prima donna.

The two of us met in 1969 when I did my first *Aida* at Covent Garden and we immediately hit it off. My middle name is James but I rarely used it nor did anyone else, except for her. She always called me Brian James; I countered by calling her Grace Anne. We were neighbours in Vienna and when there at the same time, she'd come over to my flat on Sundays to watch old videos. Sunday afternoon with Grace Anne became a ritual as did convivial dining at Aki Nuredini's Ristorante Sole. (Aki, a fervent opera lover from Macedonia, opened his establishment nearly forty years ago and Sole remains the gathering place for Vienna's musical best—singers, musicians, et al.) Professionally, we worked together on several productions including the multifaceted *Don Carlos* staged by John Dexter for the Met. Grace sang and portrayed the tortured Eboli brilliantly. As the years passed, we weren't together as much professionally, but continued to see each other socially. Whatever the motivating force, time with Grace meant time well spent. I particularly treasure the memory of my eightieth birthday party, a grand celebration in Salzburg which included cocktails, and a programme of musical selections, followed by dinner and dancing. The dance band consisted of members of the Vienna Philharmonic. During the musical programme, Grace gifted me with two Spanish songs by Joachín Rodrigo.

It grieves me to report that Grace's senior years were not as comfortable as they might have been had she not lived on the fast track for so long. Eventually, in order to sustain herself, she gave singing lessons and then, one-by-one she began to sell off her jewels. Friends rallied around her so that in those waning times, she was sustained, but barely. Who could believe that such an intelligent woman would live for the moment and then pay the price for it. In that sense, she provided a cautionary tale for any performer who "forgets" there's a future. Grace Bumbry died on 7 May 2023. It's still hard to believe that scintillating presence is gone. I miss her, terribly.

A substantial woman with a lovely face and an exquisite voice, *Montserrat Caballé* had a great sense of humour. She loved to laugh and her giggles and guffaws punctuated any production we did together. On those occasions, you'd always hear comments concerning her size. Today, with the emphasis on compassion rather than caricaturizing, such behaviour would be unthinkable. But back then no one laughed more about her girth than Montserrat herself. She delighted in telling tales about the clash of sight and sound whenever she appeared on stage in operas featuring heroines described as "fragile". One of those stories became a classic. Given the choice of what she wished to sing for a BBC television gala, Caballé chose "Addio del passato", Violetta's deathbed aria, from the last act of *La Traviata*. This did not bode well for TV viewing. The small screen would only emphasize the Spanish soprano's sturdiness. Accordingly, BBCTV tried to steer her into a more practical choice. Caballé, however, had made up her mind. The producers could stall no longer. Okay, she was told, you can do it, but only if you insist. "I enseest, I enseest", cried the singer. The BBC yielded, advising the soprano that they would have to come up with some special effects to make her look less robust. "Anything you do will be good", she cheerfully replied. The crew set to work. Employing the tried-and-true stagecraft axiom, "to make something look smaller make everything else bigger", an extra-large scaled bedroom was constructed in the studio and in the centre stood a huge four-poster with pillars of Parthenon proportions. The scene itself would be shot by a crane camera looking down through the pillars, a view guaranteed to wield miniscule magic. Sure enough, within the scale of the surrounding objects, and with her head nestled in plumped-up pillows and her form lost in loosely-lying bed linens, the singer did appear diminished. She looked like an angel and sang like one, too. When shown the video, Caballé was ecstatic. "Wonderful, wonderful. I have never been so small in my life! I am positively teeny-weeny!"

Years later, I directed a Vienna State Opera production of Donizetti's delightful *Daughter of the Regiment* in which Monserrat appeared as the Duchess of Krakenthorp. Basically, the Duchess is a non-singing part usually portrayed by a semi or fully retired opera luminary or the occasional celebrity from another discipline. (Ruth Bader Ginsburg, a United States Supreme Court Justice and opera fanatic, once essayed the role for the Washington Opera Company.) As far as my catchwords, fear and trust, the word "fear" wasn't in Montserrat's vocabulary. On the other hand, she did have an abundance of trust. I wanted to get her full personality on the screen, her sense of fun, her joy, and her overall vivacity. As was my custom, I went to her dressing room to discuss Krakenthorp. "It's a small role and in order to make an impression, you've got to sell your laugh, your sense of humour, your wicked smile, your joie de vivre." Montserrat giggled at each descriptive phrase. "And you've got to do it in close-up and you've got to trust me to give you the best close-up. Will you do it?" "Of course I do eet. Just tell me how." I sat her down in front of the dressing-room mirror, and as she spoke the words, I gave her instructions, the most relevant of which was the rock-solid recommendation to look up to the light. By so doing, the camera would capture the sparkle in her eyes and the warmth of her endless smile. The Duchess of Krakenthorp came to life in Monserrat Caballé's vivacious portrayal and small as her role may have been, she became the production's effervescent quintessence.

In 1984, when the Met mounted a production of *Simone Boccanegra* for the American baritone Sherrill Milnes, and the Bulgarian soprano, *Anna Tomowa-Sintow*, I met both of them for the first time. A powerful dramatic baritone, Milnes shone in Verdi roles, from the noble Simone to the sinister Iago in *Otello*. Tomowa-Sintow had had a fine career in Europe and I looked forward to meeting her. We really hit it off. An attractive, charming, warm-hearted woman, and an artist who thoroughly researched her roles, Tomowa-Sintow asked if she could watch the rehearsal tapes with me and would I comment? I readily agreed. Her responses to my suggestions were intelligent and appreciative and we soon became friends. Anna lived in Salzburg and did many productions there. She asked me to work on Strauss's *Capriccio* which was being mounted for her. Booked to do it, at the last minute, I got dumped when the stage director decided that he was a "television director", too. I was upset and so was Anna, but nothing could be done. Alas, even at the Met, we didn't work together as much as I'd have liked. Anna sang roles—great Mozart, wonderful Strauss, excellent Verdi, unforgettable Wagner—that were the so-called "property" of favoured Met singers. To the members of the company went the spoils, so much so that Anna Tomowa-Sintow had little opportunity to fully show and shine in her extensive repertoire. She wasn't alone in this predicament; guest singers often were brought in and underused because resident artists had certain roles sewed up. Although my professional connection with Anna ended long ago, I last recorded her at a Covent Garden Gala in 1993, we're still neighbours in Salzburg and our friendship continues.

Another international star with whom I've enjoyed a long association, the Slovak soprano, *Gabriela Beňačková*, experienced much the same treatment at the Met as Tomowa-Sintow. Following in the footsteps of the renowned Czech soprano, Emmy Destinn (Ema Destinová) Beňačková specialized in the operas of Smetana, Dvořák, and Janáček. Her galaxy of Czech portrayals included an iridescent Rusalka, a brilliant Jenůfa, and a delightful Mařenka. Equally stellar in the standard repertoire, her Desdemona was outstanding. For me, she created the perfect Margherita in the *Mefistofele* which I recorded with Sam Ramey and her in San Francisco. The sheer beauty of her singing is breathtaking. A fabulous performer yet Beňačková, too, had to yield place to the Met's house favourites. Consequently, we heard less of her luscious soprano than we were entitled to.

It was Georg Solti who told me to keep my ears and eyes open for another Slovak singer, the coloratura soprano *Edita Gruberová*. Our paths crossed during the recording of that memorable *Magic Flute* staged by Jean-Pierre Ponnelle in Salzburg. Gruberová's Queen of the Night made her a star overnight, and became her signature role. She equally dazzled in roles such as Lucia di Lammermoor and Zerbinetta in Strauss's *Ariadne*. Appearing regularly with the Vienna State Opera, Gruberová eventually became an Austrian citizen leaving Beňačková as the Slovak standard bearer. I recorded Edita's Norma and Lucretia Borgia in Munich but the opera I'm most pleased to have documented for and with her, is *Roberto Devereux*. Her portrayal of the dying Queen Elizabeth Elizabeth brilliantly combined astounding coloratura singing with genuine emotion providing a moving testimony to a remarkable artist. Edita died on 18 October 2021 after an accidental fall in her home. Yet another sad loss.

The superb Romanian soprano, *Virginia Zeani*, whom I've already cited as my template for Violetta, also suffered the consequences of being outside the Met's preferred list. She sang the Verdi heroine 648 times in her career and was said to "own the role". Indeed, when Francis Poulenc heard her in Paris, he invited her to create the part of Blanche de la Force at the La Scala premiere of his *Dialogues of the Carmelites*. Aged 41, Zeani made her belated debut at the Met as Violetta; a few days later she sang it again. And that was it. Virginia Zeani never again sang at the Metropolitan Opera House. She didn't flinch and just went on with her career. Actually, she preferred to sing in Europe where she could be nearer her husband and son in Rome. Zeani's career covered thirty-four long and productive years, during which she went from coloratura to lyric soprano and then to lirico-spinto. And when her career ended, she became an illustrious voice teacher. After she retired, I regularly visited her at her West Palm Beach home. A lovely, lively lady, she happily shared her memories. Virginia Zeani died at the age of 97 in March of 2023. During her performing years, conductor Richard Bonynge (husband of Joan Sutherland) placed her among the top four sopranos of the twentieth century and Maria Callas's former husband, Giovanni Battista Meneghini, once confided that Zeani was one of the very few sopranos that his wife "was frightened of".

In 2005, when I began working with *Anna Netrebko* on Salzburg's stunning, stark production of *La Traviata* directed by Willy Decker, I found her cold, suspicious, distant, no smiles, nada. After she viewed a rehearsal tape of what we had done, everything changed. She went from an ice queen to a warm, delightful young woman and we got along famously. Indeed, when next we met for

Anna Bolena in Vienna, she greeted me with open arms. Netrebko is the sort of person who, if she saw you across the street, would race over to give you a hug without bothering to check the traffic.

Netrebko made her Met debut in 2002 as Natasha in Prokofiev's *War and Peace*, became a regular at that house, and enjoyed a stunning international career. Today, in her early fifties, her repertoire has changed. She's doing the heavies, Lady Macbeth and the like. Her reputation has changed too. The aggressive and devastating Russian assault on Ukraine created controversy over Netrebko's fealty to her country. Consequently, she is, for now, no longer welcome at the Metropolitan Opera House. Whatever my feelings about the present situation, I cannot forget how she lit up the stage.

I've chosen to close this musical inventory with a real-life operatic fairy tale that unfolded in front of my camera and, in my opinion, perfectly reflects the enchantment of the theatrical/musical world. Once upon a time, in a country called Romania, there lived a beautiful young woman named *Angela Gheorghiu*. Gifted with a lovely, lyric soprano voice, she became famous all over the world. Her acting was as formidable as her singing and her peerless portrayals of Violetta, Mimi, Tosca, Liu, and Magda were heart-rending. In 1996, I taped Donizetti's *L'Elisir d'amore* in Lyon with Angela in the role of Adina. The Nemorino on that occasion was Angela's newly-wedded husband, tenor Roberto Alagna, the French-born son of Sicilian parents. I met Alagna in 1994 when I taped his Roméo in Gounod's *Roméo et Juliette* at Covent Garden, the role that catapulted him to stardom. A brilliant singer in his own right, the handsome, affable Alagna personified Prince Charming. During the *Elisir* taping, the idyllic harmony and spirited good humour between Angela and Roberto was infectious. They were in love and played themselves, and the resultant recording is sheer bliss. Unfortunately, all did not remain serene. Passionate and fiery personalities, Angela's and Roberto's marriage had its ups and downs. *L'Elisir* definitely mirrored the upside. In 2009, the Met brought the Royal Opera House production of *La Rondine* along with its stars, Gheorghiu and Alagna, to Lincoln Center. Thrilled to be directing, I was equally pleased to be in their company again. Perfectly cast, they played their parts convincingly. At the final curtain the parting of the two lovers was so tender, so moving, there wasn't a dry eye in the house. In truth, that was the last hurrah. The swallow had flown away and not long after, Angela and Roberto were divorced. The *Rondine* DVD remains, a bittersweet souvenir of an enchanted moment in theatrical time.

And there you have it, a sampling of the 600+ people I've known, about as outstanding a cast of characters you ever could hope to find. I'm struck by the fact that for a man who claimed to be wary of making friendships with artists, I don't seem to have followed my own advice. I am all the richer for it.

44.

The World Is My Oyster

Through the last twenty years of the twentieth century and into the third decade of the twenty-first century, I thrived in opera houses, concert halls, theatres, and television studios all over the world. My path had been determined when I answered that BBC advertisement in *The Daily Telegraph* and left the tight circle of academia for television's ever-expanding horizons. Had I not done so, I might have spent my life contentedly teaching a finite number of students at university. Instead, I experienced the exhilarating privilege of bringing music to millions all over the world.

My work was recognized, I received honours and awards in England, on the continent, and in America, but, unlike performers—singers, dancers, actors, musicians—I never took a bow. How could I? I was either sitting in a television truck parked around the corner or confined to a broadcasting booth in the depths of a theatre. The time has come to remedy the situation by humbly and gratefully acknowledging what has been the very heart and soul of my being. And so, hoping that you've learned a little and enjoyed a smile or two, I'll take my leave with a bow ... *"An die Musik"*.

Acknowledgements

Valerie Solti encouraged me to write my memoirs, but, having penned biographies of Smetana and Martinů, I didn't feel up to writing about myself. However, an invitation from Jack Mastroianni to dine with Marilyn Horne and her friend and biographer, Jane Scovell, changed my feelings. Jane, the author of an impressive list of books including collaborative autobiographies with, among others, Elizabeth Taylor, Ginger Rogers, and Maureen Stapleton, and biographies of Oona O'Neill Chaplin and Samuel Ramey, started me thinking again. At dinner that evening, the chemistry between Jane and myself clicked and, on the spur of the moment, I asked her if she would work together with me. She said yes and then found a way to tell my story in my own words with honesty, grace, and humour. I am indebted to her for the way she shared her skills, her expertise, and her rich experience to bring my story alive. Working with Jane has added an extra dimension to my life. What started as a literary collaboration has flowered into a wonderful, lasting friendship.

I also want to acknowledge other friends: Hazel Wright who kindly catalogued hundreds of programmes, Judy Flannery, producer for New Broom Sweeps Clean, Josef D'Bache-Kane who helped to collect various production photos, as well as Franz Fichtinger and Georg Falkner, who provided valuable material on Zdenka Podhajská. Sincere thanks to Véronique Firkušny for checking the Czech and reuniting me with Jaraslov Mihule, and to Renée Fleming for agreeing to write a Foreword. And finally, thank you to Mary Lou Falcone who read the manuscript, made valuable suggestions, and wrote the Introduction.

BRIAN LARGE

Thanks to my inhouse editorial board, Amy Appleton, Lucy Appleton, Bill Appleton, Jane Donahue, and Andrew Barraclough as well as the next generation of supporters, Charlotte and Ben Sarraille and Isabelle and Kate Appleton. Thanks also to Véronique Firkušny, Marilyn Horne, Lester Lynch, Fred Plotkin, Jessica Davis, Kris Monroe, and to everyone at Tarallucci e Vino UWS. A very special thank you to Mary Lou Falcone. My gratitude to the late Stephen E. Rubin who always came through for me and to the late Sydney Sheldon Welton, my friend and editor. I began this project with Shelley and I still hear her gentle, on-the-mark corrections and suggestions. Sincere appreciation to Silvia Jaklitsch, Brigitte Swoboda, and everyone at VfmK for a task not just well done but superbly done. Which brings me to Brian Large. Despite my interest in the classical music world, particularly opera, I didn't know of him because Brian worked behind the scenes. When he asked me to assist in his project, I accepted but confessed that I wasn't quite up on his provenance. "I think you're in for a few surprises", he told me. Surprises?

"Étonnez-moi!" (Astonish me!) Sergei Diaghilev famously commanded his Ballet Russe dancers. Well, I truly was astonished. What a life! What a story! And what a pleasure and privilege to work with this remarkable gentleman, my dear friend, Brian Large.

Finally, Alan Scovell introduced me to classical music in Boston's Symphony Hall a very long time ago. With the exception of Brian Large, my big brother knows more about music than anyone I've met and he's shared it with me, my children, and my grandchildren. I have him to thank for the gift of music.

JANE SCOVELL

About the Authors

BRIAN LARGE

Television director of more than 800 opera and concert performances, Brian Large began his career as a producer for BBCTV (1965 to 1980). From 1980 to 2010 he served as director of television productions for the Metropolitan Opera. For his telecasts, he won many awards including two Emmys. Among numerous international productions, Large directed the telecast of *Der Ring des Nibelungen*, the first complete video recording of Wagner's epic tetralogy (Bayreuth, 1980), the original Three Tenors Concert (Rome, 1990), Vladimir Horowitz's historic *Return to Moscow* (1986), and nineteen New Year's Concerts in Vienna's Golden Musikvereinsaal (1989–2011). In addition, he is the author of definitive biographies of the Czech composers Bedřich Smetana (1970) and Bohuslav Martinů (1976).

JANE SCOVELL

Jane Scovell has collaborated on autobiographies with major figures in the entertainment world including Marilyn Horne, Elizabeth Taylor, Ginger Rogers, and Maureen Stapleton and has written biographies of Samuel Ramey and Oona O'Neill Chaplin. Four of her books were on the *New York Times* and *Los Angeles Times* Best Seller Lists.

Photo Credits

Colour Pages

II Anna Tomowa-Sintow © Deutsche Grammophon
IV Preparation for the Live Broadcast of *La Traviata*, Salzburg Festival, 2005
    © Ali Schafler/First Look/picturedesk.com
IV Brian Large with Renato Zanella and the Vienna State Opera Ballet
    at the *New Year's Concert*, 2005 © Milenko Badzic/First Look/picturedesk.com
V   Brian Large with Peter Pears as Peter Grimes © Dave Pickthorn/BBC Archive
VI John Culshaw, Colin Graham, and Brian Large during *Owen Wingrave*, 1971 © BBC Archive
VIII Elisabeth Soderstrom on the monitor, Brian Large, and Richard Armstrong © BBC Archive
X   Brian Large, Benjamin Britten © BBC Archive
XII BBC production of *The Flying Dutchman* © BBC Archive
XIII BBC production of *The Flying Dutchman* © BBC Archive
XIV Seiji Ozawa and Brian Large © Johannes Ifkovits
XV Oleg Prokofiev and Brian Large on the set of *The Love of Three Oranges*, 1980 © BBC Archive

All other colour photos

© Private archive of Brian Large